URBAN MINISTRY

AN INTRODUCTION

Ronald E. Peters

Abingdon Press
Nashville

URBAN MINISTRY: AN INTRODUCTION

Copyright © 2007 by Abingdon Press

All rights reserved.

This book is printed on acid-free paper.

Library of Congress Cataloging-in-Publication Data

Peters, Ronald Edward.
  Urban ministry : an introduction / Ronald E. Peters.
     p.   cm.
  Includes bibliographical references.
  ISBN 978-0-687-64225-0 (pbk. : alk. paper)
1. City churches.   2. City missions.   3. Church work.   I. Title.

BV635.P48   2007
253.09173′2—dc22

2007010511

07 08 09 10 11 12 13 14 15 16—10 9 8 7 6 5 4 3 2 1

MANUFACTURED IN THE UNITED STATES OF AMERICA

To Mary

More Praise for *Urban Ministry*:

"With the intellectual acumen of a first-rate scholar and the sensitivity of a pastor and urban dweller, Ron Peters introduces the world to urban ministry. It is obvious in this book that the urban context is not simply a phenomenon to be examined dispassionately but a pervaasive reality that Peters investigates with rigor, respect, integrity, clarity, and thoughtfulness. *Urban Ministry: An Introduction* is needed by the academy and the church."
　　　　—Jason A. Barr, Jr., Senior Pastor, Macedonia Church of Pittsburgh

"Engagingly written, Dr. Ron Peters's testament is an eye-opening, mind-expanding theological journey across the rugged terrain of our modern-day city of God. *Urban Ministry* is a timely, prophetic text that deserves wide readership."
　　　　—Katie G. Cannon, Annie Scales Rogers Professor of
　　　　Christian Social Ethics, Union Theological Seminary
　　　　and the Presbyterian School of Christian Education

"This work is a *tour de force*. Peter writes with . . . a pedagogical passion for the city and the rightful place of urban ministry as a discipline of North American theological education and a ministry of the church . . . declaring that urban ministry *is* Christian ministry."
　　　　—Warren L. Dennis, Dirck Romeyn Professor of Metro-Urban Ministry,
　　　　New Brunswick Theological Seminary

CONTENTS

LIST OF CHARTS
AND DIAGRAMS

PREFACE

This book is about urban ministry values and theological outlook. Nearly half of the people on the face of the globe live in urban areas. In highly developed countries, for example, the United States, approximately 80 percent of the people live in metropolitan areas. Although these types of statistical realities have been talked about as important for understanding the global-conscious world in which we live, as a lifelong city dweller, I have long appreciated how human relationships are interconnected in ways beyond provincial characteristics of particular communities. Just as families, clans, and tribes reveal behavioral similarities, cities also bear the stamp of their human connections beyond cultural differences. I write from the perspective of a person who has lived in, been educated in, worshiped in, worked in, served as pastor of, and taught in inner-city communities all of his life. Having received Christian baptism at the age of nine in the Tulane Memorial Baptist Church of New Orleans, Louisiana, where my parents, Charles and Leola Williams Peters, had been active members and quite heavily involved in its various churchly activities long before I was born, I always knew and experienced congregational life of a city church as part of my extended family.

The reader will understand my sadness as I, along with the rest of our nation, saw in September 2005 the tragic pictures of my native city of New Orleans drowning, not only because it was deluged by water, but also by apathy and indifference. Following Hurricane Katrina, not only did levies break and fail to protect the city from the floodwaters, but also promises were broken that were supposed to protect people from the danger, sickness, and loss of life that occurred. Clearly, the vast majority of the people who could not get out of the city were poor. More pathetic than even this catastrophe are the social and economic realities that typified pre-Katrina New Orleans, which can be found in cities across the nation and, indeed, around the globe in even more profound dimensions. Other cities may not be below sea level physically, but educationally, economically, and in terms of social challenges facing poor families in urban centers engulfed by health challenges, drugs, gang violence, and unemployment, they are seriously below needed safety levels.

There is a two-pronged conceptual framework of which the reader should be aware. First, this book is not about sociology of religion, congregational studies, or urban strategy. It is about clarifying and promoting an urban theological attitude that affirms God's love of the city behaviorally. God loves the city, and those who perceive themselves called by God into any type of Christian relationship with God should love those whom God loves: people. This is the essence of the gospel of Jesus Christ. Thus, this book is about a theological attitude that characterizes the proclamation of the gospel in the city behaviorally and seeks to promote the twin goals of the gospel: love and justice.

Second, my approach to urban ministry is profoundly informed by my experience as an African American pastor who served churches in core-city African American communities for eighteen years prior to joining the faculty at a theological seminary. Frequently, the resources of the Black experience are thought to have relevance primarily only for persons of African heritage. I would argue, however, that the Black religious experience not only gives shape and substance to urban ministry for the Black experience, but also shares in the plurality of all ethnic and cultural experiences that form the urban reality. I approach urban ministry through the prism of the Black experience in America as a model of urban ministry praxis that has theological relevance to all urban contexts and cultures and from which insights concerning God-to-human and human-to-human relationships can be ascertained.

As we move through the study of urban ministry, the book is divided into three parts. Part 1 deals with challenges in urban ministry. In chapter 1, I examine some of the questions that define the task of urban ministry. In chapter 2, I review the two dominant images of the city portrayed in scripture, followed, in chapter 3, by an overview of the bridges needed to get us across some common dividing realities.

In part 2, including chapters 4–7, I examine the origins of urban ministry. I look back into the role of the city as revealed in scripture and church history and how these have informed what I call *top-down* and *bottom-up* theological approaches to urban ministry today.

"Perspectives" is the last section of the book. Chapters 8–11 deal with urban-ministry core values and how these determine how urban-ministry practitioners view the city and participate within it to enhance the quality of urban life outlining major focus areas that typically characterize urban ministry. While the city contains all manner of structures and buildings, infrastructure networks, and particular physical settings and advantages, these are not really the essence of the city. A city is composed of people. Without people, there is no city. Because God loves people, God loves the city. In order to demonstrate God's love for all people and all creation (that is, where people live), any sense of divine call to ministry has in it the potential as a call to urban ministry.

ACKNOWLEDGMENTS

Although the multiple demands of faculty and administrative responsibilities, along with local church leadership and community participation, have constrained the availability of time for research, reflection, and writing, it has been a privilege to write this book. I have been constantly encouraged in this effort by hosts of people. In a real sense, my service as pastor of the Martin Luther King, Jr., Community Church of Springfield, Massachusetts, for fourteen years is the foundation of this book. With patience and love, the people of that congregation helped me understand how faith in Jesus Christ could make a difference in a city.

Special mention must go to the Pittsburgh Theological Seminary community, where I have taught for fifteen years. The students, faculty and staff, administration, the board, and the Metro-Urban Institute Advisory Committee have been invaluable. Former seminary president Carnegie Samuel Calian, former dean John Wilson, and my faculty colleagues deserve special mention for their consistent support and encouragement. I am also deeply grateful for the support of my Metro-Urban Institute departmental colleagues, Dr. Jermaine McKinley and the Reverend Sharon Washington, and for the help of my secretary, Ms. Jacquie Sledge. Two friends, Warren L. Dennis of New Brunswick Theological Seminary and Marsha Snulligan Haney of Johnson C. Smith Seminary at the Interdenominational Theological Center in Atlanta, Georgia, must be mentioned. Warren's friendship, insights, reading portions of the manuscript, and hospitality at New Brunswick helped make this writing project much easier. Also, Marsha was kind enough to offer invaluable feedback as this work progressed. Words are inadequate to express my appreciation to Robert Ratcliff of Abingdon Press for his help and support in working with me through to this book's completion.

Family members proved to be the bedrock to the completion of this effort. My brother, Charles L. Peters, Jr., of Los Angeles and his wife, Doris, hosted me as I did some writing in their home. My sister, Zara Peters Wynn, and my adult children, Charles Andrew and Mary Lecel, who always believed in me and listened with interest as I discussed aspects of this work with them, were not only inspiration but also joy throughout this time. Peola and Vernell Smith, my wife's sister and brother-in-law, were kind enough to allow me the use of their condominium in Myrtle Beach, South Carolina, to do some writing. Most significant of all, however, I am grateful to God for my best friend in the world, Mary Smith Peters, who read the entire manuscript page by page and offered helpful critique and indefatigable patience and encouragement. Without her incredible love, this book would never have been written. My prayer is that the frailties of this piece, which are entirely my own, will be overshadowed by God's gifts of mercy through all who have helped make it a success.

PART 1

CHALLENGES

CHAPTER ONE

AN INTRODUCTION: THE INFORMATION GAP AND DISCERNING THE RIGHT QUESTIONS

If you don't know what it looks like, you won't recognize it when you see it.
—West African Proverb

In trying to define the term urbanization . . . we are confronted with the fact that social scientists themselves are not entirely agreed about what it means. It is clear, however, that urbanization is not just a quantitative term. It does not refer to population size or density, to geographic extent or to a particular form of government. Admittedly some of the character of modern urban life would not be possible without giant populations concentrated on enormous contiguous land masses. But urbanization is not something that refers only to the city.
—Harvey Cox[1]

When someone can get you to ask the wrong question, the answer you receive won't really matter because it will be irrelevant.
—Charles L. Peters, Sr.

Having met for the first time as we found our seats around the banquet table, we introduced ourselves and began making polite conversation while waiting for the meal to be served. When the young woman sitting next to me learned that I was a seminary professor who taught urban ministry, she asked me the usual questions: What is urban ministry? How does it differ from rural or suburban ministry? Her innocent queries concerning the nature of my discipline were not unlike those of students or faculty colleagues who do not live in the city, but are clear about their perceptions of urban society and, yet, are relatively vague about what it means to engage in effective and life-enhancing ministry in this arena. In an era that places so much stress on information, this lack of understanding about urban ministry represents a deep division, a chasm, in the life of the church and society that is much bigger than just an information gap. The question posed at the banquet table revealed more than an information gap about urban realities and

Christian ministry; it also exposed a need to discern how this gap can be overcome and eliminated. Her questions made me wonder why there exists so little understanding about urban ministry.

Unlike urban churches, seminary education is largely oblivious to urban ministry in spite of the fact that 79 percent of the U.S. population reside in its metropolitan centers.[2] Nearly two-thirds of all seminaries accredited by the Association of Theological Schools in the United States and Canada offer no courses related to urban ministry.[3] This situation helps explain the resilience of the vast gaps of information about urban ministry outside urban communities in general and within seminaries in particular, the longevity and vitality of its practice notwithstanding.

Conversations in Seminary and on City Streets: An Insight

Biblical scholars have debated whether Isaiah's mention of King Uzziah's death (Isaiah 6:1) was, in fact, a historical point of reference or perhaps something more, such as the catalytic event that clarified Isaiah's understanding of his prophetic vocation.[4] The death of Martin Luther King, Jr., in 1968 prompted me to view this passage as a thorough mixture of both. During that year, Dr. King was killed in Memphis, Tennessee, on Thursday, April 4, by an assassin.[5] The entire decade of the 1960s was punctuated by the assassinations of famous people in the United States: first, the nation's president; then, a radical Muslim preacher from New York; Dr. King was the third; and, fourth, a presidential candidate (the late president's brother).[6] At the time of Dr. King's death, his leadership of the civil rights movement was virtually uncontested. The difference between the response to this event on my seminary campus and on the streets of cities across the United States was startling.

The nation was in a state of turmoil. A man whose ministry was largely defined by his activities on behalf of the oppressed, Martin King had gone to Memphis in support of striking garbage workers who had taken their struggle for better wages and working conditions to the streets with public protests. Upon news of his death, urban areas large and small were engulfed in riots almost immediately. National Guard units and other military personnel and armaments of war became part of the urban landscape from Boston to Los Angeles and just about every city in between. Across the nation, religious, civic, and community groups organized impromptu memorial services and called for peace. By contrast, so far as I could see on my seminary campus, there was no mention of the incident either formally or informally. I was not a seminary student when the first two assassinations of that decade took place, so the stark contrast between the serenity of my seminary's campus with its apparent aloofness to what was happening in city

4

streets nationwide in the wake of Dr. King's death was a surprise to me. For this reason, 1968 (the year Dr. King died) became not only a historical point of reference for me, but also a key factor that inspired within me a fresh theological insight: I saw a gaping chasm between God-talk[7] in the seminary and God-talk in city streets.

More than thirty-five years since that theological insight, I now teach in a seminary surrounded by city streets. The city is not Memphis, but Pittsburgh, Pennsylvania, and there have been no mass riots in some time. No president, presidential contender, famous cleric, or other dignitaries have been killed by assassins in Pittsburgh. Indeed, unlike that transformational year in my life, the killings on this city's streets nowadays are caused not by the notoriety of the victims, but by their lack thereof. These are ordinary people: a teenage girl walking home with her friends after school, a father and his eight-year-old daughter sharing a meal while sitting in a fast-food restaurant, a postal worker delivering mail, a woman riding in the car with her sister, a man in front of his home. The deaths of people like these on city streets in Pittsburgh and thousands of others like them in cities across America are overshadowed by cataclysmic events such as the notorious September 11 attacks on New York City's World Trade Center towers and the Pentagon in Washington, D.C., and the spiral of national and international events that have followed. And, for the most part, the chasm between the nature of the God-talk in seminary and that of its surrounding city streets has remained remarkably similar to my experience back in 1968. Generally, on campus, little attention is given to these deaths. The young lady's banquet-table question, therefore, did not surprise me, but it reminded me that the deep informational and conversational gaps between seminaries and city streets that existed years ago when I was a seminary student still remain.

Conversational and Cognitive Chasms

The conversations on city streets (and their God-talk), whether about drive-by shootings, child abuse, finding and sustaining mutually fulfilling relationships in a culture of distrust, gangs, the latest in hip-hop, the growing prevalence of AIDS or diabetes, or other issues of survival, do not sound like the conversations of the seminary. Even when talk on the city streets is clearly rooted in ethical concerns about right or wrong, evil, suffering, redemption, or where God is in all of this or if there is a God, these conversations still differ fundamentally in substance, subject matter, and style from that of the seminary and its God-talk. The concerns found in city streets today—such as day-to-day lived-in realities about the cost of food and rent, redlining,[8] police brutality among poor and Black or Hispanic communities, domestic violence, or health-care challenges—are different

5

from concerns typically discussed in seminary classrooms. Overcrowded prisons and probation systems, racial profiling, unemployment, or troubled public schools are matters that rarely interrupt the major focus of God-talk in seminaries, which tends toward preoccupation with esoteric beliefs and reinforces the perception that such discussion makes for holiness and points toward ultimate truths. The chasm persists.

The seminary's propensity to cloister inside itself for the purposes of withdrawal from "the world," so as to better hear from God in quiet prayer, study, research, and meditation, is not altogether unlike similar responses of local congregations inside and outside the urban arena. While many urban practitioners criticize seminaries for being "ivory towers" of academic self-absorption far removed from the "real world" of the streets, the fact is that many urban congregations are just as out of touch with "the streets" as are the seminaries they lambaste. In reality, churches and seminaries frequently fail to recognize that they are each merely extensions of the other. Problems experienced in one sphere only mirror realities of the other. Both tend toward different types of conversations found on the other side of the divide that still seems to remain between such institutions and many urban streets.

Thus, seminaries are not alone in distancing themselves from the urban community. Many churches outside core-city neighborhoods and even congregations within metropolitan areas do not perceive urban realities as relevant to their own ministries, theological outlook, or any other aspect of their Christian witness. Indeed, there is much in society at large that reveals a reticence to acknowledge the overtly urbanized character of our world today in spite of its obvious effect on our lives. Andrew Davey, in his book entitled *Urban Christianity and Global Order*, posed several penetrating questions based on his observation of this phenomenon in the culture of the UK:

> As long ago as 1970 a sociologist wrote "Britain is physically as urbanized as any nation in the world, yet as a society we seem to be extraordinarily reluctant to accept this fact" (Pahl 1970, 1). Despite the many social changes of the past thirty years, that reluctance is as evident today as it was in 1970. What is it that makes people so disinclined to acknowledge the urbanization they witness around them? Is it an inadequate vocabulary to express the processes they are a part of? Is it a nostalgic fear of all things urban? What do cities and urban areas represent in the popular imagination that makes people so reluctant to understand themselves as part of an urban society?[9]

Growing Global Urbanization

Without question, the world is growing more populous and more urban every day. It is estimated that in 1800, the world's population stood at about one billion people, and by 1900, that figure had nearly doubled to about 1.7 billion. By 2000, however, the earth's human population had jumped to over six billion, and by 2025, it is projected that this figure will increase to more than eight billion (see chart 1 below).[10] Prior to the twentieth century, the proportion of the global population that lived in cities was relatively small, but since then the picture has changed drastically. Between 1800 and 2000, the proportion of United States citizens who lived in urban areas went from a mere 6 percent to 79 percent (see chart 2 on page 8). By 2000, nearly half of the world's population lived in cities, and it is projected that by 2050, as many as 79 percent of all people on the globe will live in urban centers.[11] In the United States, projections are that by 2025, nearly 85 percent of the nation will be urban.

Globally, 37 percent of the world's population lived in urban areas in 1975, but by 2000, the figure was 47 percent. The United Nations has projected that by 2025, more than half of all people in Asia and in Africa (54 and 53 percent respectively) will live in cities; 74 percent of the people in Oceania (including the regions of Australia and New Zealand), 84 percent of South America, 83 percent of Europe, and nearly 85 percent of all North American residents will live in urban areas, for a total of more than 60 percent of worldwide population located in cities.[12] In light of these population shifts, it is apparent that ours is an increasingly more urbanized world.

Chart 1: Global Population Projections[13]

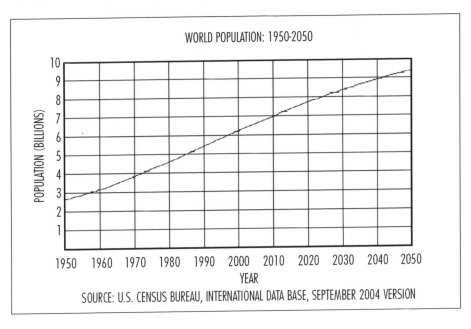

WORLD POPULATION: 1950-2050

POPULATION (BILLIONS)

YEAR

SOURCE: U.S. CENSUS BUREAU, INTERNATIONAL DATA BASE, SEPTEMBER 2004 VERSION

Chart 2: U.S. Population, 1800–2000[14]

Year	Total U.S. Population	Urban Population	Urban % of Total U.S.	Rural Population	Rural % of Total U.S.
1800	5,308,483	322,371	6.1	4,986,112	93.9
1900	76,212,168	30,214,832	39.6	45,997,336	60.4
1930	123,202,624	69,160,599	56.1	54,042,025	43.9
1960	179,323,175	113,063,593	63.1	66,259,582	36.9
1990	248,709,873	187,053,487	75.2	61,656,386	24.8
2000	281,421,906	222,360,539	79.0	59,061,367	21.0

The urbanization of our world and the closely related issue of Christian ministry in this urbanized context, however, are much more involved than mere statistics about population shifts or other demographic profiles. It is a subject essentially concerned with human relationships and divine realities as these are experienced in the ecology of the social, spatial, and spiritual context we refer to as the urban environment and what the urban arena reveals to us about God. As such, urban ministry is a way of understanding God based upon the dynamics of the city and involves a theological praxis that seeks to enhance the quality of life for all creation. Still, the questions arise: What about suburbia, edge cities, or rural areas? Aren't these also viable resources for seeking to enhance the quality of life for all creation? Cannot insights gleaned from these areas, along with information from the urban setting, also give us a clearer picture of divinely inspired life-enhancing realities?

There is no attempt here to suggest that revelation is limited to or enhanced by one particular frame of reference, such as an urban context, over another. Such a strategy would only lead to deepening already-existing chasms. Scripture is replete with teachings informing us that divine revelation certainly can and does occur anywhere (Genesis 3:8-9; Isaiah 6:1; Jonah 2:1-10; Psalm 139:7-12; Mark 9:2-8; Acts 9:3-7; Revelation 1:9). The point here is simply that, overwhelmingly, the vast majority of resources aimed at developing Christian leaders is drawn from or directed toward contexts *other than* the urban setting. By contrast, it is the urban setting that is underrepresented in a ubiquitous array of Christian resources that are suburban or rural in outlook, ethos, and theological orientation, displaying little attention to nagging justice issues so prevalent in the city or to the ethnic or cultural pluralism that characterizes city life. Yet, these resources are generally presented as being universally applicable. In order to obtain a clearer picture of divinely inspired strategies for realizing goals that affirm life and reduce strife, injustice, and want, Christian focus on the urban context needs to be bolstered. Harvey Conn and Manuel Ortiz have stated the problem well:

> Most Christians know of books and materials written to help local church leaders who serve in a suburban or rural setting. . . . They often focus only on the local church and fail to address sociological and missiological implications. . . . Matters of style and methods that reflect contextualization are universalized without the provision of any caution. . . . If the context is mentioned, it is only for the reader to know its geographical location. . . . Therefore, even though a book is geared toward Christian leadership in the context of a nonurban environment, there is no mention of this uniqueness. In reality the content of the book is geared for leadership in a suburban/rural community. The assumption is that all Christian leaders come from a non-urban context and are serving outside of the urban reality. There is also an assumption that since scriptural principles are universal they fit anywhere without contextualization. These assumptions are invalid and need redirection.[15]

Addressing the Issues

The gap in clarity in theological schools concerning urban ministry poses several other problems, three of which warrant attention if this situation is to be resolved. First, lack of clarity in seminary curricula regarding urban ministry encourages confusion because practitioners and teachers of the discipline tend to define it in different ways, usually rooted in their own venue of ministry. While there is certainly overlap among various definitions that have emerged, the sheer variety of definitions and approaches inhibits concentration on core values in urban ministry. More focus on these core values would not only clarify understanding among those rooted in urban churches or other areas of urban ministry, but also would make more visible the nexus between urban ministry and other theological disciplines for those outside the field. Also, there has been a tendency to define urban ministry by citing best-practice examples.[16] This method of approach to urban ministry definition, although extremely helpful in prompting ideas, essentially leaves it to the learner to discover applicable insights on one's own rather than concentrating on core values that inform all contexts of urban ministry.

Second, vagueness concerning the precise nature of urban ministry as a discipline taught in a theological school frequently leaves people engaged in this type of ministry isolated in theological discussions and forums on practical theology (pastoral care, ethics, homiletics, and so on) that appear more concretely defined. Integration of theological study suffers as the interrelatedness of various disciplines as reflected in the urban arena is overlooked in the curriculum design and course offerings. The urban-ministry practitioner, then, is left to adapt the central focus of other disciplines to the particular needs of the urban context. Given the relatively wide variety of interpretations concerning the nature of urban ministry, this adaptation can be a rather daunting task, especially for the newcomer to the field.

Third, imprecision about urban ministry as essentially a branch of theological study (rather than as a segment of sociology or urban public policy or planning, topics more suited to research universities) tends to render the seminary an unwelcoming environment for those interested in urban ministry. The continuing but unfortunate practice of dichotomizing theological education into "traditional/classical" and "nontraditional/other" spheres, with those involved in urban ministry always categorized in the latter sphere, is not helpful as it promotes a schismatic and unrealistic theological paradigm that will be of little value for twenty-first-century ministry. It is no surprise, then, that several spiritual zealots in the urban context view a seminary as a "cemetery" for those seriously interested in effective work in the city and shy away from formal theological education in such a context. Recruitment of individuals from urban churches or other urban contexts into theological schools, therefore, remains more difficult than it should be.

The aim of this text is to examine briefly the nature of urban ministry and thereby to propose a concrete working definition of the discipline and its core values and principles. It would be foolish to suggest that such an undertaking could eliminate all questions concerning urban ministry's definition, nature, or useful strategies. Clearly, there are many valuable resources that already address these issues, yet questions remain. The aim here is to assist the readers, both in seminary classrooms and in congregational or other community-based settings, in framing better and more relevant questions concerning urban ministry and to help overcome huge information gaps about the city, the church and seminary, and urban ministry.

CHAPTER TWO

PITFALLS AND POTENTIALS: THE CITY AS A PARADIGM OF HUMAN RELATIONSHIPS

Then the LORD came down to see the city and the tower which those men had built, and he said, "Now then, these are all one people and they speak one language; this is just the beginning of what they are going to do. Soon they will be able to do anything they want! Let us go down and mix up their language so that they will not understand each other."
—Genesis 11:5-7, GNT

When the day of Pentecost came, all the believers were gathered together in one place. Suddenly there was a noise from the sky which sounded like a strong wind blowing, and it filled the whole house where they were sitting. Then they saw what looked like tongues of fire which spread out and touched each person there. They were all filled with the Holy Spirit and began to talk in other languages, as the Spirit enabled them to speak.
—Acts 2:1-4

Admittedly, there are several instances in scripture that seem to portray the city in a bad light. Yet, closer examination reveals that there are two distinct images of the city lifted in scripture: one good and one bad. On the negative side, the first builder of a city mentioned in scripture is Cain, the murderer who killed his brother (Genesis 4:17). There is also the story about the construction of the Tower of Babel (Genesis 11:1-9), which identifies human ambition and arrogance as key factors in the construction of the city, incurring divine wrath and spawning confusion and misunderstanding.[1] Collectively mentioned 260 times in scripture as a city or an empire, Babylon is second only to Jerusalem as the most frequently referenced urban setting, and its image in this context is virtually synonymous with wickedness. From the prophet Habakkuk's complaints to the unflattering descriptions in Revelation (chapters 17–18), it is clear that the image of Babylon is one that connotes rebellion against God. This is the city as a sinful pitfall in society. It symbolizes a bad city in which moral dysfunction, injustice, violence, and oppression reign.

By contrast, there are more than one thousand references to the city of Jerusalem in scripture, and it is frequently portrayed as "the holy city" where God resides (see Psalm 46:4; Zechariah 8:3; Matthew 4:5). Illustrations of Jerusalem such as the ones found in the prophecy of Isaiah (65:17-25) and the

11

related vision outlined in Revelation 21:1-4 reveal idealistic images in which God's presence in the city renders it a safe, healthful, and happy environment. The record of the Pentecost event (Acts 2:1-12), which occurs in Jerusalem, stands in marked contrast to the Tower of Babel event. In this case, the quest to seek God's guidance replaces human arrogance and results in divine blessing and understanding. The image of Jerusalem in scripture, thus, comes to symbolize what can happen when God's presence among people is rightly acknowledged and affirmed. In this image of the city, God's glory manifests itself in the abundant evidence of social, spiritual, and material well-being found among the city's inhabitants who enjoy the ambience of God's omniscient and omnipresent love, mercy, and protection. Here one finds scripture's view of the city's divine potential. It represents a good city in which the presence of God is reflected in right relationships among all residents, and love, justice and righteousness, peace and praise of God are the fruit of this city's divine character.

This scriptural outline of "a tale of two cities"—one good and one bad—is one way to understand the larger divine paradigm or model of human relationships and faith in God. Those whose lives are governed by faith in God will live in such a way as to inspire right relationships in which love, justice, and praise of God are evident, qualitatively elevating the entire environmental atmosphere (see Isaiah 4:2-6; Micah 4:1-4). Here the divine potential of faith in God is revealed. Where there is no faith in God or where such faith is tentative or of secondary importance, the pitfall of such doubt is made plain: human relationships suffer, as do surrounding environmental conditions (see Genesis 4:8-12; Luke 19:41-44). As such, the significance of the city in urban ministry goes beyond its uniqueness as merely a geographic location or a specific type of sociological reality. In urban ministry, the city stands as a symbol or paradigm of human relationships and environmental conditions based on faith in God. It is against this scriptural and theological backdrop that the key challenges in urban ministry at the beginning of the twenty-first century may be succinctly defined and to which we now turn our attention.

The Challenge in Urban Ministry

In order to understand the core values in urban ministry, it is helpful first to look at the challenging context in which urban ministry, broadly speaking, is done. One of the biggest challenges facing practitioners in urban ministry has less to do with the geographical or sociological context of the city itself than with pervasive realities that define the era in which we live. Realities that define the context in which urban ministry is carried out today can be summed up in three words: *alienation, fear,* and *violence.* These are relational realities that are found in all communities, but their characteristics are more obvious in urban society.

Alienation, fear, and *violence* in the urban context are relational manifestations of the far deeper issue pondered throughout the history of human theological reflection: the problem of evil. Entire volumes in religion and philosophy in addition to works in popular literature have dealt with this perplexing reality. While it is beyond the purpose of this volume to engage in an in-depth analysis of this vexing theological reality, suffice it to note that the phenomenon traditionally known as evil cannot be defined but has been variously described in the literature in its effects and characterizations (that is, sin, human doubt and disobedience of God, the fall of man, and so on), all of which generally associate the presence of evil with varying interpretations of human complicity. Consistently, evil is malevolent, deceptive, and destructive. It is also contagious. Evil warps the spiritual perspective, distorts material vision, and dulls the ethical senses in a manner that often belies its sinister and ultimately fatal qualities. Inevitably, evil's unpleasantness causes pain and facilitates physical, emotional, and spiritual corruption on both personal and group levels.

Although evil is clearly acknowledged in scripture, it is not explained. It is just there to be dealt with. The Bible opens with a wonderful story of an ideal world created by God. The two biblical accounts of the creation story recorded in Genesis (1:1–2:4a and 2:4b–3:24) are beautifully intertwined in a way that conveys to the reader not only God's eternal existence but also sovereign generative abilities that ultimately placed human beings in the Garden of Eden in which everything was good. There is no hint of anything unpleasant, dangerous, or evil. The environment is so idyllic that the temperature and ecological balance is such that all vegetation, fish, birds, insects, and animals live together in harmony among the two human beings who also inhabit this gorgeous setting. The intimacy with God and nature is such that not even clothes are required of the human beings as part of this spiritual and physical paradise. Mysteriously, without warning and with no explanation whatsoever, evil just simply appears out of nowhere hanging in a tree (chapter 3) in the form of a serpent that communicates doubt and misinformation.

The results of evil's unexplained presence in this setting lead to disastrous consequences. The unclothed bond between the woman and the man suddenly becomes shrouded in shame, and the intimacy of the spiritual relationship among the human beings and God gives way to human efforts to hide from God. The oneness of the human family with the ideal setting of their paradise is replaced by a give-and-take relationship that requires toil and sweat and ends with diminished powers and physical death. Enmity comes to characterize the relationship between human beings and serpents, and pain becomes a part of parenting, even at its very beginning in the act of childbirth. Worse still, this diminished quality of life gives rise to sibling rivalry between the first two children of the original couple and leads to the murder of an upright man, Abel, by his own jealous brother, Cain. In short, without any reason given for its presence, evil not only has always been a part of reality from the beginning of creation but also has always introduced dysfunction into a setting in which none previously existed. The result is always the same in the human environment and produces the same relational manifestations: *alienation, fear,* and *violence.*

Alienation as represented by economic, group, or ideological difference is present in all communities. Yet, in suburban and rural areas, class, group, or ideological differences are often mitigated by social and economic factors (primarily economic and ethnic) that tend to discourage or filter out elements considered significantly dissonant from community norms. Suburban and rural areas, therefore, tend to be more homogeneous in composition with regard to socioeconomic status, ethnic composition, and cultural and ideological norms. The overt appearance of conformity to group norms common to these areas sublimates, to a large degree, the alienation that is present.

Cities, by contrast, are pluralistic by nature and generally reflect the presence of persons from a variety of socioeconomic levels, ethnic groups, and ideological and cultural orientations in comparatively close spatial juxtaposition to one another. Where individual group norms are observed, they are observed in the context of competing norms from other groups. Ethnic neighborhoods (Chinatown, the Italian section of town, the Jewish community, the White Anglo-Saxon, Latino, or Black communities, and so on), common to all cities, are reflective of this principle. In this context, class, ethnic, and cultural differences shape the cosmopolitan setting and competing interests, and values reveal sharp contrasts to a degree that is rare in the more homogeneously populated suburban and rural environments. Nonurban areas, on the one hand, tend to structure relationships and lifestyles in light of social and public similarities within the environment. Urban settings, on the other hand, tend to structure relationships and lifestyles in light of social and public differences in the environment.

Sadly, this juxtaposition in urban settings, which should be the context for mutual enhancement and collaboration, frequently establishes the setting in which competing interests among differing segments of society (class, ethnic, religious, cultural, or ideological) reflect behaviors that exhibit alienation rather than cooperation toward the proverbial "other." This can be seen in conflicts in which oppositional postures abound (ideological confrontations, culture wars, one ethnic group vs. another, rich vs. poor, Democrat vs. Republican, Christian vs. Jew vs. Muslim, Catholic vs. Pentecostal, Conservative vs. Liberal, Bloods vs. Crips, and so on). The emphasis is on how we are different from one another rather than on what we have in common.

This type of alienation is overt in the city. Although people are geographically close to one another in the urban setting, their emotional proximity can be quite distant, a reality fueled by what Howard Thurman, mentor to Martin Luther King, Jr., long ago identified as "contact without fellowship." Thurman noted how such a paucity of understanding nurtured fear and even created the seedbed for hatred:

> Hatred often begins in a situation in which there is contact without fellowship, contact that is devoid of any of the primary overtures of warmth and fellow-feeling and genuineness. . . . Contacts (awareness and social exposure) without fellowship tend to express themselves in the kind of understanding that is strikingly unsympathetic. There is understanding of a kind, but it is without the healing and reinforcement of personality.[2]

In the urban arena, this "strikingly unsympathetic" *alienation*, which is part of all society, reveals such realities as walled-in neighborhoods, the virtual abandonment of public schools by middle-class residents, and incidents of random drive-by shootings. The prevailing sense of alienation encourages a response of fear on the personal level, as well as in society at large.

Few will argue with the proposition that *fear* is one of the prevailing characteristics in society today that influence human relationships. Fear always has to do with the basic issue of survival: how can I make it through this? Because of our alienation from one another and our concentration on our differences and the uniqueness of our own group or issues, we lack sufficient understanding or appreciation of those who are different from ourselves or are "outside" our own particular group, neighborhood, and economic or ideological camp. Even when the other person poses no real physical threat, our lack of mutual understanding makes us afraid. Because of alienation, it is perceived that the proverbial "other" has the potential to do harm, and the fear of that potential is sufficient to move us to extraordinary lengths to protect ourselves from that which is threatening.

The process by which our fears become entrenched is simple: it is a process called labeling and generally proceeds in the following manner. After noting how others are "different" from ourselves, first, we assign to their dissimilarity an oppositional label that codifies their difference (and emotional distance). In other words, we objectify them, reducing their status from human beings to an assigned label or stereotype to which our fear is attached. Instead of seeing other people in our environment as human beings, they are assigned objectified labels: immigrants, criminals, suburbanites, Muslims, Republicans, liberals, hillbillies, straight, gay, Negroes, Gen Xers, and so on.

The response to fear can be seen in society's political penchant for "get tough" sentencing policies such as "three strikes and you're out" judicial practices, and in the ever-growing security industry, the preponderance of locks and alarm systems being installed in homes, vehicles, and businesses, or the metal detection and X-ray systems now present in most public facilities, buildings, and airline travel venues. Unfortunately, this alienation and the fear produced inevitably lead to some manifestation of violence.

Violence in society represents the nadir of failed human relationship. Social indicators amply document the widespread lack of relationship that violence represents in every sector of society today, most vividly in the urban arena. Violence is evident on the personal level (self-inflicted: suicides, homicides, substance abuse), in the home (domestic violence), in the public square (at schools, in crime statistics, or the type and severity of law enforcement in so-called high-risk areas), and in national or international conflicts (civil and international wars, terrorist or guerrilla-type activities). The numbing violence reflected on television and in cinema and computer games and expressed in the lyrics and videos of popular music has been exacerbated in the post–September 11, 2001, terrorist attacks, greatly increasing already well-entrenched public fears. Nowhere in society are these fears more vividly displayed or expressed than in the urban arena. The reality that violence has become such a matter-of-fact phenomenon in society epitomizes the functional spiritual deprivation in human interactions and the virtual absence of meaningful relationships. In sum, the realities of alienation, fear, and violence not only characterize all society but also especially shape the context of the city in which urban ministry is practiced.

The Charge in Urban Ministry

In this context, the pitfalls of the "bad city" are clearly evident. Babylon is alive and well with its paradigm of moral dysfunction, injustice, violence, and oppression appearing to be firmly in control. Yet, it is the purpose of urban ministry constantly to lift the vision of the "good city's" potential to become a "new Jerusalem," and of a new Atlanta, a new Los Angeles, a new Paris, a new Mexico City, a new Cairo, a new Calcutta, and a new Johannesburg. In contrast to the negative realities of *alienation, fear,* and *violence,* urban-ministry practitioners are called to exemplify the alternative vision of the "good city" and to emphasize the potential of divine realities embodied in *reconciliation, love/justice,* and *cooperation.*[3]

Scripture is clear that the response to alienation is *reconciliation* (Genesis 3:8-9; Matthew 5:23-24, 43-46; Romans 5:6-11). Second Corinthians 5:17-20 puts the matter plainly, interpreting efforts at human-to-human reconciliation by believers in Jesus Christ as evidence of their new and divinely inspired right relationship with God:

So if anyone is in Christ, there is a new creation: everything old has passed away; see, everything has become new! All this is from God, who reconciled us to himself through Christ, and has given us the ministry of reconciliation; that is, in Christ God was reconciling the world to himself, not counting their trespasses against them, and entrusting the message of reconciliation to us. So we are ambassadors for Christ, since God is making his appeal through us; we entreat you on behalf of Christ, be reconciled to God.

In this passage, reconciliation becomes the behavioral representation of faith in God and a key evangelistic component in enabling human beings to be spiritually reconciled to God. Conflict resolution rather than conflict exacerbation must be the goal. In this context, reconciliation is a divine mandate that does not ignore or gloss over real motivational/situational factors that define the oppositional relationship between contending parties. Rather, as a divine mandate, reconciliation involves the implementation of conciliatory strategies and behaviors that seek to affirm the human dignity of all opposing sides and undo the harm that fosters the oppositional relationship so as to underscore the unity of all parties as children of God.

Urban ministry must also reflect the potential of *love* as the most effective alternative to *fear*. More will be said about this later in chapter 8, "Core Values in Urban Ministry"; however, it suffices to note at this point that reference here is to *agape* (or self-effacing and sacrificial love, which seeks nothing in return, but only the enhanced situation of the object of said affection). According to theologian James Cone, Martin Luther King, Jr. insisted that it is impossible to demonstrate this type of love without a corresponding commitment to *justice*. While many Christians are quick to focus on *agape*, King noted that the functional implementation of agape is, in fact, justice and that there is no evidence of love without just and fair treatment of others:

As God's justice is grounded in God's creative and redeeming love, so human justice is grounded in love. Neighborly love, especially for the enemy, defines the means by which justice is established and also the goal of the struggle for freedom, namely the beloved community.[4]

In other words, it is *compassion demonstrated through justice* that has the power to undermine fear's effectiveness, the fear that always lacks concern for the welfare of the other, but is concerned only for the self. This type of genuine compassion (*agape*) always has the potential to place the well-being of others as a priority and, thereby, limit the capacity for injustice. Again, the apostle Paul explains love as the evidence of just treatment of others, which fulfills the requirements of the law (Romans 13:8-10):

Owe no one anything, except to love one another; for he who loves his neighbor has fulfilled the law. The commandments, "You shall not commit adultery, You shall not kill, You shall not steal, you shall not covet," and any other commandment, are summed up in this sentence, "You shall love your neighbor as yourself." Love does no wrong to a neighbor; therefore love is the fulfilling of the law. (RSV)

The writer in 1 John 4:13-20 goes even further in equating love of neighbor as evidence of love of God. The writer says "God is love" (1 John 4:16) and identifies an indwelling spirit of agape within an individual as evidence of God's presence in the life of that person. This loving spirit eliminates fear ("Perfect love casts out fear" [1 John 4:18]) and renders anyone who demonstrates hateful (fearful) behavior toward others as being ungodly: "If anyone says, 'I love God and' hates his brother, he is a liar" (RSV).

Right relationships with others, therefore, are always based on faith in God as evidenced by agape/love toward the neighbor. Urban ministry must stress the potential of agape/love and its companion behaviors, justice and mercy, in the face of an overwhelmingly fearful and oppositional social context. With a focus on reconciliation and love with justice, the oppositional framework that spawns and emphasizes difference, avoids compassion, denies justice, and gives rise to violence will be dismantled. In place of confrontation, opposition, and violence, the potential of *cooperation* increases, and the paramount virtue reflects intentional efforts at making positive connections with others and reaching out to seek collaborative opportunities.

The potential of the good city embodies the relationship-building process as part of its ministry. Instead of manifesting behaviors that mirror social alienation from other people or fear of others or that bow to rampant violence in society, urban-ministry practitioners become the incarnation of reconciliation efforts, compassionate in demeanor, and advocates for justice. They seek all opportunities to build cooperation among previously alienated and competing parties. The pitfalls of negative and dysfunctional relationships are replaced with behavioral paradigms of human relationships that demonstrate the potential of reconciliation, compassion, and justice and emphasize cooperation, connecting, and collaboration. In this way, behaviors redeem the image of the city not merely by means of rhetoric but by activities that seek to create and strengthen positive relationships. Although popular society may view the city as a "bad" and morally corrupt pitfall, the focus of urban ministry is always to lift the divine paradigm of the city's potential for right relationships grounded by faith in God. In this way, the city's divine potential for ameliorating negative realities of *alienation, fear,* and *violence* can be realized by demonstrating the divine qualities of *reconciliation, compassion,* and *justice,* emphasizing *cooperation, connecting with others,* and *collaboration.*

CHAPTER THREE

BRIDGING THE CHASMS IN URBAN MINISTRY

The central urban ministry premise is the need to bridge the gulf between learning, faith, and practice by implementing faith commitments through public policy in the academy, church, and community. . . . A conversation is taking place about faith and public participation. The dialogue is about teaching and learning, curricula development, credentialing, and the economic well-being of the community.

—*Warren Dennis*[1]

With reconciliation as one of the primary goals in urban ministry, the task of addressing this goal in principle should be clearly stated if it is to be accomplished in practice. We will not be able to move from just rhetoric about "saving our cities" toward the reality of behavioral outcomes that actually produce systemic change that strengthens the quality of life for the most vulnerable in society until we overcome some powerful divisions or chasms that continue to plague our efforts in urban ministry. A chasm is a deep cleft or depression, a gorge, that constitutes a huge division in an otherwise relatively unbroken stretch of landscape and, as such, symbolizes much that characterizes challenges to be addressed in urban ministry.

Chasms and Bridges as Symbols in Urban Ministry

The city of Pittsburgh is located in southwestern Pennsylvania, a region so mountainous and full of uneven terrain that moving from almost any point to another in this area involves going down or up some slope or crossing a ravine, gully, river, or other type of chasm in the earth's surface. Three rivers (the Allegheny, Monongahela, and Ohio) carve up the major regions of center-city as they make their way to join together in downtown Pittsburgh, along with innumerable streams, tributaries, and ravines that separate neighborhood from neighborhood throughout the broader metropolitan region of Allegheny County. Given this geographic context, it is no surprise that Pittsburgh is a city characterized by its many bridges. With topography such as this, bridges are a virtual requirement for making the landscape amenable to host the interrelated networks of this metropolitan area that accommodates the region's 2.4 million residents.[2] "One count reports over 2,000 bridges of 8 feet span or greater. . . . It's virtually impossible to travel any notable distance without crossing a bridge."[3] Pittsburgh's physical landscape and the resulting network

19

of connecting bridges symbolize the challenge before all seminaries and churches as they seek to span the informational and conversational chasms that reflect even greater social, political, and economic cleavages characterizing urban life and the extraordinary physical and spiritual investments of faith that must be undertaken to get across them.

There are at least four chasms that must be bridged if what we have come to call urban ministry is to enable an enhanced quality of life in cities through a more effective witness of faith in Jesus Christ. In order to be able to produce real "fruit" that can be enjoyed (outcomes of ministry that change people and society for the better), first we will have to bridge the following chasms that challenge some of our current approaches to urban ministry. These include the chasms between:

1. urban ministry and Christian ministry
2. urban and rural
3. ethics and evangelism (among Christian theologians)
4. urban as code word and urban as theological symbol

1. The Urban Ministry and Christian Ministry Chasm

The first chasm to be overcome is crossing (*removing*) *the artificial barrier between urban ministry in particular and Christian ministry in general.* For most people, "urban" refers to an experience of challenging realities and mixtures of people, cultures, and economies as well as political and social phenomena in a particular spatial context that can be overwhelming when considered as a whole. Understandably, few people consider any metropolis as a whole, concentrating instead only on those aspects of city life that give meaning to their own lives. The term *ministry* in the Christian tradition, by contrast, is essentially a holistic concept. Its roots come from the idea of service (*diakonia*) for the general welfare of society (especially those most vulnerable within it, in all aspects both material and spiritual) and are considered within the appropriate service framework of the church's concern. This concern, in turn, emanates from God's love as revealed in Jesus Christ and can be seen in the behavior of believers who, through faith, reflect God's love in their compassion for others (see Matthew 6:25-34; Mark 10:13-16; Luke 4:18-19; John 3:16-17; James; 1 John 4:7-21). As such, spatial, social, or political characteristics comprising the uniqueness of any context (urban, suburban, or rural) all become irrelevant in the face of an omniscient, omnipresent, and immutable God, who is the same yesterday, today, and tomorrow and is more than capable to handle any and all situations. Since God is the same for all contexts, many Christians have understandably approached ministry as if it, too, can be the same for all contexts. Hence, there has always been a certain level of confusion about urban ministry, which, by definition, seems to focus divine concern on a particular context when, in fact, God's concern and interest are universal.

Beyond the matter of theological focus, there is another challenge in some quarters that skews thinking about the city. Unfortunately, when issues of urban ministry are considered among many well-meaning Christians, a strange perceptual dichotomy frequently emerges. Urbanization prior to and during the time of Jesus of Nazareth is often separated out from the otherwise normal consideration of social, economic, or political events characterizing human history. It is as if matters of faith, religion, and history are one thing while the phenomena of city life in the modern urban context, somehow, are another matter. This separation is especially well represented in the thinking of many Christians outside core-city areas (as well as within the minds of some living in the city) and is unfortunate because it allows warped perceptions of urban realities to persist unchallenged. Largely supported by negative and sensationalized media images, the notion of the city as a hopelessly secular place in need of people who are willing to be "bold for God" in these citadels of iniquity, atheism, and apostasy is promoted in many Christian circles.

There is no denying that the city is the scene of much that is lamentable about the human condition and creation. Unspeakable poverty exists amid unimaginable wealth in cities with blatant oppression, illness, and pollution carefully segregated so as not to disturb neighboring communities of privilege, tranquillity, and comparative opulence. Yet, artificially pristine answers laced with theological language that reduce the world to competing spiritual spheres—in which rural/suburban is represented in middle-class or wealthy imagery portrayed as uniformly good, and urban/city is reflected as exotic, unsafe, and generally bad—do not solve these vexing human and ecological problems. Buttressed by doctrinal verbiage not intended for mass consumption (creation, election, soteriology, eschatology, and so on), this flawed view often represents Christian faith to the wider public as essentially concerned only with spiritual matters, while urban ministry, so concerned with temporal issues of society (poverty, injustice, health, education, and so on), is viewed more as social work with a slight religious twist.

What is needed is a frank acknowledgment that Christian ministry, the proclamation and living out of the gospel by the inspiration and empowerment of the Holy Spirit, when it occurs in the city, is urban ministry. It is not psychology, social work, criminal justice, or community organizing with a veneer of the cross pasted on the front. Clearly, its methodology will differ from nonurban contexts as urban Christians seek to be authentic in their faith as well as contextually appropriate in their witness. Nonurban Christians will do well to understand their visceral connection with urban ministry, as should urban practitioners acknowledge the unity of their anointing in Christ along with those outside the city limits.

2. The Urban and Rural Chasm

Closely related to the above misperception is the regrettable practice of ignoring the fundamental unity that exists between the urban and rural venues of ministry. Divisive tactics as a means to thwart uplifting actions that empower and free people from debilitating realities have long been standard practice among those comfortable with injustice so long as it does not touch them. The practice of building new prison facilities in rural areas as opposed to urban centers is but one example of the principle. This tactic not only separates the incarcerated from their families but also takes jobs and important census statistics away from heavily populated areas in favor of rural districts. Another example of the urban versus rural chasm could be seen in reports about Hurricane Katrina's destruction in 2005. For example, the Mississippi Gulf Coast cities of Biloxi, Gulfport, Waveland, and the more rural surrounding areas were in the direct path of the hurricane. Overwhelmingly, however, news accounts of the devastation tended to focus on the city of New Orleans, taking relatively little notice of the common denominator that characterized those left most vulnerable to tragedy and loss in both venues: poverty. Although analysis of the tragically inadequate response of all levels of government to this tragedy must involve considerations of politics, race, land use, and emergency planning, the fact remains that both urban and rural areas of this region were characterized by the poverty that exacerbated this crisis.

The reality is that urban and rural areas have many problems in common, and we must avoid the tendency to ignore the fundamental unity that exists between these areas. In any field of human endeavor, whether in business and economics, politics, education, art and entertainment, health care, or in matters of faith and religion, the reliability of this ancient method of subversion is well proven. In several places, scripture exposes the dangers of allowing selfish or other types of narrow interests to undermine faithfulness to a more broad-based or common good. This is the basic point of the story about Cain's murder of his brother Abel (Genesis 4:1-16). Also, the Old Testament books of Exodus through Deuteronomy document how the perpetual lack of a genuine faith consensus among the liberated Hebrews resulted in the death of an entire generation and doomed them to wandering in the wilderness rather than realizing divinely inspired dreams. In the New Testament, the story of Judas Iscariot's betrayal of Jesus (Matthew 26:14-16; Mark 14:10-11; Luke 22:3-6) stands for all time as testimony to the horror that can be wreaked by the old "divide and conquer" strategy if unchecked.

It should not surprise us that although the challenges of the urban context have their counterparts in rural settings—whether poverty, poor housing, inadequate access to quality health care, poor academic performance in public schools, substance abuse, domestic violence, unemployment, or other forms of economic exploitation—these two venues often have been positioned as competing rather than complementary sectors of ministry. Although the ghettos of cities such as Calcutta, Houston, Lagos, London, New York City, Rio de Janeiro, or Sydney may have the same types of deprivation seen in Appalachia, the Mississippi Delta, on some western Native American lands of North America, or in some rural villages of Tanzania, the urban versus rural paradigm of approaching challenges seems altogether too prevalent.

Of course, methodologies that reflect the clear differences between urban and rural contexts cannot be ignored. The typically homogeneous social nature and the physical expanse of the rural setting as compared to the socially plural constituency and comparatively dense land-use realities of the urban area are some obvious examples of the need for approaches that are contextually competent. Yet, the need for a difference in strategy should not obfuscate the reality of challenges that are common to both venues.[4] That decisions made by big business or by media magnates originate in urban centers and affect both urban and rural consumer markets globally is a fact that informs ministry, both urban and rural. A reduction in the level of drug trafficking in the city will not be effective or long sustained without similar results in outlying rural areas, nor will health care improve in rural contexts without a complementary improvement thereof in the city. We must get to the point at which practitioners in urban as well as rural areas recognize the essential unity of purpose insofar as ministry is concerned: improving the quality of life in cities and rural areas is a goal that cannot be accomplished by isolation of either of these venues, one from the other.

3. The Ethics and Evangelism Chasm

A third challenge to be addressed is *bridging the artificial chasm between urban ministry's roots in justice advocacy (ethical agency) and evangelistic mission.* As an academic discipline, urban ministry is a branch of theological inquiry and practice within the broader spectrum of Christian ethics that focuses on life in the city and its diversity from the perspective of society's most vulnerable populations. This is a very important point of emphasis because far too many discussions of urban ministry approach it as if it is primarily a matter of Christian missionary endeavor with evangelistic intent only. The culturally pejorative attitude of "let's go in and convert the heathen" that characterized much in missionary endeavor of previous eras simply will not do in today's urban ministries. Sadly, this approach has tended to gloss over or miss entirely the point regarding the visceral connection between "love of God and love of neighbor," which requires the inseparable responses of *praise to God by means of justice to neighbor*. The reality that each aspect of this response, *praise to God/justice to neighbor*, is invalid and without merit in the absence of the other is a fact often lost in mission/evangelism-only or justice/ethics-only approaches to urban ministry.

Many of these efforts engage the urban reality from a skewed perspective of missionary endeavor that often implies an artificial separation of evangelistic proclamation of the gospel from ethical considerations involving justice advocacy, as if one could be effectively undertaken without the other. Frequently, such approaches are represented in the perspective of one who is not a native, but who has come to the city from a rural or suburban setting, has become intrigued by it, and now sees his/her "mission" (divine calling) as bringing "Christ to the inner city." Regrettably, these *relocated persons*[5] (nonnatives who have moved into the city and view it as an urban mission field) are often unable to sufficiently shed the us/them mentality, so crucial to understanding the ethos and values of any context. Although many of these efforts are well intended, they often overlook the reality that Christ is very much alive and well in the social, economic, political, and cultural matrix of city life, in which ethical considerations, justice advocacy, and evangelism are inseparable aspects of urban ministry. *Indeed, urban ministry ordinarily is not urban ministry for Christians who are native to city life: it is ministry, period.* Having been born and reared in the city and having been a part of city-based churches all my life, it is significant for me that the first time I heard the phrase "*urban* ministry" as a specialized area of Christian endeavor (mission, evangelism, ethics, or otherwise) was in connection with graduate theological education.

This division of evangelism from ethics by some missiologists and ethicists that is found in some seminaries smacks of cultural fetishes that typify socioeconomic and intellectual elitists in academic guilds, but that are irrelevant to people struggling to make sense out of the nonsense that often characterizes the realities of everyday life. The apostle Paul understood the irrelevance of exotic debates among privileged groups as he stood before the council in Jerusalem (Acts 23:6-9) and took advantage of the situation to address a critical life-threatening reality. Clearly, it was the intensity and vigor of the differences between the Pharisees and Sadducees in that instance that derailed their focus from the practical issue they sought to address unfortunate concerning Paul and rendered their efforts useless. In like manner, the continued intellectual schism bifurcates ethics and justice issues from evangelism and seeks to locate urban ministry exclusively in the realm of some sort of spiritually oriented misapplied "zeal for Christ" that ignores justice for those for whom Christ died.

While the theological assumptions of urban ministry do not significantly contrast with those of nonurban contexts, urban ministry views the socio-economic, cultural, and ethnic pluralism of the city as indicative of divine presence. As such, urban ministry interprets negative social and political challenges as obstacles to faith that are best addressed through worship rituals and social activities that reflect a bias in favor of the city's most vulnerable populations. Issues of ethical agency and evangelism are addressed in tandem from a perspective that underscores the inseparable nature of *agape* (unselfish) love and justice advocacy. Generally, urban ministry addresses one or more of at least eight public issues in city life: *economic life*, *educational systems*, *family life*, *public health*, *ethnic/racial relations*, *religious culture*, *restorative justice* (civil and political rights), and *the environment*. Few urban-ministry practitioners will address all eight, but most will address some combination of these. We will return to discussion of these foci later.

4. The Urban Code-Word and Urban Theological Symbol Chasm

Finally, the chasm between *urban as code word* and *urban as theological symbol* must be addressed. In the United States, the reality is that *urban* is often a code word for Black, Brown, or whoever "those people" (the non-White people) happen to be, depending on whether the city is Atlanta, Los Angeles, Seattle, New York, Chicago, or Miami. This reality is not entirely unrelated to the issue of ethical agency and warped evangelistic efforts that see people of color in urban centers or in general as somehow intrinsically inferior, whether the context is in the United States, Africa, Asia, the Caribbean, Oceania, or South America. It is a well-established fact that the notion of race is a social construct and has no genetic significance biologically.[6] Yet, the cultural conundrum of ethnicity plagues all social contexts and generally plays out in ways that leave economic and political disenfranchisement unequally located among people of color. The stamp of these social realities is seen, for example, in health statistics regarding HIV/AIDS, the unfortunate fact that two-thirds of world debt is owed by poor southern nations to affluent northern nations, or in the disproportionate incarceration percentages of U.S. prisons.

In a social context in which race is such an emotionally and politically charged public issue while, at the same time, it is customary to publicly affirm pluralism and the equality of all, code language is often used as a means of remaining evasive about the subject of race in an effort to draw attention away from thorny realities such as group stereotyping or racial profiling.[7] Evasion via code language is often perceived as the less-threatening and more broadly acceptable way to cope with the nettlesome topic of race in U.S. society. Like many people in society, denominational leaders and seminary officials frequently use the code language of *urban* to diffuse focused attention from issues of concern to various ethnic and cultural groups represented in society while attempting to engage the task of cross-racial dialogue and theological reflection. Phrases such as "urban context" or "urban society" are familiar code-language handles that help give perceptual shape and form to a complex matrix of juxtaposed and competing realities in the ecology of the city involving ethical issues of race, gender, and class. This is an important point in understanding urban ministry because it underscores the reconciliation challenge implicit in this discipline that involves bridging not only informational, but relational and spiritual gaps as well.

There is another aspect of the word *urban*, however, that must be considered if urban ministry ultimately is to produce the spiritual fruit that is evident in substantive and tangible ways, that is, outcomes of change in the city that are positive and systemic. Reference here is to the understanding of the word *urban* as a *theological symbol*. Urban areas are typically defined in one of three ways: *spatially* (in terms of the uniqueness of geography and/or environmental characteristics), *socially* (identifying realities that shape the context and caliber of social interactions: population demographics, and so on), or *symbolically* (referring to the ethos or metaphorical meaning assigned to the metropolis based upon its perceived or projected characteristics, for example, "the Big Apple" or "the Holy City").[8] While all three meanings can connote aspects of *urban ministry*, the most common uses of the phrase focus on the *social* and *symbolic* meanings.[9] Although the social and spatial aspects of urban ministry are lifted throughout this book, the symbolic meanings involved in urban ministry are emphasized because it is the religious symbolism of the gospel that leads to a clearer understanding of the theological significance of the city.

Many Christians overlook the theological significance of the urban context. Urbanization is typically understood as the process of interrelating social, cultural, economic, political, religious, and spatial characteristics that reflect the environment and ethos of the city.[10] Yet, as in antiquity, the city's usefulness as an eschatological paradigm and symbol of hope for a better reality than currently exists is one that should inform urban ministry today. It was from the humiliation and horror of exilic relocation and exploitation (Lamentations 1–5) that eventual pictures of a new communal urban reality were envisioned in Isaiah 65:17-25 as well as Jeremiah 31:31-34; 32:38-39; and 33:6-9. Against a similar backdrop of oppression and incarceration in the New Testament, one finds this same element of the urban context as a symbol of hope in Revelation 21:1-4. These writings serve to sustain the oppressed and inspire hope that could serve to motivate reality-changing behavior among the readers. Scriptural writers were not the only ones to employ the city as a symbol of political idealism and altruistic possibility. Plato's *Republic* is a clear example of the urban reality as social and political idealism, and Augustine's *City of God* is a classic example of the urban context lifted as a divine symbol of hope. The titles of several resources in urban ministry today, such as Walter Earl Fluker's *They Looked for a City: A Comparative Analysis of the Ideal of Community in the Thought of Howard Thurman and Martin Luther King, Jr.*; Ray Bakke's *A Theology as Big as the City*; Eleanor Scott Meyers's *Envisioning the New City: A Reader on Urban Ministry*; Robert Linthicum's *City of God, City of Satan;* or Eldin Villafañe's *Seek the Peace of the City: Reflections on Urban Ministry*, all include the theological symbolism of the city reflected in the Scriptures.

Urban as code word does not refer to the spatial or symbolic context of ministry, but tends to zero in only on negative social dimensions. When we limit our perceptions of urban ministry to its social dimension, devoid of theological symbolism and reduced to code word for negative realities, we inhibit its practical usefulness as well as its potential for positive outcomes. Ministries physically located in a given metropolitan context, for example, purely from a spatial consideration understandably qualify for the identification of urban ministry. From the limited code-word perspective that considers *urban* only in light of negative social perceptions, however, this may not be the case.

This perceptual reality helps explain why many congregations or faith-based organizations that are physically located in the metropolitan context actually do not view themselves as being urban ministries. Those of European ancestry, who do not fit the implied ethnic or social stereotypes related to the code-word interpretation of *urban*, frequently shy away from identification with the language of urban ministry with regard to their own activities. Such behavior usually involves social, psychological, or even economic reasons for desiring to maintain a perception of difference from "the urban reality," although they may be physically located well inside the city. It is important to understand this social dimension of *urban* ministry that, in effect, views this type of ministry as being either primarily targeted toward or conducted by *urban* constituencies, meaning visually identifiable ethnics who are *not* "WASPs" (White Anglo-Saxon Protestants). Yet, people of color in the city also rarely define their ministries generically as "urban," but for different reasons. They tend to describe their efforts in keeping with the particularity of their endeavors (tutoring ministry, substance-abuse ministry, and so on) because their descriptions are socially coded not by race, but by the ministry function.

This social understanding of *urban ministry* as code word for "those people" generates two versions of ministry over time, each with different outcomes. First, there is the *benevolent model* of urban ministry. In this type of ministry, many social services are provided by secular and religious agencies or community groups whose policy-making, administrative, and service-delivery personnel do not reflect the constituency of those receiving the services. In many instances, the "helpers" may not even reside in the areas in which the ministries are located and are not typically connected socially, economically, culturally, or ethnically with service recipients. Such efforts qualify as *urban ministry* because the targets of their efforts are visible ethnics, poor, live in socially challenged communities, and the like (*urban*). The benevolence of the "helpers" or relocated persons motivates the ministry, which, more often than not, tends to be a dependency model.

The second version of a social understanding of *urban ministry* as code word is the *belonging model*. It is characterized by service providers who are indigenous to the areas they serve and who draw their human resources from these areas.[11] While they may draw upon resources or coaching from others, the policy-making, administrative, and service-delivery personnel are reflective of the recipients of ministry. This model of indigenous involvement and leadership tends to foster urban ministries that are able to transcend stereotypical attitudes and create an environment in which self-sufficiency can take root. Issues of socioeconomic class, culture, and ethnicity, therefore, are involved in the characterizations that distinguish congregations or other faith-based organizations doing *urban ministry* from other such groups located in the city, but whose social ethos and religious experience are different from those of indigenous urban-ministry practitioners. As such, social location (Wilson, 1996) is a factor in defining urban ministry.[12]

In summary, code words function to convey an essential meaning without using the overt reference. Although the word *urban*, in this usage, is overtly a covert reference for racial or ethnic stereotyping, it also carries other social meanings involving class and gender. Such a perspective on urban ministry functionally serves to describe and define urban ministry in such a way as to limit it to stereotypically prescribed constituencies and not other urban dwellers. This view takes no cognizance of the theological significance of the urban context as reflective of the believer's eschatological hope revealed in Jesus Christ that is both all-inclusive and hopeful about the city.

Bridging the chasm between urban as code word and urban as theological symbol is possible. It is not unlike the symbolism of the Crucifixion that initially reflected rejection, defeat, shame, punishment, and disgrace, but ultimately has been transformed into an emblem of divine redemption and empowerment (1 Corinthians 1:18-25; Philippians 2:6-11). When we are able to take the word *urban*—with its narrow and socially coded meanings that only conjure up pejoratively understood ideas about who lives in the city and what constitutes the city—and reframe its meaning with an understanding of urban as a theological symbol of eschatological hope (Revelation 21:5-7), then our urban ministry will truly bear fruit that has a divine stamp affixed upon it.

PART 2
ORIGINS

CHAPTER   FOUR

LOOKING BACK: ANCIENT AND MODERN URBAN MINISTRY

It is not taboo to go back and get what you have forgotten.
— *West African Proverb*

At the outset, Christianity was predominantly urban. It moved along the trade routes from city to city. By the second decade of its second century in at least some parts of Asia Minor, it had spread widely into towns and even into the countryside, but its strength was in the cities which were so prominent a feature of the Roman Empire.
— *Kenneth Scott Latourette*[1]

In the previous chapter, we noted that one of the barriers to effective Christian witness in the city involves bridging the perceptual chasm between Christian ministry, on one hand, and urban ministry, on the other, which is frequently viewed as something different, perhaps as social work with a religious twist. So pervasive is this misperception of urban ministry as being something other than "regular" Christian ministry that urban Christians will have to address it in some fashion whether dealing with other Christians (some urban and nonurban Christians) or with non-Christians. Nowhere is this perceptual chasm more evident than in examining traditional interpretations of biblical history and the postbiblical record of church history. It is as if the issues of life that most obviously characterize urban settings (such as housing, poverty, crime, and politics) all fall exclusively into a mythic social or anthropological arena, while matters of faith in Jesus Christ (conversion, discipleship, stewardship, and so on) are fantasized as essentially spiritual or as theological considerations isolated from the mundane realities of daily living.

This is an old misperception found in many churches, urban and nonurban, as well as in most seminaries. Those beguiled by this artificial dichotomy tend to interpret the events of postbiblical church history with a hermeneutic that pits religion against reality, piety against pragmatism, or spiritual versus social approaches in ministry. According to this hermeneutic, the eleventh-century split in 1054 between the Latin-speaking Western and Greek-speaking Eastern portions of the church was only a religious matter if political realities were not a factor. Similarly in this view, the quarrel of the sixteenth-century Protestant

Reformer Martin Luther with Pope Leo X was only a religious matter with no attendant political realities. Likewise, John and Charles Wesley's pietism of the eighteenth century is spoken of as if it basically involved few practical consider- ations, and Martin Luther King, Jr.'s ministry in the twentieth century is regarded as having been fundamentally a social movement that involved no serious spiri- tual or theological essence.[2] This divisive hermeneutic interprets the Bible as if the social, economic, and political contexts from which the Scriptures sprang were irrelevant to the functioning of the Holy Spirit in the lives of the people contained in its pages. Although Christianity was essentially born in cities, this fact rarely receives the emphasis it deserves because of this perceptual chasm that says urban ministry is something different from *regular* Christian ministry.[3]

One of the best ways to correct this situation is to examine some key events in the unfolding story of Christianity that reveal the unity of its social and spiritual development in the urban context. In the Akan culture of West Africa the pop- ular proverb that states *"It is not taboo to go back and get what you have forgotten"* is symbolized by a mythic bird, the *Sankofa*, which flies forward while looking back- ward. In this chapter, this is exactly the metaphorical procedure we shall strive to follow as we attempt, by *looking back*, to discern insights that will enable us to *move forward* in bridging this perceptual chasm that continues to view urban min- istry as something other than traditional Christian ministry. Although analysis of the entire scope of Christian history is beyond the scope of this volume, we shall look back to consider some historical realities with an *urban-focused hermeneutic* drawing attention to the role of the city in these events. None of the information here is new, but its urban character is often sublimated or ignored. The aim here is to better understand urban ministry as an integral part of Christian ministry and the city as a place of divine presence and revelation.

Looking Back in Order to Go Forward

Given the fact that, less than two hundred years ago, London was the first city in modern times to reach even one million people and now megacities numbering in the tens of millions can be found on every continent, it is not hard to understand how current perceptions of antiquity invoke pastoral and rural images in our thinking. With the exception of a few well-known ancient cities, Rome or Athens, for example, most people in U.S. cities evidence rela- tively little knowledge (or interest) concerning life in ancient times. Except for a few popular myths or fragments of historical fact that are attached to various contemporary cultural or religious commemorations (Thanksgiving, Christmas, Hanukkah, Ramadan, Easter, Memorial Day, Fourth of July, and the like), not much thought is given to social and political realities of the past. Issues that define urban life today such as economic opportunity, affordable housing, crime and public safety, recreation, or public health were also part of city life in ancient times. City planning considerations such as land use, environmental concerns, water distribution, road construction, and sewer and garbage disposal are facts of municipal life that occupy each generation's attention. Strange as it may seem to people today, these represent many of the same realities that shaped life before the Scriptures as we know them today were penned.

If there is any one characteristic that typifies the city, it is its plural nature. As far back in Western culture as the writings of Aristotle reveal in his *Politics*, the urban context was noted for its diversity: "a city is composed of different kinds of men; similar people cannot bring a city into existence."[4] Although the diversity and complexity of the city's plural nature are often perceived as problematic or challenging for those unaccustomed to city life, it is the thesis of this chapter that throughout the Scripture and Christian history, God's presence is often revealed in the midst of urban diversity. In *looking back* in order to *move forward*, we shall examine six aspects of the plural dimension of city life that reveal divine presence and the indivisibility of urban from Christian ministry. These aspects will be examined under the following categories: *the city as sacred place; urbanism by the numbers; urban politics and group dynamics; the urban impact of culture and language; class and cultural stratification;* and *the city in church history.*

Looking Back: The City as Sacred Place

The notion of the "Holy City" did not originate with Jerusalem. Long before the "City of David" gained its popularity in this regard, the idea of particular geographic locations having special religious significance was well established in human history. Yet, the prevailing stereotype of the city found in many churches and in the academy regards the city as a secular and impersonal domain. This understanding of the city, argued Harvey Cox, was forged by the forces of technology and the postmodern and impersonal values it engendered that replaced the sacred and made cities essentially secular:

> Secularization simply bypasses and undercuts religion and goes on to other things. It has relativized religious world views and thus rendered them innocuous. Religion has been privatized. It has been accepted as the peculiar prerogative and point of view of a particular person or group. . . . The gods of traditional religions live on as private fetishes or the patrons of congenial groups, but they play no significant role in the public life of the secular metropolis.[5]

Not only did the role of religion in the city become culturally insignificant in this view, the urban context transformed into an environment marked by bureaucracy and a lack of valued relationships as well:

> Urbanization means a structure of common life in which the diversity and the disintegration of tradition are paramount. It means an impersonality in which functional relationships multiply. It means that a degree of tolerance and

anonymity replace traditional moral sanctions and long-term acquaintance-ships. The urban center is the place of human control, of rational planning, of bureaucratic organization. . . . The technological metropolis provides the indis-pensable social setting for a world where the grip of traditional religions is loos-ened, for what we have called a secular style.[6]

John Inge and Edward Casey are among those who argue that this perspec-tive is not only dehumanizing, but also that its high regard for science and technology undermines the continuing importance of particularity in human experience and, more pointedly, of the religious significance of special places.[7] In this connection, Inge suggests that it is the divine-human encounter in a particular geographic setting that identifies a specific place as sacred:

God relates to people in place, and the places are not irrelevant to that rela-tionship but, rather, are integral to divine human encounter. . . . It is not that some places are intrinsically holy, but that this self-revelation on the part of God is then built into their story.[8]

Looking back to recover what has been forgotten concerning the role of the city in human relationships, we find that it was the interplay of human social organization and quests to fathom the divine that gave rise to critical roles of cul-ture, economics, and political development that defined the city as a place where God could be found. Several writers[9] have documented the intimate power relations that defined the role of worship as a means of social organization and political development of the city. As such, religion, social organization, and civil administration have been intertwined components of what we have come to call the city since its inception. More specifically, the city started as the gath-ering place for a community experience of the divine-human encounter.

Lewis Mumford suggested the origin of the city reaches as far back as the Paleolithic era, during which human beings gathered together in or around caves as worship sites. According to Mumford, "The Paleolithic cave brings to mind many other venerable shrines that likewise embodied sacred properties and powers, and drew people from afar into their precincts: great stones, sacred groves, monumental trees, holy wells."[10] Mumford identifies the beginnings of the city as the gathering of the ancient clans and their various tribal units around the family cult deity:

The first germ of the city, then, is in the ceremonial meeting place that serves as the goal for pilgrimage: a site to which family or clan groups are drawn back, at sea-sonable intervals, because it concentrates, in addition to any natural advantages it may have, certain "spiritual" or supernatural powers, powers of higher potency and greater duration, of wider cosmic significance, than the ordinary processes of life. And though the human performances may be occasional and temporary, the struc-ture that supports it, whether a Paleolithic grotto or a Mayan ceremonial center with its lofty pyramid, will be endowed with a more lasting cosmic image.[11]

As early as 4000 BCE, human beings self-identified not so much as a family (as would later be the case with "the children of Israel"), but more as those related to or connected to particular sites of gathering or urban areas or shrines.[12] Each city was defined by its own deity. There was no such thing as distinct spheres of the sacred and the secular. The functions of worship leadership and civil administration had not yet been separated, and social organization was structured along the lines of city-state arrangements that were supported by religious underpinnings:

> At the heart of power's expression in the city-state was its religious role. The temple was central to the life of these cities. . . . "Every feature . . . revealed the belief that man was created for no other purpose than to magnify and serve his gods. That was the city's ultimate reason for existence" (Mumford 1961:74-75). Citizenship was defined in terms of service to the gods. Family, agriculture, and economy were bound together by their religious commitment to the local gods in a seamless experience of everyday life.[13]

These shrine sites, in which divine-human interaction in worship was revered, served as central gathering places and as nodes facilitating all manner of social, economic, and political contact. They became the destination of religious pilgrimages. In scripture, several such sites are mentioned in Israel's early history and are notable for their significant roles in that people's self-understanding, including Bethel (Genesis 28:19; 35:14-15); Shiloh (Joshua 18:1; 21:2); Mizpah (1 Samuel 7:5-6); Gilgal (1 Samuel 7:16); and Ramah (1 Samuel 7:17).

Social organization was centralized within the ancient city, and its worship site, to which surrounding areas of hinterlands would give their allegiance. This model would eventually be evidenced far beyond its cultural cradle in the northeast area of Africa and the greater Mesopotamian region, but would also be representative in cities such as Mohenjo Daro and Harappa in the Indus Valley of present-day Pakistan as well as the cities of Anyang and Zhengzhou in the Huang-Ho Valley of China.[14] In the beginning, however, the city was more the self-contained city-state model.

Ancient cities often were identified with myths or cults that shaped city life, explaining its origins, social structure, economic or political functions, and the personality of the city. In describing the social, political, and economic organization, including class stratification that characterized ancient cities, Cheikh Anta Diop described the role occupied by the ruling class in ancient European culture, the *Eupatridae*, whose power included religious, economic, and civil authority:

> This first class is that of the "haves." From the very beginning, property had a divine character and only members of this class could possess the land in the sacred sense of the term. They alone, having ancestors, could have a domestic cult and a god, without which one had no political, judicial, or religious

personality and was thus "impure," a plebeian. They alone knew the sacred rites, the prayers which for a long time had remained unwritten and were transmitted orally from father to son.[15]

This situation is also reflected in the ancestral stories of Genesis. One such example is the narrative about Rachel's pilfering the domestic gods of her father, Laban, when she, husband Jacob, and their family initiated their escape from her father's household and property to return to Jacob's homeland (Genesis 31:19-35). Religious belief was a critical factor in ancient social organization and in city life, defining who held power and authority as well as property rights. Diop goes on to discuss how lower social classes of these city-states, the *plebs* of Europe or the *untouchables* in India, constituted restricted groups, whose social location placed them not only on the margins of society, but also at the margins of or outside the city.[16] The urban ethos, therefore, involved the way people, regardless of their status in society, understood themselves to be in relationship socially, economically, politically, and religiously. Whatever else the city might provide for its residents, it also was the place that symbolized the presence of the divine.

It is against this backdrop that we can better see how the city of Jerusalem came to occupy its central role in ancient Israel's articulation of its faith in God. Once he became king, David's zeal to reorganize the social, civil, and military structure of Israel around the city of Jerusalem was adroitly orchestrated within the religious heritage of the nation. With great pomp and pageantry, he brought the ark of the covenant, the religious symbol from the days of Israel's tribal confederacy, to be housed in the new administrative capital of his monarchy, Jerusalem (2 Samuel 6). The capstone of his military and civil leadership of the nation was intimately defined and interwoven with its religious heritage, thereby giving his reign not only military and police authority, but also moral and religious respectability with the official establishment of the state religion headquartered in "David's City." The seeds of a "royal theology"[17] were sown. The Davidic dynasty's influence on the theological outlook of Israel's self-perception and expression of its faith in God is seen in the poetic literature of the Psalter (examples include 2:6-9; 46:4-5; 48:1-3; 68:28-29; 87:1-3; 122:1-9; 125:1-2; 147:1-2, 12-14) and throughout the historical and prophetic writings of the Old Testament and in the New Testament that view the city of Jerusalem as symbolic of divine presence in the community of faith. The city was affirmed as a sacred place because God's presence was symbolized there, and this reality had implications for the nature of human relationships among its residents.

Looking Back: Urbanism by the Numbers

It is a well-documented fact that cities existed long before the time of Jesus, and at the time of his birth, there were numerous cities of significant size and influence guiding the culture in which he lived. It is assumed that Palestine and Galilee, where Jesus functioned as an itinerant preacher and healer, were culturally off the beaten track of the major seats of power and influence in the Roman Empire and, therefore, bore little resemblance to anything of urbanized society. This is a notion that is badly in need of reexamination if we are to grasp more precisely the significance of Jesus' ministry as it relates to the culture of the city.

In its initial stages, Christianity was a basically urban phenomenon.[18] Rodney Stark, a sociologist who analyzes the rise of Christianity from an obscure sect in the Roman Empire to the imperial religion in three centuries, examines many factors that set the stage for this relatively swift and profound religious shift. In doing so, like other observers with kindred interests,[19] Stark found that the intensely cosmopolitan context of Hellenistic culture within the Roman Empire as reflected in its cities was a major sociological factor definitely contributing to the spread of Christianity. The sheer number of metropolises of significant size and the excellent means of travel and communication among them were a prominent factors. Drawing on the work of other researchers, Stark identified twenty-two ancient cities and posited conservative population estimates for each. He included Athens, although by the time the message of Jesus was circulating among various cities of the empire, its population had been in decline for many years. Listed below (chart 3) are ten of the cities referenced within the Scriptures, along with their estimated populations during the first century and comparisons of U.S. cities with their 2003 population figures.

Chart 3: Population Figures of Biblical Cities & U.S. Cities[20]

	Biblical City	Population	U.S. City	2003 Population
1.	Rome	650,000–1,000,000	Detroit, MI San Francisco, CA	911,402 751,682
2.	Alexandria	400,000	Atlanta, GA	423,019
3.	Ephesus	200,000	Richmond, VA	194,729
4.	Antioch	150,000	Dayton, OH	161,696
5.	Sardis	100,000	Cambridge, MA	101,587
6.	Corinth	100,000	Trenton, NJ	85,314
7.	Smyrna	75,000	Silver Spring, MD	76,540
8.	Damascus	45,000	Concord, NH	41,823
9.	Salamis	35,000	Jefferson City, MO	37,550
10.	Athens	30,000	Wheeling, WV	31,429

From the figures in chart 3, one is able to gain some appreciation of the urbanized environment in which the earthly ministry of Jesus took place. In terms of sheer numbers, the metropolitan nature of the context in which Christianity was born is not unlike most cities today. The highly organized, economic, political, multicultural, and urban setting of the Roman Empire—the culture into which Jesus was born and lived—is an essential factor in shaping Christian history. Any attempt, therefore, to engage in urban ministry that does not understand the intimate relationship of the divine within the mundane realities of the urban context will surely miss the point of the gospel story and its relevance for cosmopolitan situations.

The Bible is very much rooted in the urban setting and has numerous references to large cities of antiquity including Babylon, Nineveh, Susa, and ancient Rome. Robert Linthicum has pointed out that cities antedated as well as existed during the era that framed the biblical period. Indeed, Linthicum suggests some were larger during the time of Jesus of Nazareth and the apostle Paul than they would be for another thirteen centuries following this period.[21] Linthicum states that

> when Abraham migrated from Ur (approximately 2000 B.C.), that city had a population of 250,000 people. . . . Nineveh was so large, it took three days for Jonah to cross it on foot. . . . Babylon has eleven miles of walls and a water irrigation system. . . . (At the time of Christ) Rome had more than a million people . . . 46,000 tenement houses with many 8–10 stories high. Its streets were so crowded that wheeled traffic was banned during the day. . . . Ephesus had nightlights (and) Antioch had 16 miles of colonnaded streets.[22]

Some of the Bible's most vivid examples of God's intervention on behalf of the oppressed took place in urban centers. Moses began his long liberating and teaching ministry in the seat of ancient Egyptian power by confronting the pharaoh. Isaiah and Jeremiah saw the focus of their ministries directed toward their nation's administrative capital, Jerusalem. Nehemiah was a city planner and community organizer. According to scripture, Daniel was appointed by Nebuchadnezzar to be chief of the nation's administration, hardly a task that could be done in isolation from the city.

Although the bulk of Jesus' ministry was focused in and around places such as Cana in Galilee (John 2:1), Capernaum (Mark 1:21), the district of Tyre and Sidon (Matthew 15:21), or the villages of Caesarea Philippi (Mark 8:27), it is a misperception to construe these as exclusively nonurban regions. Several writers have called into question our twenty-first-century understandings of urbanization and how these have been projected back in time onto people and places of another era, during which notions of social organization and land use were interpreted differently. The definition of exactly what constitutes an urban area has changed over time and even today varies greatly:

Some national statistics, such as Iceland's, will consider settlements with a population of a few hundred as urban; others will set various minimum levels: 1,500 (Ireland), 10,000 (Malaysia). Some add extra criteria . . . the majority of inhabitants depending on nonagricultural activities, population densities within a given land area, existence of municipal government, etc. The U.S. defines "urbanized areas" as being the fully developed area of a city . . . and the adjacent built-up areas with a minimum population of 50,000.[23]

Even by these standards, it would appear that our perceptions concerning the population density of the regions where Jesus spent most of his days on earth in the flesh are far too modest and should probably be reevaluated. Some researchers have taken the time to address this misperception. According to one writer, the province of Galilee included "an area of about 750 square miles [and] supported a population of about 200,000 during the reign of Herod Antipas."[24] Indeed, it has been argued that this general area was one of the more highly populated areas of the Roman Empire:

In lower Galilee, a geographical zone roughly fifteen by twenty-five miles, we enter "one of the most densely populated regions of the entire Roman Empire" . . . Through this area Roman road systems ran, placing lower Galilee at the center of trade and travel in the entire region.[25]

In the writings of the ancient Jewish historian Josephus, there is also some indication that Galilee reflected much more of an urbanized character than is generally appreciated: "The cities lie very thick and the very many villages that are here are everywhere so full of people by the richness of their soil that the very least of them contained about 15,000 inhabitants."[26] While these population figures have been questioned,[27] the point remains that the region probably reflected urban realities to a much higher degree than has been typically acknowledged.

Using Antioch as an example of the urbanization that characterized the first century of nascent Christian growth when Paul began to write letters to young churches in various cities of the Roman Empire, Stark described the spatial and social realities of this city as representative of urban challenges that bedevil many a twenty-first-century metropolis. According to Stark, problematic issues such as overcrowded and cramped living spaces, crime, pollution, poverty, fierce competition for economic survival, and a highly diverse, if economically stratified, society were found in Antioch of the first century:

When founded in about 300 B.C.E., its walls enclosed slightly less than one square mile, laid out along a southwest-to-northeast axis. Eventually Antioch grew to be about two miles long and about one mile wide. . . . Like many Greco-Roman cities, Antioch was small in area because it was initially founded as a fortress. . . . Once the walls were up, it was very expensive to expand.

Within so small an area, it is astonishing that the city's population was as large as it was: at the end of the first century Antioch had a total population of about 150,000. . . . This population total applies to inhabitants of the city proper—those living within, or perhaps immediately against its walls. . . . Given this population and the area of the city, it is easily calculated that the population density of Antioch was roughly 75,000 inhabitants per square mile or 117 per acre. As a comparison, in Chicago today [1996]: there are 21 inhabitants per acre; San Francisco has 23, and New York City overall has 37. Even Manhattan Island has only 100 inhabitants per acre—and keep in mind that Manhattanites are very spread out vertically, while ancient cities crammed their populations into structures that seldom rose above five stories. . . . Keep in mind too that modern New Yorkers do not share their space with livestock, nor are their streets fouled by horse and oxen traffic. . . . Within these tenements, the crowding was extreme.[28]

Stark goes on to emphasize other realities that accompanied such cramped conditions in Greco-Roman tenements such as the absence of furnaces, fireplaces, or indoor plumbing. Cooking was done over wood or charcoal braziers, which served as sources of heat, but also were the cause of rapidly spreading fires. Although Stark understands the impressiveness of certain conveniences of the period frequently noted among historians, he also notes that sanitation, under these living conditions, inevitably proved to be a serious issue:

Aqueducts are, of course, often mentioned, as are the public baths and the public latrines often constructed next to the baths. It is all well and good to admire the Romans for [these accomplishments], but we must not fail to see the obvious fact that the human and animal density of ancient cities would place an incredible burden even on modern sewerage, garbage disposal, and water systems. Keep in mind too that there was no soap. Hence it is self-evident that, given the technological capacities of the time, the Greco-Roman city and its inhabitants must have been extremely filthy.[29]

Many of the spatial and social realities that typify many modern urban contexts of ministry have their counterparts in the spatial and social realities that form the background of many portions of the scriptural witness.

The pervasive notion that the origins of the gospel were framed almost exclusively in bucolic settings finds little support from numerical realities of these ancient cities. Although scripture has many examples of the "voice of God" being discerned in nonurban settings, the sheer numbers and often cramped living conditions of the urbanized world in which the early church emerged attest to the reality that God is also revealed in the crowded and noisy diversity that is the urban context. That scripture records the birth of Jesus taking place in an urban setting so jammed with people that he who was ultimately to be revealed as *the Savior of the world* initiated his earthly sojourn as a homeless infant underscores the reality of what God can do in the midst of the crowded city.

Looking Back: Urban Politics and Group Dynamics

The plural nature of urbanization inevitably forces upon society the realities of power politics wherein various groups contend and negotiate competing interests. Even the most cursory examination of the context in which Jesus' ministry took place reveals a cultural and religious context that typifies tensions prompted by the diversity of urban arenas today. For early believers in Jesus Christ, however, the contexts of politics and group dynamics were ultimately reinterpreted to be a human stage upon which they would dramatize the healing and sustaining presence of God in the midst of challenge.

The Gospel of Luke gives special attention to the sociopolitical realities typically influencing the ebb and flow of urban life of the day. For example, in discussing Jesus' birth, Luke identifies the event with references concerning various civil administrations of the era: Jesus was born when a census had been ordered by Emperor Augustus (Luke 2:1) and when "Quirinius was governor of Syria" (Luke 2:2). The beginning of John the Baptist's ministry is similarly recorded with language that calls attention to particular civil and religious administrative authorities: "In the fifteenth year of *the reign of Emperor Tiberius* [14–37 CE], *when Pontius Pilate was governor of Judea, and Herod was ruler of Galilee, and his brother Philip ruler of the region of Ituraea and Trachonitis, and Lysanias ruler of Abilene, during the high priesthood of Annas and Caiaphas,* the word of God came to John son of Zechariah in the wilderness" (Luke 3:1-2, emphasis added).[30]

Palestine was heavily caught up in the urbanized web of economic, social, political, and religious forces spawned by its locus as a nexus point along important trade routes connecting Africa with Arabia and Asia in the Mesopotamian terrain. This fact accounted for its long history of tension and conflict as various superpowers vied for its control. For centuries, a succession of empires ruled Palestine following the collapse of the divided kingdoms of Israel (721 BCE) and Judah (587 BCE). Over time, the region took on its distinction as a hotbed of civil resistance owing to the stubborn adherence of Jewish theocratic leadership to their monotheistic religious rituals. As far back as 331 BCE, when Alexander conquered Syria and took control of the area as part of his ambitious scheme to "unify the world" through the spread of Hellenistic culture and language, such ideas were not universally welcomed in Palestine. After the great conqueror's death, Palestinian resistance to the colonizing practices of foreign powers eventually reached its peak under the orchestration of a devout family of Jewish insurgents who became known as the Maccabees (hammer). Anchoring their activities in Jerusalem, the region gained a century of relative religious and political independence until, in

63 BCE, the Romans, under Pompey, intervened and essentially set up their own puppet leaders for the region, including Herod (74 BCE–4 CE). By the time Jesus came along, political and social tensions in the area were quite intense. The weight of political and economic oppression and taxation, combined with the overlay of hellenizing cultural pressures, spawned many pockets of religious and cultural resistance in the Jewish community. These pockets included groups such the radical Zealots, the Pharisees, the aristocratic and conservative Sadducees, and the more withdrawn Essenes. While the differences between them were substantial, their unifying core involved their fundamental resistance to religious syncretism. It is into this political, cultural, and religious setting that Jesus was born and reared.

In their video titled *Portrait of a Radical: The Jesus Movement*, theologians Huston Smith, Richard Rohr, and Allen Dwight Callahan describe the ministry of Jesus as much more practical, countercultural, and antiestablishment in its focus than most aspects of Christian tradition typically suggest. Behind the vague and spiritualized divine figure of Christian tradition, they see a very practical and human Jesus, whose earthly ministry focused on helping people understand that God was much more accessible, less threatening, and affirming of the human spirit than legalistic religious rituals of the day implied. In stating their thesis they summarize, in sharp relief, the underbelly of urbanized political realities that exploited the poor, both urban and rural, and set the stage for widespread popular acceptance of Jesus' ministry:

> With Roman imperialism, there were a lot of big cities with wealth concentrated in urban areas. . . . [This] produced a drain on the countryside [and exerted pressure] on agrarian areas to produce more and more surplus to pay for theaters they could not attend, games and amusements they could not afford, and palaces they did not live in. . . . [Religiously,] debt and purity codes . . . controlled the behavior of the people. . . . There was complaint that the Temple Code and priestly establishment no longer represented the interests of the people and [that priests] were enriching themselves at the people's expense. By the time that Jesus came . . . ninety-percent of the economy of Jerusalem had to do with the buying and selling of animals, panning of animals, the butchering of animals by priests, and the hauling of the animals out by the tens of thousands after every feast-day. . . . The priestly establishment, according to Mosaic law, "got their cut" right off the top: ten percent. On top of that, there was taxation by secular authorities. . . . None of those tiers of government were interested in anything but taking things from the people. So the people were looking for a way out; they were looking for God to do something.[31]

Jesus' ministry struck a chord with the political, social, and spiritual restlessness of his era. His teachings were not based on musings about fine points of law or philosophy or other concepts borne of high attainment in formal education. Rather, Jesus spoke the language of ordinary people and based his teachings on the typical experiences of common people. His teachings clearly reveal more of an intimacy with the masses of poor and working-class people struggling to survive oppressive circumstances characteristic of urban culture than is usually recognized. According to one analysis, the range of topics addressed in Jesus' teachings definitely bears the stamp of situations, issues, and institutions that are quite characteristic of the city. These include court systems, policing, and prisons (Matthew 5:25); city market squares (Matthew 23:7; Mark 12:38), financial analogies built on interest-bearing accounts (Matthew 25:27; Luke 19:23), descriptions of absentee landlord behavior (Mark 12:1-12), situations involving military personnel (Matthew 8:5), desperation caused by bad health, poverty, and anonymity (Mark 5:25-26; Luke 8:43-44), and bureaucratic tax collectors (Matthew 9:10; Luke 5:27).[32]

Following the Resurrection, the witness of the first believers became essentially lodged in cities owing to the religious, social, and political circumstances of the cradle into which the church was born. Christianity began in Jerusalem as no more than a family squabble among contending factions within Judaism. Church historian Justo González summarized the origins of the faith in this way:

> The earliest Christians did not consider themselves followers of a new religion. All their lives they had been Jews, and they still were. This was true of Peter and the twelve (Mark 3), of the seven (Acts 6), and of Paul (Acts 9). Their faith was not a denial of Judaism, but was rather the conviction that the Messianic age had finally arrived. Paul would say that he was persecuted "because of the hope of Israel" (Acts 28:20). The earliest Christians did not reject Judaism, but were convinced that their faith was the fulfillment of the age-long expectation of a Messiah. That was why Christians in Jerusalem continued keeping the Sabbath and attending worship at the Temple.[33]

It was the initial success of the apostles' ministry in Jerusalem that fomented the perceived threat to local civil and religious power brokers and forced public policy decisions that had violent outcomes and prompted immigration to other areas. With the apostles gaining new converts and evidences of healing among the sick, the situation was proving problematic for the religious leaders. The apostles' activities bore classic signs of community organization efforts growing out of residual political and theological problems related to the recently crucified Jesus of Nazareth (Acts 3). From the perspective of Jerusalem's religious leadership, this emerging "new wing" within Judaism was not only heretical, but also clearly evangelistic. When the boldness of these working-class and uneducated men in promoting their ideas (Acts 4:13) did not yield to intimidating threats or incarceration alone, the religious and political establishment responded swiftly, first, with the execution of Stephen and, second, with severe persecution of anyone associated with this seditious group (Acts 6–8). As a result, the increasing numbers of converts to the new way were forced to leave Jerusalem, seeking refuge in other cities where synagogues could be found whose leadership, hopefully, was less hostile than in Jerusalem. Thus, in the earliest days of Christianity, whenever the believers went to a new area, they always sought out a synagogue to begin their activities.

Rather than squelching this new interpretation of faith, the machinations of power politics and group dynamics fostered by hostile religious and political leaders actually promoted the spread of early Christianity. Among the first believers, the urban challenges of politics and intergroup dynamics, far from being a hindrance to faith, proved to be a catalyst to the proclamation of the gospel. If Acts 2 reveals nothing else about the early church, it exposes a people who clearly perceived difference and diversity as powerful manifestations of the presence of God in their midst, manifestations that they were determined to share with others. Once again, the city was the place where God was found and God's presence proclaimed.

Looking Back: The Urban Impact of Culture and Language

Cultural resistance to change is a huge factor supporting the misperception that urban ministry is something other than Christian ministry. Long-established traditions, even when they have little remaining social significance, are usually relinquished with great difficulty. This is one of the major reasons individuals or families new to the urban context find it easier to become accustomed to its variety by first locating themselves within communities of similar constituencies and values as themselves. From this base within the culturally or ethnically familiar, it is easier to interface with wider and much more varied urban cultural reality. Yet, in the competing mix of cultures, ethnic groups, religious beliefs, and economic strata that comprise city life, change is inevitable. Cross-fertilization of ideas and values is intrinsic to negotiating the social, political, and economic variety of the city.

From its very inception, the plural nature of the urban community affected the culture and even the language used to express faith in Jesus Christ. In fact, the embrace of new ways of relating to one another and the means of sharing the gospel quickly became a distinguishing characteristic of the early church. As the early believers scattered from Jerusalem to other areas, even when seeking out synagogues in these areas, use of the Greek language became more prevalent. The Hellenistic culture of the Roman Empire had some influential effects on the millions of Jews living throughout its environs; Aramaic, the language used by Jesus in the Palestinian subculture in which he matriculated, became less common, particularly outside that context. By the time the apostle Paul began writing his letters (the oldest documents of the New Testament) to the scattered and growing numbers of the faithful in different cities, it is not surprising that they were written in Greek. Paul was clearly one of the Hellenistic Jews. He was a Roman citizen, he wrote in fluent Greek, and, when quoting from the Scriptures, he used only the Septuagint, the Greek translation of the Hebrew text. Although there has been some suggestion that certain New Testament writings originated in Aramaic prior to being translated into Greek,[34] all the earliest canonical books extant from church history were penned in Greek, including the synoptic Gospels of Mark, Matthew, and Luke.

Roman imperialism illustrated another aspect of urban diversity that impacted the origins of the Christian faith and its openness to others previously outside its original religious, cultural, and ethnic base. With its military and economic grip controlling Palestine, Roman imperialism also brought with it a measure of greater travel facility with less threat from marauding bandits by land or pirates by sea. This enabled easier connection and communication with other areas via the overlay of Hellenistic culture that encouraged use of Greek as the preferred connecting language among the various other cultures and languages under Roman control. While both Latin and Greek were spoken throughout the empire, it was the latter that proved to be the language of commerce. Therefore, the spread of the gospel message was facilitated among masses of people simply by virtue of ordinary economic or social interaction rather than exclusively through targeted evangelistic activity:

> The missionary task itself was undertaken, not only by Paul and others whose names are known—Barnabas, Mark, et al.—but also by countless and nameless Christians who went from place to place taking with them their faith and their witness. Some of these, like Paul, traveled as missionaries impelled by their faith. But mostly these nameless Christians were merchants, slaves, and others who traveled for various reasons, but whose travel provided the opportunity for the expansion of the Christian message.[35]

Stark is representative of a group of scholars[36] who suggest that most traditional assessments of the rise of early Christianity greatly undervalue the response of the hellenized Jews to the gospel in spite of the eventual death of the early church in Jerusalem and the destruction of Jerusalem by Rome CE 66–70. Indeed, Stark argues that this segment of the Roman Empire's Jewish Diaspora may have accounted for a significant portion of the earliest respondents to the gospel. He also stresses that not all of the earliest Christians, especially among its hellenized Jewish converts, were among the lower economic classes:

> It is important to keep in mind how greatly the Hellenized Jews of the diaspora outnumbered the Jews living in Palestine. . . . [Some estimates place] the population of the diaspora at five to six million. It is also worth noting that the Hellenized Jews were primarily urban—as were the early Christians outside Palestine. Finally, the Hellenized Jews were not an impoverished minority; they

had been drawn out from Palestine over the centuries because of economic opportunities. By the first century, the large Jewish sections in major centers such as Alexandria were known for their wealth. As they built up wealthy and populous urban communities within the major centers of the empire, Jews had adjusted to life in the diaspora in a way that made them very marginal vis-à-vis the Judaism of Jerusalem.[37]

Although there was an obvious ethnic and religious connection among Jews within the social and political structures of urban environments both in Palestine and throughout the Diaspora, what started out as a dispute within Judaism related to the activities of Jesus of Nazareth and claims among his followers about his resurrection eventually would result in complete rupture into separate religions. The religious argument soon moved out of its religious origins and took on cultural, social, and political aspects of its metropolitan context. That which began as a dispute "primarily among groups of Jews, those who kept the customs and language of their ancestors, and those who [in light of the Resurrection] showed more openness to Hellenistic influences,"[38] would widen, with the latter group embracing more and more non-Jews. In Acts 6:1-6, all seven men appointed to help the apostles in the early church were Jews with Greek names. Within a century after the Resurrection, leadership among Christians would be almost entirely among those of non-Jewish birth. These realities did not occur in a spiritual vacuum. Clearly, the impact of culture and language had its influence upon the spread of the gospel and framed the early Christian movement as, in fact, an urban phenomenon.

Looking Back: Class and Cultural Stratification

Another urban reality that typified both Jesus' ministry and the early days of Christianity was the class stratification of the wider society and its related issues of political oppression. Although there were certainly exceptions (Jarius in Mark 5:22; Joanna in Luke 8:3; a Roman military officer in Matthew 8:5; Zacchaeus in Luke 19:1-9; Nicodemus in John 3:1; Joseph of Arimathea in Mark 15:42-43; Lydia in Acts 16:14-15, and so forth), the first respondents to the gospel message were overwhelmingly drawn from those on the economic, social, political, and public health fringes. The Scriptures note this at various points (Matthew 3:4; Mark 1:6; Luke 1:46-52; Acts 4:13; 1 Corinthians 1:26-29). Indeed, after the inglorious death of Jesus, the humanly inexplicable Resurrection event, followed by the post-Ascension faith of the irrepressible disciples, the growth of the early church was remarkable, in spite of growing public hostility toward its new converts. The fortunes of new believers worsened amid growing public hostilities within the empire.

In 64 CE, a terrible fire raged through the imperial city of Rome, destroying much of it. The unpopular Roman emperor Nero chose to use Christians as political scapegoats for this tragedy in an effort to deflect negative public attention away from himself. Rumors suggested that he had ordered sections of the city torched. An unprecedented era of torture and persecution was initiated against the Christians, owing to their social vulnerability and relatively low status in the city. It is during this era of Nero-spawned persecutions that the apostles Peter and Paul are believed to have been executed. This era of persecution lasted for centuries but was not universal throughout the empire or uniform in its severity. It reflected, nonetheless, the social and political vulnerability of the early Christians. González described the political and social vulnerability of confessing Christians when brought before the governor of the Roman province of Bithynia, Pliny the Younger, in 111 CE:

> When somebody sent the new governor a list of Christians, Pliny began inquiries, for he knew that this religion was illegal. The governor had the accused brought before him, and thus began learning of the beliefs and practices of Christians. Many declared that they were not Christians, and others said that, although they had followed the new faith for a time, they had abandoned it. Of these Pliny required only that they pray to the [Roman] gods, burn incense before the image of the emperor, and curse Christ, something that he had heard true Christians would never do. Once they performed these rites, he simply let them go. . . . Those who persisted in their faith were executed not so much for being Christians, as for their obstinacy. If they were Roman citizens, he had them sent to Rome, as the law required.[39]

Class bias along with religious bigotry formed another element of prejudice against the early Christians among the social and intellectual elites of the Roman Empire:

> Although [the social and political elite] attacked Christianity on numerous counts, this criticism boiled down to a main point: Christians were an ignorant lot whose doctrines, although preached under a cloak of wisdom, were foolish and even self-contradictory. This seems to have been a common attitude among the cultured aristocracy, for whom Christians were a despicable rabble. . . . Their main objection was that Christianity was a religion of barbarians who derived their teaching, not from Greeks or Romans, but from Jews, a primitive people. . . . As to Jesus, it should suffice to remember that he was a criminal condemned by Roman authorities.[40]

It was during these oppressive times of political and social vulnerability, when it was illegal to discuss matters of faith and ethical behavior openly in language and religious patterns that did not conform to the prevailing religious practices of the day, that the teachings of the Christian faith began to be crystallized. The writings of many church leaders who themselves were martyred during this period (Ignatius, bishop of Antioch, condemned c. 107; Polycarp, bishop of Smyrna, c. 155; Justin Martyr, c. 165, to name but a few) laid the foundation for an understanding of God upon which Christian theology would eventually be framed. It was from the midst of this type of cultural, social, and economic oppression, all located in the press of urban politics and power, that the tenets of the Christian faith were born.

It should be noted, however, that while assessments over time generally interpret the earliest respondents to the gospel as being from among the more-marginalized elements of the Roman Empire, there is also a school of thought that posits the early church was more socially and economically diverse.[41] Wayne Meeks, who is of this opinion, argues that it is not possible for people today to understand the major differences between contemporary society and the social structure of the Roman Empire. Current social descriptions such as "lower middle class" or "middle class" have no relevance to the hierarchical culture of the first century CE, wherein society was stratified in keeping with "household codes" of male patriarchy that determined the social privileges of women, children, servants, and slaves within the household[42] and in society at large.[43] In keeping with such observations, it is argued by Meeks and others[44] that the profound success of Christianity in moving from obscurity and oppression to acceptance and legalization in a relatively short time frame could not have been achieved without the participation of some of the more socially and economically influential elements of society. Indeed, E. A. Judge concluded:

> Far from being a socially depressed group, then, . . . the Christians were dominated by a socially pretentious section of the population of big cities. Beyond that they seem to have drawn on a broad constituency, probably representing the household dependents of leading members.[45]

Whether primarily drawn from the margins of society or inclusive of more plural social strata reflecting the broader range of constituents in the cities of the empire, the fact is that converts, in spite of the tremendous odds, were brought into the Christian fold. As time went on, circumstances required early church leaders to address the issues of new converts in their gatherings in distant places. More and more, gatherings (*ecclesia*) were being ostracized from the synagogues in these urban centers and tended to include non-Jews. This reality prompted the emergence of several letters that were written to congregations in these major urban centers, such as Rome, Corinth, Ephesus, Philippi, Colossae, and Thessalonica, and their eventual inclusion in what has become the New Testament. The urban plurality of the New Testament, in terms of the various ethnicities, and economic strata as well as the numbers of cities represented in the canon, essentially defines the intrinsic unity of urban and Christian ministry as one.

Looking Back: The City in Church History

It is difficult to escape the fact that most of postbiblical church history has been shaped in the spiritual crucible of city economics, culture, education, social life, and politics and has been profoundly influenced by those on the sociopolitical margins. Believers in Jesus Christ, in an effort to respond to the practical issues of life involving survival and human relationships, attempted by various means to share the gospel as best they could given the realities of their often precarious context. Various social and political challenges gave rise to theological questions that had to be addressed. In the first three hundred years of church history, all manner of social and political challenges arose, growing out of the illegal nature of Christianity at the time and, especially during the end of the first and second centuries, the persecution of the believers and resultant martyrdom of many.

Prominent heretical beliefs associated with the faith arose. Notable among them was the challenge of Gnosticism (from the Greek for "knowledge"), which, in effect, denied the physical incarnation of Christ, viewing as it did all creation as fundamentally evil and, therefore, could not conceive of the Savior as physically part of the corrupted material world. Closely associated with it was an interpretation of Jesus' life called Docetism (from the Greek for "to seem"), asserting that Jesus only "seemed to be" human, but really was not. There was also a very serious heretical challenge posed by an anti-Semitic believer named Marcion, who in 144 CE went to Rome and gathered a following that became quite substantial and whose teachings held sway in certain quarters for centuries.[46] While it is not the purpose of this study to fully document his or any of these early heretical teachings, the story of Marcion and the movement he spawned is reflective of the competing nature of urban diversity and group dynamics that gave rise to our understanding of Christianity. Marcion, a member of one of the churches in Rome, sought to convince church leaders that the Old Testament was at variance with what he perceived as the undiluted truth about Christ. His disdain for Judaism led him to such extremes as the denial of the bodily birth of Jesus as the son of a Jewish mother, Mary (Marcion claimed that Jesus simply appeared as a grown man), and repudiation of the Septuagint (the Greek version of the Hebrew Scriptures, commonly used in the early church) as authoritative in matters of faith. Marcion's views were rejected by church leaders, and he was excommunicated, but this did not restrain his focus. Instead, he compiled a new list of books he felt should replace Hebrew Scriptures, including only his amended version of Luke's Gospel and ten of the epistles written by Paul. In his version of the Scriptures, all references to Judaism or to the Hebrew Scriptures were deleted.[47]

The challenge posed by Marcion is significant primarily because of its emergence as one of the competing religious philosophies in the diversity of the urban culture within which Christianity developed. Until Marcion, various churches generally appealed to the Septuagint as the authoritative source of scripture along with one or more of the various Gospels and a certain few epistles, particularly those of Paul. Once Marcion began spreading his own version of the Scriptures and an alternate understanding of the faith, one that attracted substantial response in the urbanized and plural culture of the day, Christian leaders needed to respond. It was at this time that churches started informally assembling a list of sacred Christian writings by consensus in response to Marcion.[48] These urban-based events were catalytic in prompting the long process that would eventually lead to creation of the Christian canon as we know it today and stand as testimony to the inherent inseparability of urban and Christian ministry.

Early church leaders framed the nature of Christianity's early struggle to define and clarify the faith in a hostile social environment and produced theological tenets affirmed by the church today. These teachings were shaped by the cultural, political, ideological, and economic pluralism that constitutes city life. Among these early urban church leaders were Irenaeus (bishop of Lyons, 130–200), whose pastorate was critical to the refutation of early heresies; Origen (Alexandria, Caesarea, c. 185–c. 254), whose long and prolific career also countered popular heresies and broke new ground for the early church in biblical interpretation; Tertullian (Rome, Carthage, 160–225), regarded as the father of Latin theology/the Western wing of the church, whose strong witness against heresy laid the foundation for what eventually became the church's principle articulation of the Holy Trinity; Athanasius (Alexandria, 296–373): mocked as the "black dwarf,"[49] was the theological giant whose writings were eventually determinative in the church's understanding of Christology; and Augustine of Hippo (354–430), who, without question, was one of the most influential theological writers in the Christian church.

Throughout history, key elements of Christian doctrine have been forged out of the human interaction in the city. Indeed, articulation of the divinity of Jesus Christ, the very essence of the Christian faith, is an understanding of God that was borne in the context and political challenge of the urban context. For example, the emergence of the Nicene Creed in 325 CE, the first universally accepted statement of Christian faith, grew out of the peculiarly urban-based theological challenges and political tensions grounded in an urbanized culture. Let us briefly consider the urban, political, social, and ecclesiastical realities that produced this document.

Arius, a popular church leader from the city of Alexandria in Northern Africa, was teaching that Jesus was not equally God as the Father, but rather was the first of all creation. This was a position that was vigorously opposed by the Alexandrian bishop (Alexander), who relieved Arius of all ecclesiastical responsibilities. Supporters of Arius protested and even participated in public demonstrations on his behalf. What has become known as the "Arian controversy" soon began spreading throughout churches across the empire as Bishop Alexander and backers of Arius sought to advance their respective positions by gaining broader support from other areas, primarily in the Greek-speaking eastern sectors of the empire. Just after Christianity had gained legal recognition and freedom from political persecution, it seemed immediately threatened by rupture from within over doctrinal interpretation as church leaders in various urban centers took sides.

Against this background, the newly converted head of the state, the Christian emperor Constantine, decided to convene a meeting of Christian bishops from throughout the empire to settle the matter. As a result, in 325 CE the first ecumenical council of the Christian church was held in the city of Nicea, not far from Constantinople (now Istanbul in Turkey), with some three hundred bishops from Africa, Asia, and Europe gathered to settle a growing religious dispute that threatened serious schism within the church. It was out of this gathering that the Nicene Creed was fashioned, affirming the intrinsic unity (*homoousios*, Greek for "of one substance") of God the Father and God the Son:

> We believe in one God, the Father Almighty, maker of all things visible and invisible.
> And in one Lord Jesus Christ, the Son of God, the only-begotten of the Father, that is from the substance of the Father, God of God, light of light, true God of true God, begotten, not made, of one substance with the father, through whom all things were made, both in heaven and on earth, who for us humans and for our salvation descended and became incarnate, becoming human.[50]

Sadly, this did not end the controversy, which continued to fester amid political maneuvers in both the church and by the civil authorities for years. In 381 CE, a second ecumenical council was convened in the city of Constantinople to deal with the same issue, reaffirming the Nicene Creed. Challenges to it persisted on various grounds, yet another council was convened, this time in the city of Ephesus, in 431 CE, which also affirmed the actions originally taken in Nicea nearly a century earlier. It would be another twenty years before the matter would be broadly settled within Christianity with the convening of the Fourth Ecumenical Council, held in the city of Chalcedon in 451, which once again affirmed the Nicene Creed.

To suggest, therefore, that the city is somehow foreign to the Christian faith and that urban ministry is a relatively new concept in Christian mission or theological and ethical focus flies in the face of historical fact. Critical events throughout the history of the church have largely been framed against the backdrop of the city and the social, economic, ethnic, and political realities that define urban life in all its glory and tragedy. There were clearly periods of glorious "triumph," as in the conversion of Constantine, the ending of political persecution in the Roman Empire, and in his building a "new Rome" (Constantinople). There also were times of tragedy as in the regional, ethnic, cultural, and language-difference factors that lay below the surface of "theological" differences that ultimately led to the East-West split of the church in 1054 (Constantinople). Later, there was the tragic period of violence along with ethnic, cultural, and theological animosities that were fostered with religious blessing, as reflected in the centuries when "the Crusades" took place (1095–1270), with the city of Jerusalem and its environs figuring prominently. These were urban-related events. A new understanding of urban ministry must involve appreciation of the reality that God is at work in the city even in the midst of social conflict and the dynamics of power politics.

The sharp philosophical and theological scholasticism of Thomas Aquinas (1225–1274), which ultimately became the theological cornerstone of Roman Catholic theological exposition for centuries, was honed in the urban centers of Naples, Italy, and Paris, France. The act of an audacious priest (Martin Luther) in Wittenberg, Germany (1517), and the public ministry of John Calvin, the legal mind who authored the classic treatise on Protestant Christianity known as the *Institutes of the Christian Religion* (1536) and who served as city manager in Geneva, Switzerland, are both examples of urban ministry. Calvin's chief theological formulations anchored the Reformed traditions in Protestantism and were born in the everyday lived-in experience of urban politics. The condemnation of Galileo by the Roman Catholic Church for his Copernican theory took place in the city of Rome in 1633. In the later period that came to be known as the Age of Enlightenment in Europe (1688–1879) with its inclusive events of the Glorious Revolution in England and the French Revolution, the role of the city figured prominantly.

In the unfolding history of the United States, again the centrality of the city has figured prominently in the church's witness amid the plurality of issues facing the emerging nation. Great social movements have found some of their clearest expression in the city. From the signature of the Reverend John Witherspoon on the Declaration of Independence (Continental Congress meeting in Philadelphia), through the abolitionist movement against the slave trade, to major public issues involving women's suffrage, workers' rights, the settlement house ministries of the early twentieth century in response to the mass migrations into Northern cities, to the civil rights movement of the 1950–1960 era, urban ministry has been a key factor in these social and theological events. In looking back, we find that the notion of urban ministry as a new wrinkle in the landscape of Christian endeavor simply does not hold up under scrutiny.

As such, the early theological framework that ultimately became the orthodoxy of the Christian faith as we know it today was carved out within the challenges and opportunities of the urban setting. Christian faith, piety, and spiritual discipline did not develop in isolation from social, economic, and political events of the city, with its overcrowded dwellings, issues of poverty, crime, intertribal animosities, and squalor amid great wealth, privilege, refined culture, and learning. On the contrary, it developed in the midst of these urban realities. There was no separation of piety from the pragmatism of pressing issues of political decisions, no division of religion from reality, or separation of spiritual concerns from social circumstances of the believer.

Conclusion

To properly understand urban ministry and bridge the perceptual chasm that appears to separate it from regular Christian ministry, we must look back to the origins of the Christian movement with an urban-focused hermeneutic. With this approach, we are better able to see how the human quest for answers to life's greatest questions, deepest fears, and loftiest aspirations found some of its clearest expression in the cosmopolitan setting of the city. However imperfect its methodology, the aim of this quest was always grounded by an abiding sense that something divine could be revealed in the diversity of the urban setting. The city was at the center of this quest: its religious rituals were integral to the social, economic, and political ordering of life.

According to history, the city has never been bereft of divine presence; on the contrary, it was always understood as a place where God's presence could be discerned. In the contrasting biblical stories that discuss, on the one hand, the human tragedy of disunity and alienation (the Tower of Babel [Genesis 11:1-9]), and on the other hand, the divine triumph of human unity and reconciliation (Pentecost [Acts 2:1-12]), both take place in the city, and both clearly reflect God's presence therein. Although not the only context, the plural setting of the city figures prominently as the place from which many important events in scripture emerge. Mundane and often unattractive struggles of human day-to-day survival formed the urbanized context into which Jesus was born, lived, and died. Following the Resurrection, it was in the urban environment of stress and conflict that the apostles preached and believers responded to the gospel message. For the first believers in Christ, all of this bore witness to God's presence with them in the city.

Linthicum argues that the nonurban bias that crept into Christianity's theological formulations is a result of the collapse of Rome (c. 410) and much of the social, political, and literary disintegration in Europe that followed for the next six hundred years. According to Linthicum, Rome's population declined from his estimate of approximately one million people at the time of Christ to about twenty-five thousand by the fifth century (at which time it was still one of Europe's largest cities) and it would be well over a thousand years before Europe saw cities of that size again (not until London reached the one-million mark in population in 1820).[51] It was during this time, says Linthicum, that a nonurban bias crept into Western culture's God-talk, owing largely to the lack of large urban settings as a context from which theological reflection might take place as was the case prior to Rome's collapse.

With this antiurban bias came an interpretation of Christianity as essentially bucolic in origin, with little attention to the urban social crucible into which the gospel message was first received. Yet, throughout church history, the core beliefs that distinguish recipients of the gospel as, in fact, Christian were forged to no small degree out of the challenges and complexities of the urban context. As such, the perceptual chasm that views Christian ministry in general as fundamentally nonurban and foreign to city life is not one that has basis in the facts of church history. Looking back at the development of Christianity with an urban-focused hermeneutic reveals that Christian ministry is urban ministry that occurs naturally in the city. The plural nature of the city, with all its diverse complexities of social, cultural, economic, and political exchanges, constitutes the place where God's presence and revelation in Jesus Christ are affirmed and celebrated.

CHAPTER FIVE

URBAN THEOLOGY: A BOTTOM-UP PERSPECTIVE

If the world from you withhold of its silver and its gold, and you have to get along with meager fare, just remember, in God's Word, how God feeds the little bird, take your burden to the Lord and leave it there.
                                                              –Charles A. Tindley, 1916

Theologians do not normally reveal the true source of their theological reflections. They often tell us about the books that are similar and not so similar to their perspectives, but seldom do they tell us about those nonintellectual factors that are decisive for the arguments advanced on a particular issue. More often than not, it is a theologian's personal history, in a particular sociopolitical setting, that serves as the most important factor in shaping the methodology and content of his or her theological perspective. Thus, theologians ought to be a little more honest, and let the reader know something about those nonintellectual factors that are so important for the opinions they advance.
                                                              —James H. Cone[1]

According to Luke 4:16-22, Jesus' public ministry began with his overt identification with those on the fringes of society as he quoted from a scripture in the book of Isaiah:

"The Spirit of the Lord is upon me, because he has anointed me to bring good news to the poor. He has sent me to proclaim release to the captives and recovery of sight to the blind, to let the oppressed go free, to proclaim the year of the Lord's favor." (Luke 4:18-19)

This scriptural narrative is reflective of a consistent biblical theme that encourages believers in God to show special care for the welfare of those whose circumstances or situations in life make them vulnerable to disrespect and abuse in society. In scripture, these people are represented in terminology consistent with prominent social vulnerabilities of ancient times: widows, orphans, strangers, prisoners, the lame, or the blind. Further, scripture stresses that this concern/respect for vulnerable people results from God's sovereign compassion for the believer whose faith in God, in turn, obligates him or her to show compassion for society's less fortunate (Exodus 22:21-27; Deuteronomy 26:12-13; Psalms 37:14-15; 112; Proverbs 29:13; Isaiah 3:14-15;

Jeremiah 7:5-10; Ezekiel 22:6-13; Amos 2:6-7; 4:1; Matthew 18:23-34; 25:31-46; Luke 1:46-53; 10:29-37; Acts 6:1; Philippians 2:4-8; James 2:1-8).

This special concern for the welfare of the socially, economically, politically, or culturally vulnerable people is what I refer to in this chapter as a "bottom-up" theological perspective. This is a theological orientation that seeks to understand God's revelation in Jesus Christ from the perspective of those whose context in life locates them "on the bottom" socially and, therefore, renders them vulnerable to disrespect and abuse. Howard Thurman referred to such people as those with "their backs against the wall,"[2] distinct from those whose situation in life defines them as more sociopolitically and economically secure, those at "the top" socially. As we shall see in this chapter, the phrase "bottom-up theological perspective" is primarily concerned with *behavioral outcomes* of articulated theology rather than with doctrinal statements. Further, as we move through this section dealing with origins, we shall see how bottom-up theology is not a new theological orientation in Christian ministry, but is one that historically seeks to emphasize how faith in Jesus Christ *should function in society.*

Universal God-Talk from Particular Situations

Theology is no more and no less than "God-words" (from the Greek *theos*, meaning "God," and "logos," meaning "word") or "words about God." These *words about* God (theology) are generally the result of reflection on human experience and the perception that there has been something divine involved in that experience. All theology or God-talk is contextual; that is, it arises out of the context and experience of the believer. Because God is beyond human ability to comprehend, human assertions about God that have any claim to validity are typically understood as resulting from divine self-disclosure, revelation, or inspiration. The reality of divine self-disclosure or revelation in human history generally helps, though not always immediately, to clarify human experience in some way, but does not negate that experience. At its best, theology aims to point beyond the particular circumstances of its origin toward realities that are transcendent, universal, ultimate, and eternal.

While no one will argue the universal nature of the theological focus on the divine, one of the unique characteristics of Christian theology is its insistence on the particularity of God's revelatory behavior, that is, God's habit of creating epiphany experiences through particular situations in human life. Within the Judeo-Christian heritage, divine reality is often revealed in specific situations, contexts, and events wherein human beings somehow discern that something beyond mere human origin has occurred or is occurring. Examples of this principle can be found in Abraham and Sarah's perception that there was divine significance in their departure from Ur "to a place where God would show them" or in the birth of their son Isaac (Genesis 12:1-5; 18:1-15). Moses' encounter at the burning bush (Exodus 3:1-6), the blessings that come to Ruth and Naomi once they enter into the land of and community of Judah (Ruth 2–4), and the birth narratives of Jesus of Nazareth (Matthew 1:18-25 and Luke 2:1-20) are all framed in scripture as examples of the particularity of God's revelatory behavior. Although God is clearly understood by scripture writers as omniscient and omnipresent in capacity and universal in concern, God is nevertheless revealed in particular situations, contexts, and/or events. The particular (situational, contextual) aspects associated with the uniqueness of urban ministry are not foreign to Christian theology, but are very much within its scope.

The broad goal of Christian ministry is to assist human beings to better understand God's involvement in their lives. This goal is aided in a variety of religiously motivated behaviors that find their origin in Jesus Christ of the Holy Scriptures. Three typical—but not exclusive—expressions of this religious behavior that seek to point people toward faith in Jesus Christ include *religious rituals* (prayers, liturgies, worship), some form of *benevolent service* (addressing social, educational, emotional, or physical need), and *advocacy* (increasing public awareness concerning the welfare of society and its most vulnerable populations). The difficulty in comprehending the significance of a modifier to the phrase "Christian ministry," especially one like "*urban* Christian ministry," has to do with understanding the unique character, gifts, needs, and goals of the city. Yet, before the scope of *urban* Christian ministry can be fully appreciated, its relationship to the more inclusive character of Christian ministry in general should be noted.

The divine impetus (God's call) within the life of the individual believer always involves the welfare of the wider covenant community (or model community). This divine call/claim upon the covenant (or model) community, however, is ultimately directed toward the betterment of the wider and more global social order (of the world). In this understanding of "call" (impetus or motivation to engage in ministry), scripture and Christian tradition teach that the believer cannot be in "right" relationship with God apart from the welfare of the wider community. In the prophetic tradition of the Old Testament and in the Gospel writers as well as throughout other New Testament writings, concern for the welfare of the neighbor is evidenced as divine mandate (Psalm 15, 37; Amos 5:21-24; Micah 6:6-8; Matthew 5:23-24; James 2:1-14). Holiness, personal piety, and moral virtue are defined by compassion and justice toward those who are most vulnerable in society. It is against this spiritual backdrop and the witness of history and tradition that the Christian church in the wider society has become, in its best incarnations and examples, a symbol of caring and right relationships (justice) in society. Thus, urban ministry seeks to engage the assets and resources of the church to empower right relationships and values of compassion in the urban arena and beyond.

Not only must urban theology elucidate an understanding of God that is applicable to city streets and urban neighborhoods, it must also have relevance that speaks to the human quest for eternal meaning in life, regardless of context. Urban theology may arise out of the context and experience of the city, but it has universal applicability. The egalitarian metropolis refers to the urban arena but speaks to all social contexts. Urban theology refers to an understanding of the divine-human encounter that ultimately results in a social order that reflects egalitarian behaviors. By egalitarian metropolis, I refer to a social, political, and spiritual context that is preoccupied with justice, the mutual affirmation of persons, ecologically uplifting and safe, and where love and respect are the order of the day. It is an environment in which true compassion, reconciliation, restitution, and right relationship are taken seriously as public policy. In the egalitarian metropolis, the atmosphere is so thoroughly permeated with compassion and justice that the existence of evil is unknown because the presence of the divine is so tangibly present in the lives of its inhabitants. This is the goal of urban ministry and the goal of the urban theology that inspires this vision.

Yet, to add the modifier "urban" to the phrase "Christian theology" is to open the proverbial Pandora's box among the various types of Christian theologies: Eastern Orthodox, Roman Catholic, Protestant, Pentecostal, Anglican, Anabaptist, Reformed, Wesleyan, Charismatic, Fundamentalist, Liberal, Womanist, Liberation, Black, Asian, Reconstruction, and the list goes on and on. Is there any such thing as a uniquely urban theology that is different from other theologies? Of course there is. All human reflection on experience is conditioned by the particularity of the one doing the reflection, including reflection concerning the divine.

Sources and Norms in Theology

If we agree that the word *theology* is no more than words about God, then the writings or "God-words" based upon the central personality described in the Gospels of Matthew, Mark, Luke, and John (namely, Jesus of Nazareth) define the core of Christian faith, that which sets Christianity apart from other types of god-words or "theologies." Alister McGrath clarifies the point in this way:

> Christianity came into existence in a polytheistic world, where belief in the existence of many gods was commonplace. Part of the task of the earliest Christian writers appears to have been to distinguish the Christian god from other gods in the religious marketplace. At some point, it had to be asked which

god Christians were talking about, and how this god related to the "God of Abraham, Isaac, and Jacob," who figures so prominently in the Old Testament. The doctrine of the Trinity appears to have been, in part, a response to the pressure to identify the god that Christian theologians were speaking about.[3]

Involved in any discussion about the content of god-words is the notion of how people perceive or become aware of divine presence. Generally, Christian theologians speak of the concept of *revelation*: divine self-disclosure to human sensibilities. Closely allied with the concept of revelation is the notion of its *sources*: "formative factors"[4] that shape the fundamental concepts attributed to a particular theology and its assertions about the divine. Typical sources for discernment of divine revelation in Christian theology include at least scripture, tradition, and experience. By *scripture,* reference is typically made to those writings believed to be divinely inspired and generally affirmed by the community of faith that draws its understanding about God, in part, from these writings. *Tradition* refers to the repository of spiritual insights and theological reflections of believing communities, including creeds, confessions, or covenantal statements as well as broadly affirmed practices and customs that are transmitted from one generation to another. *Experience* as a source in theology is the abbreviated reference to reflection on human experience, including intellectual or rational evaluation, along with prayer and meditation concerning events of one's life and context in light of perceived divine activity.[5]

James Cone argues that in addition to identifying sources from which divine revelation may be perceived, there is the question of the criteria by which these sources are evaluated. Cone suggests that the norm (criteria used to evaluate sources) is equally important in theological discourse about discerning divine revelation:

> Sources are the relevant data for the theological task, while the norm determines how the data will be used. It is often the case that different theologies share the same sources, and it is the theological norm which elevates one particular source (or sources) to a dominating role.[6]

Cone's analysis of the role and function of sources and norms in Christian theology is helpful in suggesting a methodology by which different sources are emphasized by different people in formulating their theological rhetoric. The norm among Roman Catholic theologians, for example, has typically valued tradition quite highly among the several theological sources. Protestant norms gravitate more toward scripture as a preeminent source for God-talk. Nonetheless, Roman Catholics and most Protestants alike affirm both scripture and tradition as legitimate sources for theological rhetoric.

In *Christian* theology, God-words necessarily revolve around human experiences interpreted through the prism of Jesus Christ and what he reveals to us about the metaphysical reality we commonly understand as Almighty God, Creator of the universe. Christian theology that is urban, therefore, identifies what is revealed about God through Jesus Christ in the context, experiences, and unique characteristics of the city. Yet, urban Christian theology, like the best in all theological reflection, ultimately seeks to point people toward realities that transcend the particularities of its own immediate situation and context and seeks to give insights into the ultimate questions of life that are universal for all experiential contexts and give meanings that, in fact, have eternal merit.

Social Location and God-Talk

As you ride the bus or train or drive through the various sections of any North American city, one of the first things that you notice about the city's landscape is the wide divergence between wealth and poverty that exists. Some neighborhoods are pristine with lovely homes and well-kept vehicles, cultural and educational facilities, welcoming parks and playgrounds or other public spaces, while other neighborhoods consist of vast areas of vacant lots, abandoned buildings covered with graffiti, dilapidated housing, abandoned vehicles, and dirty streets. Still other places in the city are alive with impressive business complexes, entertainment centers, and inviting shopping areas, with no signs of physical decay or economic distress. More than fifty years ago, Howard Thurman decried the frequency with which so much of Christian preaching and its underlying theological assumptions tended to identify, either subliminally or overtly, with wealth and privilege in society while benignly neglecting realities facing those who are marginalized:

> Many and varied are the interpretations dealing with the teachings and the life of Jesus of Nazareth. But few of these interpretations deal with what the teachings and the life of Jesus have to say to those who stand, at a moment in human history, with their backs against the wall. To those who need profound succor and strength to enable them to live in the present with dignity and creativity, Christianity often has been sterile and of little avail. The conventional Christian word is muffled, confused, and vague. Too often the price exacted by society for security and respectability is that the Christian movement in its formal expression must be on the side of the strong against the weak.[7]

Sadly, the observation made by Thurman more than a half-century ago is still relevant to the articulation of the gospel and current theological tendencies to conform to culture rather than to engage in serious attempts to transform it for the better.[8] The perspective and voice of the poor and the powerless in society are often muted in theological discussions in favor of more respected and acceptable voices. While the city is home to a broad range of social, economic, political, and theological constituents, the perspectives of the socioeconomically marginalized are typically drowned out by the prerogatives of the more affluent.

William Julius Wilson has called attention to the *social location* of those most economically and physically marginalized in the city and to the fact that their context continues to grow more precarious. Using Chicago as the context of his investigations, Wilson documented a phenomenon that characterizes many inner-city neighborhoods in the United States. He noted that as industries have moved away from core-city areas and relocated in suburban industrial parks, vast expanses of abandoned urban landscape have been left behind. The poor remaining in these and adjacent neighborhoods, according to Wilson, have been left at a physical handicap in that they often have little or no access to employment opportunities located in distant locales outside the city in these industrial parks or shopping malls; he notes the difficulty of maintaining a job when public transportation is not available or, where it is present, that it may require inordinate amounts of time (sometimes more than two hours of connecting bus or train routes one-way) to get to and from work. Wilson discusses the situation among poor Blacks in some of Chicago's hardest-hit neighborhoods as he correctly observes that their physical location is but one index of their social location. In many instances, he observes, those left behind in core city areas are persons who are second- and third-generation poor and unemployed, making them what he calls "the underclass."

> The social structure of today's inner city has been radically altered by the mass exodus of jobs and working families and by the rapid deterioration of housing, schools, businesses, recreational facilities, and other community organizations, further exacerbated by government policies of industrial and urban laissez-faire that have channeled a disproportionate share of federal, state, and municipal resources to the more affluent. The economic and social buffer provided by a stable black working class and a visible, if small, black middle class that cushioned the impact of downswings in the economy and tied ghetto residents to the world of work has all but disappeared. Moreover, the social networks of parents, friends, and associates, as well as the nexus of local institutions, have seen their resources for economic stability progressively depleted. In sum, today's ghetto residents face a closed opportunity structure.[9]

Not infrequently, people from such neighborhoods are those whose social location has effectively severed them not only from the broader society's economic opportunity, but also from its theological dialogue. This separation diminishes the quality of human understanding concerning God, not just for the marginalized, but for society as a whole. Although there is God-talk in disenfranchised communities and reflection upon divine revelation in the context of their experience, ordinarily such reflection is not factored into the wider society's articulation of theology. Speaking of the poor in Briton, Michael Northcott argues that the reality of social and economic marginalization in society should not, in fact, neutralize the validity of the God-talk of the poor or the seriousness with which their assertions about God are considered:

> Are there not signs that, in (urban areas) as elsewhere in this country, small groups of people are beginning to follow their own style of theological reflection and to deepen their Christian understanding in ways that spring naturally from their own culture and abilities? May such groups not have a contribution to make to the theological thinking of the wider Church as a whole? . . . Such a theology would start, not from a conventional academic syllabus of Christian knowledge or biblical study, but from the personal experience, the modes of perception and the daily concerns of people themselves—priorities which might well be different from those of people of a more intellectual background.[10]

Obviously, one's social location or position in society is a significant determinant of one's theology or God-talk and inevitably factors into theological discourse that shapes the witness of the whole church in the wider society.

Cultural Value Assessments and Theology Sources

Value is the word we use to refer to the importance attached to something: an object, a service, a concept, or even our opinion of an individual. The esteem in which something, someone, or some ideal is held qualifies as its value, its worth or significance to us. Since all things are not considered as equally important, values are relative. Our homes, for example, are ordinarily more valuable or important to us than a pair of shoes. We are taught from childhood that telling the truth is better than lying. Thus, the concept of truth-telling is given a higher value than lying. Some situations, such as being on vacation at a wonderful place with those we love most, are realities that, for most people, would be more highly valued while other situations, like being in jail, would not be an experience considered as desirable or valuable at all. The point is that values are simply those ideals or goals in life that we consider so important that they motivate us to do whatever we can in order to achieve them. Values are the *priorities* that inspire the choices we habitually make in managing our lives.

The geometric figure of the triangle provides a helpful way to explain cultural values affecting all of society, including the urban context. The values triangle symbolizes the way in which cultural values in society are evident and reveals the relationship between highly regarded and less-valued realities in society. The economic principle related to marketable goods and services known as the law of supply and demand is useful in explaining the values triangle. According to this principle, products or services that are found in abundance are generally regarded with less value than those that are scarce (see diagram 1).

Diagram 1: Top-Down "Supply/Demand" Material Values

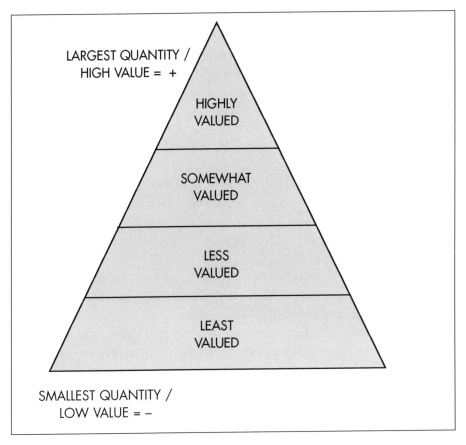

Somewhat like the economic principle of supply and demand, the greater the supply or availability of a product, the less value; and the less available an item, the more valuable it is deemed. Even important resources that are critical for survival, like the air we breathe, are taken for granted and generally ignored until they become dangerously polluted or scarce. Then their value rises as availability lessens. Rolls-Royce automobiles, for example, are not as plentiful as are Toyotas and are valued more highly because they are out of the economic reach of most people. In academic settings, the letter grade of A (excellent) is more prized than the letter grade of C (average) and is perceived as more difficult to attain. As scarce and highly prized items become more available to the masses, usually their value diminishes.

Unfortunately, the values we assign to relationships and even to people sometimes conform to the "supply/demand" material resources triangle rather than the "human value" triangle. While the espoused public rhetoric in society generally affirms adherence to valorizing the importance of all people and human life, frequently social, economic, and political realities reveal that materialistic assessments have been assigned even to human beings. In this "information age" in which we are currently living, it is interesting to note how information is disseminated. Instead of making accessibility to voting something that is as easy to comprehend as dialing 911 or finding the nearest exit sign in a public building, often the process of access to the ballot is made quite difficult for certain people. For example, due to legal prohibitions, fully 13 percent of African American men in the United States are currently or permanently unable to vote (seven times the national average) as a result of a felony conviction.[11] This fact suggests that their votes are not valued in society as much as those from other sectors of the voting populace. The cumbersome and unnecessarily complicated process for voting also limits access to the ballot for millions of other mostly poor people, suggesting that votes from this sector of society also are not highly valued.

Examination of the economic and racial constituencies most frequently expelled from public schools, arrested, without adequate employment or access to health coverage, and living in substandard housing conditions reveals some statistical realities that suggest poor people and those of certain racial groups, that is, Blacks or Latinos, are apparently less valued in society as reflected in their overrepresentation in these debilitating social conditions. Compare these constituencies with those graduating from college, never arrested, highly paid CEOs, and living in the most affluent neighborhoods. These types of comparisons suggest that the supply/demand *material* values of society have a *human* value corollary involving economics and race that seems to place certain human beings in society at a higher value level than others. In many ways, this was the real value assessments that were revealed in wake of the U.S. government's lack of effective response to the 2005 Hurricane Katrina disaster in New Orleans. In many instances, it appeared that the people who were pictured on television sets across the nation and around the world begging for help had been abandoned, as if their lives counted for little.

Jesus inverted the typical understanding of cultural values in his teachings through his perpetual lifting as important people or situations that society, in most instances, viewed as having lesser value. This is what is meant by the bottom-up perspective of urban theology. It is the ability to place a high value on people and situations in our God-talk that society typically values as being of lesser value. Consider the value orientations evident in Jesus' teaching:

> Consider the lilies of the field, how they grow; they neither toil nor spin, yet I tell you, even Solomon in all his glory was not clothed like one of these. (Matthew 6:28-29)

> As he came out of the temple, one of his disciples said to him, "Look, Teacher, what large stones and what large buildings!" Then Jesus asked him, "Do you see these great buildings? Not one stone will be left here upon another; all will be thrown down." (Mark 13:1-2)

> People were bringing little children to him in order that he might touch them; and the disciples spoke sternly to them. But when Jesus saw this, he was indignant and said to them, "Let the little children come to me; do not stop them; for it is to such as these that the kingdom of God belongs. Truly I tell you, whoever does not receive the kingdom of God as a little child will never enter it." And he took them up in his arms, laid his hands on them, and blessed them. (Mark 10:13-16)

Other examples of Jesus' iconoclastic teachings that inverted cultural values perspectives abound in the Gospel narratives (see Mark 10:42-45; Luke 7:36-50, 18:9-14; 21:1-4; John 13:3-17). In this, Jesus was well within the prophetic tradition of ancient Israel, which is full of castigations of those who were held in high esteem in society because of the low value they placed upon those who were less fortunate (see Isaiah 3:13-15; 10:1-4; Jeremiah 7:5-11; Amos 5:10-13; Micah 7:2-4). Because life and human beings are considered so important, the material-oriented value-assessments triangle of what is highly prized is inverted in scripture.

In the bottom-up orientation, the goal is to emphasize that all should be saved, with no, or at least the fewest possible, losses of people. This expansive vision was clearly reflected in the early church that interpreted Jesus Christ as no less than the "Savior of the world" whose aim was to save the whole world. One of the clearest expressions of this vision is found in John's Gospel (3:14-17), in which everyone who sincerely believes is to be saved:

> And as Moses lifted up the serpent in the wilderness, so must the Son of man be lifted up, that whoever believes in him may have eternal life. For God so loved the world that he gave his only Son, that whoever believes in him should not perish but have eternal life. For God sent the Son into the world, not to condemn the world, but that the world might be saved through him. (RSV)

In addition to the very inclusive goal of global salvation, according to the apostle Paul, those who, by human priorities, would not be ranked very highly in terms of their scholastic and intellectual acumen are often the very individuals whom God chooses because of their faith (1 Corinthians 1:21-25):

> For since, in the wisdom of God, the world did not know God through wisdom, it pleased God through the folly of what we preach to save those who believe. For Jews demand signs and Greeks seek wisdom, but we preach Christ crucified, a stumbling block to Jews and folly to Gentiles, but to those who are called, both Jews and Greeks, Christ the power of God and the wisdom of God. For the foolishness of God is wiser than men, and the weakness of God is stronger than men. (RSV)

In both of these examples, the very inclusive social and spiritual values that undergird the proclamation of the gospel and its goals for salvation are the inverse of the society's hierarchical and exclusive values (see diagram 2):

Diagram 2: Bottom-Up "Salvation" Human Resource Values

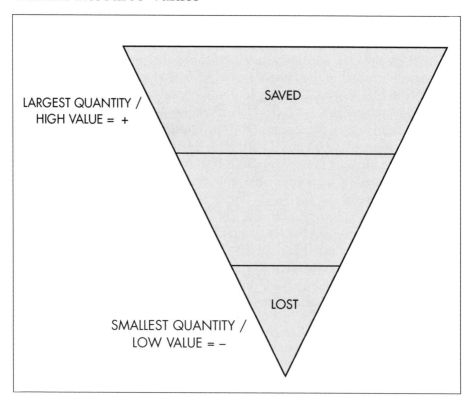

There also are situations in culture in which the high-volume/low-value assessments are replaced by high-volume/high-value assessments. This is the principle that prompts laws governing public safety in public buildings, for which preventing loss of life is the goal. In such instances, lifesaving procedures and strategies are made obvious so that the vast majority of people exposed to danger will be able to escape unharmed. The goal is that all (high volume) should be saved and none (low volume) should be lost. It is mandated in public structures that exit signs be clearly marked, lighted, and prominently displayed so that in case of fire, there can be minimal or no loss of life. Also, the public is taught to dial the 911 emergency number in order to contact help, rather than dialing a complicated seven- or ten-digit phone number. Again, the goal is to save as many people in crisis as possible.

Learning from the Poor

Taking seriously the "bottom-up" perspective of those whose social location in poverty defines them as less important or even expendable in society (housed in ghettos or jails and placed out of the economic mainstream through underemployment or unemployment) is a vital step in order for seminaries and churches to be able to engage in effective ministry in the city. Ordinarily, this is not a perspective that is reflected in most seminaries. Although discourse in seminaries from time to time certainly includes reference to the poor and socially less fortunate or their plight, less frequently are their theological articulations and perspectives seriously considered as fit subject matter for academic theological inquiry. It is primarily the social location of the more affluent and the academically trained theologians that is taken into account in accredited theological schools. Arguing for an Africentric approach to theological education as one means to incorporate some of society's underrepresented perspectives, Warren Dennis emphasizes a similar point. Dennis views the need for academic theologians to engage with community-based practitioners in urban ministry to define a theological framework that would not only benefit Christian witness in the community, but also enhance the caliber of theological dialogue within the academy itself:

> The reflection and action method seeks to empower persons and communities, that have been victimized by systemic oppression and violence to speak to the realized presence of God's affirming acts in their lives, to collaborate with the church and the community and justice-seeking institutions on common, faith-based, community development concerns. The goal is to transform the spirituality of the community by synthesizing the faith expressions of grassroots people with the insight of the academy with the consequence of producing an Africentric paradigm for liberating education and action.[12]

67

Emphasizing the importance of the poor from all sectors of society as theological contributors, right along with academic theologians, as partners in discerning what God is doing in the city, Northcott argues that

> affirming the poor as the makers of their own history and as theologians in their own right is an essential part of urban theology. . . . This new way of doing theology involves a recognition that theology is the work of the people of God, and not just of academic theologians, priests and preachers.[13]

Clearly, poverty is not a new phenomenon, nor is it unique to the urban context. Yet, it is the vast percentages of urban poor in our cities and the human suffering caused by it in the urban context that make theological reflection on this reality a central factor in any type of urban theological reflection. As such, one of the real challenges in talking about urban theology is that it has as much to do with social positioning and economic realities as with faith and belief in God. In 1948, long before writers such as James Cone[14] or Gustavo Gutiérrez[15] raised social location issues of ethnicity or economics as factors affecting the theological interpretation of the gospel in society, Howard Thurman put the matter this way:

> This is a matter of tremendous significance, for it reveals to what extent a religion that was born of a people acquainted with persecution and suffering has become the cornerstone of a civilization and of nations whose very position in modern life has too often been secured by ruthless use of power applied to weak and defenseless peoples. . . . The masses of (people) live with their backs constantly against the wall. They are the poor, the disinherited, the dispossessed. What does our religion say to them?[16]

When God-words are written down in some type of organized fashion to explain epiphany experiences and resultant insights for behavior (theology/ethics), this typically involves the capacity to read and write as well as time to withdraw from the ongoing activities required of daily survival in order to meditate and record. Such theological reflection and writing necessarily imply some semblance of a formal educational process and even professional associations and academic guilds. All of this has economic or social-class implications that can alter the perception of events shared by those whose social location does not afford them the prerogatives of formal education or release time from daily survival chores in order to contemplate the ethereal and write down their theological reflections about such.

Again, Northcott reminds us that just as Western Christianity has had to cope with its cultural bias in order to understand and explicate the gospel in non-Western cultures by learning from those cultures; effort will also be needed to incorporate the insights of the urban poor into theological analysis.

He argues that academic theology and community-based dialogue with the urban poor are critical ingredients to substantive theology that empowers urban ministry that is effective, life enhancing, and productive of systemic transformational change in urban society:

> Urban Christians and urban theologians need to be alive to the action of the Spirit which "blows where it wills" and to the spiritual yearnings present in the inherent creativity of the cultures, languages, stories and struggles of those who are on the margins of our society. For too long the Western Church has excluded non-Western peoples from full participation in the household of God because of their cultural traditions and styles. Non-Western Christians have only in this century begun to make the Gospel and the Church their own as Christianity becomes rooted and inculturated in their own contexts. There is a similar challenge in relation to the urban poor in the West. We need a church *of* the poor, not a church *for* the poor. Such a church will not look like the churches of the rich or even of the comfortable. . . . Affirming the poor as the makers of their own history and as theologians in their own right is an essential part of urban theology.[17]

People in urban centers who are poor ordinarily do not use terminology such as "theology," much less phrases akin to "urban Christian theology." They just talk about their faith in God, leaving the more sophisticated descriptions and analyses of God-talk to the more educationally or socially privileged. It should be no surprise, therefore, that even today in urban churches, the idea of a uniquely *urban* theology is, at best, an exotic concept. Urban ministry practitioners outside seminaries and other academic communities seldom use such terminology, and even those who do tend to give a variety of interpretations to its use.[18] Most people living in cities, including those most consciously involved in urban ministry, are relatively unaware that there is any such thing as a specifically urban theology. Remember that use of the term *urban* in reference to the city is often as a code word to distinguish nonurbanites from those living in the city. Although there are definite and unique theological assumptions that give rise to the ethics and moral decisions that characterize urban ministry, many practitioners of urban ministry typically view any suggestion that a uniquely urban theology should be taken seriously as something primarily for academicians and scholars to discuss. Thus, the "in the hood"/"on the ground"/"in the trenches" type of theological activity frequently remains separated from academic/theoretical reflection of seminaries and other academic settings. As a result, the theological unity needed for transformational praxis that strengthens the quality of urban life continues to suffer.

A *Bottom-Up* Theological Perspective

In light of these social location issues and their effect on God-talk in society, one of the best descriptions that may be given to an urban theological perspective is one that is a *bottom-up* approach to theology. By using the term *bottom-up*, reference is to an approach to discerning divine revelation from the perspective of the most sociopolitically and economically vulnerable segments of society represented in the city: those who are "at the bottom" socially, culturally, economically, and politically. William Pannell, in discussing the issues involved in evangelism among the socially and economically marginalized of society, employed the term *bottom-up* as a means of differentiating between the theological perspectives and interpretations of scripture found among the poor (those doing theology from "the bottom up") as compared with those of dominant society's power brokers (those doing theology from "the top down").[19] He describes the suspicion with which marginalized persons hear the theologizing of society's economically privileged articulators of Christian teaching:

> Victims of injustice, when exposed to Christians whose theories seem not to address their situation, begin to realize that a distance exists between their "experience" of the [scriptural] text, and the interpretation of similar texts by those of the dominant culture.[20]

The differences in theological orientation that are shaped by social location can be found in every context. John De Gruchy, in delineating the theological challenges posed during the awful years of South Africa's apartheid regime, identified how, throughout history, theology has often been co-opted in service of political and ideological elites:

> So-called "theologies from above" . . . reflect the ideology of those in power, those who rule from above, and thereby reinforce structures of domination. They are the theologies of the court theologians and prophets who serve the interest of the state and the cultus. They are theologies of uncritical patriotism, theologies which are not committed to hearing the living word of the Lord today in our present crisis and context.[21]

Denominationally, those "at the bottom" socioeconomically may be Catholic, Baptist, Methodist, Pentecostal, nondenominational, or any of the variety of religious traditions. The articulation of their Christian beliefs may reflects a wide diversity: charismatic, evangelical, or highly liturgical worship style. Occasionally, varieties of the dominant culture's theopolitical ideologies (that is, conservative or liberal rhetoric) may be reflected in worship. Yet, there remains a basic difference in the theological analysis of the bottom-up social context as compared with its more affluent denominational counterpart of top-down theological variety. Denominational labels, theopolitical schools of thought, as well as conservative or liberal ideologies, become irrelevant in the context of social and economic disenfranchisement that characterizes the social location of the chronically poor. That which most clearly identifies the *bottom-up* theological perspective of urban theology has more to do with social, economic, and political vulnerability and the praxis of faith-beliefs in the implementation of strategies that address injustice and systemic toleration of inequities.

Perspectives in the Bottom-Up Theological Approach

Bottom-up theology, then, is the expressed faith in God of socially, economically, and politically vulnerable people. It is an understanding of scripture and church tradition that focuses on searching out what is best for the disenfranchised in society. In our overtly individualistic culture, urban ministry's theological emphasis on communal well-being is often difficult to translate. Moreover, analysis of the theological hermeneutic that interprets scripture toward an individual and noncommunal-nonurban perspective is often manifested in characteristics that are very different in their behavioral outcomes from those having urban-focused or community-centered interests. Much of society's current approach to its God-talk—well endowed with rhetoric and platitude-laden resolutions that bespeak compassion, justice, and reconciliation—fails to reflect these values in its behavioral outcomes. Public policies, for example, which take no action against wealthy thieves who defraud investors and bankrupt retirement plans, yet incarcerate the poor in record numbers while ignoring the withering misery and survival hazards that define ghetto life, is behavioral evidence of this flawed theological approach.

In urban ministry, core values are largely defined, not by theological rhetoric, but by behavioral outcomes. According to scripture, Jesus taught, "Beware of false prophets. . . . You will know them by their fruits" (Matthew 7:15-16), and in other teachings placed heavy emphasis on behavioral outcomes that reflected reconciliation, justice, and compassion (Matthew 7:21-23; Mark 3:33-35; 11:12-14). Thus, bottom-up theology is largely shaped by practical activity aimed at alleviating injustice rather than idle academic analysis motivated by intellectual curiosity.

The bottom-up theological perspective, therefore, is based upon a behavioral orientation that reflects compassion, justice, and a concern for society's most vulnerable (economically, educationally, ethnically, culturally, physically, and spiritually). This theological orientation is the basis of effective urban ministry. Since those most vulnerable ("the least of these" [Matthew 25:31-45]) are typically on the bottom rung of society's economic/political/cultural ladder, a theological perspective that is able to include them as a priority and to see life from their perspective is one that I refer to as the *bottom-up* theological perspective. Conversely, a perspective that results in diminished focus on the needs of the most vulnerable by virtue of its elitist behavior is one that I call the *top-down* theological perspective.[22]

Chart 4: Characteristics of Top-Down versus Bottom-Up Theology

TOP-DOWN THEOLOGICAL PERSPECTIVE	BOTTOM-UP THEOLOGICAL PERSPECTIVE
Tends to emphasize: **DISTINCTIONS** (ALIENATION THEOLOGY) Genesis 2:4–4:26; Matthew 23:1-33	*Tends to emphasize:* **COMMONALITIES** (RECONCILIATION THEOLOGY) Ruth 1:16-18; 2 Corinthians 5:16-19
Truth, orthodoxy tends to be defined with observable, objective "proofs" or formulas. Starting point is sin (that which misses the mark or deviates from the standard; preoccupied with what is prohibited). Emphasizes regulatory aspects of faith; propositional or doctrinal is valued over relational or affective; legalisms, rigid boundaries are paramount; territorial. Conformity prized over variation or context.	Truth, orthodoxy tends to be defined experientially, contextually, relationally. Starting point is salvation (that which empowers the needy; preoccupied with what is possible). Emphasizes relational aspects of faith; narrative, affective valued over propositional, doctrinal; while consensus is affirmed, boundaries are flexible. Contextual sensitivity viewed as creative, capacity development.
Tends to emphasize:	*Tends to emphasize:*
1. INDIVIDUAL/PERSONAL SALVATION	**1. COMMUNAL/GROUP SALVATION**
Salvation typically defined in terms of self or personal virtue(s) or attributes; relationship to others (i.e., the group) is second to this first concern. Emphasis is on the quality of the personal/individual "relationship to Christ."	Salvation typically defined in relationship with and accountability to other persons as well as in context of the wider environment. Emphasis is on the quality of group well-being and how it reflects Christlike behavior/actions.
Scriptural examples: Luke 18:9-14	Scriptural examples: Exodus 3:5-10; Luke 4:18-19
2. MATERIAL SENSITIVITY	**2. SPIRITUAL SENSITIVITY**
Righteousness tends to be defined in terms of personal moral benchmarks that can be overtly quantified with relational impact of secondary importance; individual performance of certain rituals, attainment of certain possessions, overt conformity to sets of behavioral norms, or other tangibles are prized.	Righteousness is defined in terms of responsibility to the group as a primary spiritual barometer concerning the personal relationship with God; the megaphysical is emphasized in understanding reality, and the value of relationships is prized as an indicator of spiritual well-being and right relationship to God.
Scriptural examples: Philippians 3:5-6; Luke 12:13-21	Scriptural examples: Isaiah 6:1-8; Acts 9:10-19
3. EXCLUSIVE ORIENTATION	**3. INCLUSIVE ORIENTATION**
Tends to be overtly judgmental and status conscious. Language often reflects an "I-Thou" (Martin Buber) or "us/them," "in-group" and "out-group" perspective. Status is emphasized in identifying worthiness or unworthiness: saved/damned, members/non-members, disciples/non-disciples, ordained/non-ordained.	Tends toward affirming, welcoming, non-judgmental attitudes concerning status. Open and comfortable with unanswered questions and able to live with difference, dissonance, and unclear boundaries. Worthiness or unworthiness is not a function of status (member/non-member; in-group/out-group, etc.). Discipleship/ordination viewed as a "lifestyle."
Scriptural examples: Acts 8:1-3; 9:1-2	Scriptural examples: Acts 8:1-3; 9:1-2

This is not to suggest that the theological perspective of the socially less vulnerable or the privileged and politically well connected in society has no meaning in urban ministry. On the contrary, it is often the language and imitated dogma of the *top-down* theological approach of society's ruling classes that undergird the status quo and define the parameters of socially acceptable theological discourse that influences urban and non-urban society. As with the bottom-up reality, top-down theologies include all the varieties of Christian denominations, theopolitical rhetoric, and worship styles. As such, the top-down theological perspective inevitably is part of the urban theological dialogue. It is the officially sanctioned theology (or theologies) of the culture that is taught in seminaries, universities, and churches. It enjoys the protection and security of the state in keeping with the protections accorded to those who are economically and physically secure in society. It is preached in the cathedrals of wealth as well as in the storefront worship centers of the poor; it is likewise broadcast on airwaves of electronic media. It is a theological approach and a social ethic supported by privilege and power. It is articulated in creeds and confessional statements drawn from long-established traditions that have been enshrined and codified by power and wealth.

By contrast, the bottom-up theological approach reflects a perspective and corresponding social ethic framed out of social, economic, and political powerlessness and vulnerability. Shut out of society's economic, political, and cultural mainstream, the bottom-up theological perspective emerges from the faith insights of those in homeless shelters, those abandoned by government bureaucracy in 2005 following Hurricane Katrina's devastation on New Orleans, and those deserted by friends and family when it is learned that they are HIV-positive. Although the witness of history has attested time and again to the theological validity and substance of reflections of poor and socially marginalized persons as resources for spiritual resilience and survival against oppression, this bottom-up theology is typically written off by the socially secure and affirmed by many in academia as being ephemeral and without intellectual depth.

Conclusion

I want to emphasize that the aim of this distinction between the bottom-up and top-down theological approaches is not to contribute to continued social fragmentation and so-called social-class animosities. Indeed, society is already quite polarized by the prevalence of suspicions and hostilities between rich/poor, suburban/urban, elite/proletariat, one ethnic group/another ethnic group, and numerous other social, cultural, religious, and ideological segments and interest groups. The politics of division, whereby some seek to gain advantage for themselves by encouraging rivalries among others (in other words, divide and conquer), is already well attested in our time and needs to be counteracted rather than promoted. Moreover, simple group identifications and category characteristics do not sufficiently explain the range of complex factors that cause people to "split hairs" theologically.

The purpose of noting the differences in characteristics of these two differing theological perspectives is to clarify the theological focus in urban ministry and its philosophical and ethical debt to society's marginalized as well as mainstream sectors. Privilege and power, in and of themselves, do not automatically nullify the theological validity of the statements contained in the creeds, confessions, and traditions of the top-down theological perspective. Likewise, poverty and sociopolitical marginalization are not synonymous with moral virtue. The fact cannot be ignored, nonetheless, that social location is a key factor influencing an individual's or group's perspective of theological discernment and, in the course of history, has been known to woefully distort theological insight. Often, it is the interpretation (or misinterpretation) and application (misapplication) of time-tested creedal statements that enable the plight of "the least of these" to be tolerated rather than transformed by power brokers, revealing the ethical and missiological "blind spots" of the top-down theological approach. As previously stated, poverty and powerlessness are no guarantee that justice and compassion will be the goal among the vulnerable. Exploitation and violence among the poor are rampant. The quest to better understand and articulate the gospel of Jesus Christ in a manner that will inspire a more morally and spiritually uplifting social environment is the goal of urban theology. In order to achieve this goal, a more inclusive and holistic approach to doing theology will be necessary than is presently done. The bottom-up theological approach represents one effort to do just that.

Effective urban ministry, therefore, is found among a variety of denominational traditions, theological traditions, and ecclesiastical structures whether church governance is of an episcopal (hierarchical), congregational (democratic), or reformed (representative democracy) type. The distinctions between the *bottom-up* and *top-down* theological approaches, however, are basically identified in their behavioral outcomes with regard to how one or the other theological perspective engages the remediation of social vulnerability in the city. As scripture reports concerning the words of Jesus, the "bottom line"/top value of all God-talk is not so much what is said, but what is done:

> *"Truly I tell you, just as you did it to one of the least of these . . . you did it to me."*
> —Matthew 25:40

CHAPTER SIX

ANTECEDENTS OF A *TOP-DOWN* THEOLOGICAL PERSPECTIVE

Faith of our fathers! Living still
In spite of dungeon, fire and sword;
O how our hearts beat high with joy
When-e'er we hear that glorious word!
Faith of our fathers, holy faith!
We will be true to thee til death!

—*Frederick William Faber*

In order to understand the roots of the twenty-first-century brand of *bottom-up* theology that informs urban ministry today, it is helpful to look at the foundations of both the *top-down* and *bottom-up* theological perspectives. While the bottom-up theological perspective refers to persons whose social circumstance is relatively weak economically or politically, rendering them vulnerable to abuse and disrespect, the top-down theological perspective refers to those whose social situation is comparatively secure, broadly affirmed, and supported by the culture. That which now constitutes a top-down theological framework influencing urban realities actually began as a bottom-up theological orientation. In fact, antecedents of contemporary top-down approaches in urban ministry and the intellectual orientations that inspired them are traceable to emerging trends in Europe growing out of the Protestant Reformation that first challenged the authority of the Roman Catholic Church. This spirit of *"protest"-ism* profoundly affected Western culture, especially as it evolved in the United States. Although by no means exclusively a Protestant phenomenon today, with Roman Catholic, mainline Protestant, and nondenominational churches involved, the origins of what we now refer to as *top-down* theological perspectives in urban ministry are inextricably involved with the unfolding story of Protestant theology's effect on Western society.

In this sense, the story of urban-ministry praxis in Western culture is a case study in how those who originally started out in a position of social and theological vulnerability (*bottom-up*) gave rise to a new social and theological paradigm in which their *protest reformed* the society in which they lived. The result

75

of this new paradigm left those who were at one time socially vulnerable now with their theological and social positions broadly affirmed. They then assumed a new *top-down* status of theological and social dominance within the culture. Yet, the phenomenon of social vulnerability within culture and in its urban arenas continues as a factor in society and in Christian ministry. Urban ministry, therefore, continues to address the role of the church in society from its *bottom-up* theological perspective. A review of the background of these *bottom-up/top-down* theological orientations and their interactions with each other will help us in understanding the dynamics of urban ministry today.

Top-Down Theological Perspective Origins

During the period from the Reformation through post-Enlightenment Europe and, later, in the "New World" of North America, there was increasing philosophical interest in ideas about personal freedom and individual experience supported by strong intellectual currents that suggested science was outmoding Christianity. With insightful clarity, Cornel West succinctly described the broad sweep of issues that characterized this period:

> The basic features of early modern European culture were the increasing acceptance of the authority of science, the appearance of a new kind of pagan neoclassicism [fascination with Greek culture], and the subjectivist turn in philosophy. The intellectual defense and institutional support of practices of scientists became more and more persuasive to the literate population. These practices were guided by an adherence to a new paradigm of knowledge, an experimental method that attempted to test hypotheses and yield objective conclusions by appealing to evidence and observation. The increasing acceptance of the authority of science resulted in assaults on the authority of the church and on its theology and religious practices.[1]

In Europe and especially in the United States, the industrial revolution was drawing people into cities in unprecedented numbers, and the plight of the new urban dwellers in seeking out survival in these industrial centers was precarious. Family life suffered. Increasingly, seventeenth- through nineteenth-century philosophers and theologians sought to give rational interpretation and scientific explanation concerning economic, political, and social dynamics and outcomes earlier grounded in religious belief.

By the fourteenth century in the Latin or Western wing of Christendom, the Roman Catholic Church had come to occupy the socially and politically affirmed position of the top-down theological perspective. It was against this backdrop that the early Reformers such as Martin Luther (1483–1546), Huldrych Zwingli (1484–1531), and John Calvin (1509–1564) took umbrage with the papacy and other Roman Catholic traditions because of their deference to persons of wealth and privilege. Although Pope Leo X and the bishops acted within the prerogatives of church tradition, according to Luther, their actions could not be supported by scripture. While rejecting the scriptural legitimacy of church traditions and papal actions, these initial Reformers held fast to other orthodox norms of Christian theology. Taking the position that eternal salvation was achieved *sola fide*, by "faith alone" in Jesus Christ as revealed through scripture, as opposed to submission to ecclesiastical councils, bishops, or other religious superiors, these radicals carved out a new independence for the individual in the face of then-existing Roman Catholic religious tradition. In spite of their individualist tendencies, they did value the community of faith's importance as a validating entity representing the presence and authority of God in the life of the individual believer.

The emphasis of early Protestant Reformers on individual conscience, despite the resulting charges leveled against them by then *top-down* Catholic leaders, was not a basis for anarchy born of heresy. The Reformers, Luther, Zwingli, and Calvin, in genuine *bottom-up* theological fashion, felt their convictions to be a more just or pure expression of the gospel drawn directly from the teachings of scripture. As such, these early Reformers affirmed ancient Augustinian and Athanatian theological concepts that were central in shaping Christian dogma regarding sin and salvation imbedded in the prevalent top-down theological framework. Tenets such as the authority of scripture and the acceptance of the miracles included therein, with particular regard for the Incarnation and Jesus' resurrection, the doctrine of the Trinity, among other teachings, were affirmed without question. In the minds of the early bottom-up and socially vulnerable protest-oriented Reformers, it was the uneven application of these beliefs, encumbered by superfluous tradition, that was corrupting the church. Such a position defined them as both theologically and socially outside the dominant cultural norms, making theirs a bottom-up theological perspective at that time.

The socially and politically affirmed top-down authority of Catholicism, however, continued to hold sway throughout most of Western Europe even as secular political events conspired to lend support to the Reformers. Generally, nobility vied to protect their own power interests by either supporting the pope or protecting the Reformers. Moreover, other social, intellectual, and political events throughout urban centers on the Continent were posing serious problems for church tradition, long-held Christian dogma, and the place of the church society. In 1533, for example, when Pope Clement VII refused to grant England's Henry VIII a divorce from his wife, Catherine of Aragon, in order that he might marry Anne Boleyn, the frustrated king retreated from his earlier support of the pope against Germany's priest, Martin Luther. Instead, the English monarch responded by taking a series of political steps that, in 1534, resulted in the English Parliament's declaring the king to be the

"Supreme Head of the Church in England." The origins of Protestantism in England, thus, were very much entangled with overt signs of political motivation. On the Continent, religious fervor often collaborated with political expedience in bloodthirsty fashion to determine whether bottom-up Protestant activism or top-down Roman Catholic traditions would prevail in a given area. The infamous Thirty Years' War (1618–1648), in which there were several military campaigns designed to stamp out various outbreaks of Protestantism, was a terrible example of this reality. In this fashion, Geneva, Switzerland, became one of the early centers of Protestant safety.

Although it started as a Lutheran-inspired phenomenon in Germany, through a series of political intrigues and nationalistic tendencies, the bottom-up reformist spirit of religious protest-ism caught on in Switzerland and the Netherlands, and eventually made its way to Scotland, England, and North America. As it spread, each new local context brought a unique character to its brand of Protestantism under the influence of the various clergy joining the cause. Under the influence of leaders such as Huldrych Zwingli, John Calvin, and Theodore Beza in Switzerland, John Knox in Scotland, Jacobus Arminius in the Netherlands, John Wesley in England and North America, Jonathan Edwards in the North American English colonies, and Charles Finney in the young Republic, Protestant theology underwent substantial modifications in response to its differing social, political, and economic contexts. The urban character of this movement's spread as well as its growing social acceptance were undeniable.

Over time, however, it was John Calvin's stamp on Protestant Christian orthodoxy—with his interpretation of irresistible or unchanging divine grace, whereby God elects certain people to eternal salvation while damning others to eternal destruction—that became a dominant influence in early Protestant individualist thinking. In this, the seeds for Protestant transformation from a bottom-up social location to a position of top-down theological affirmation were sown. Calvin's doctrinal position on this matter of predestination is clearly stated in chapter 21, book 3 of the Institutes:

> All are not created on equal terms, but some are preordained to eternal life, others to eternal damnation; and, accordingly, as each has been created for one or other of these ends, we say that he has been predestinated to life or to death. This God has testified, not only in the case of single individuals; he has also given a specimen of it in the whole posterity of Abraham, to make it plain that the future condition of each nation was entirely at his disposal.[2]

In spite of Calvin's apparent intentions that this doctrine be understood as a catalyst to inspire humble gratitude and righteous behavior among those who recognized their status as recipients of this unmerited divine favor, unfortunately, less-noble results followed in the interpretation of this teaching. In areas where Protestantism became numerically dominant and less socially and politically vulnerable, it became possible for Calvinists and followers of other variations of Protestant thought to function in society with impunity. In time, the responses of humble thankfulness, modesty, and frugality that Calvin claimed as appropriate to the status of the elect gave way to other less-virtuous characteristics. Although scripture-based spiritual reform was a prime motivator among core Protestant leaders, in the wider society among an emerging new bourgeoisie, more-mundane considerations were prevalent. As later ethicists and theologians have observed, interpretations of Calvin's doctrine significantly affected the outlook on society as a whole by giving more attention to its assertion of inequality among human beings rather than focusing on calls for humility and thankfulness for divine favor.[3] Preston N. Williams's comments are representative of conclusions about the ethical outcomes of this warped understanding of Calvin's teachings on this point:

> This way of understanding God's household has had enormous consequences for the manner in which stewardship was established in respect to all things . . . [and has] left its mark upon our ideas of community. Troeltsch captures the historical consequence accurately when he states that Calvinism has no doctrine of abstract equality. It affirms instead an inequality of earthly vocations and an essential inequality of human life.[4]

This growing sense of political security, combined with the new emphasis on individual freedom and a warped sense of divine favor (election via predestination), became a theological template for a new understanding of society that redefined the thinking in Calvinistic Protestantism from its bottom-up perspective to the more privileged intellectual and spiritual status of top-down.

The Influence of Science on Faith

Concurrent with these events, intellectuals began promoting ideas that also seemed to test long-held religious traditions. This period witnessed a subjectivist turn in European philosophy in which the influences of René Descartes (1596–1650), Baruch Spinoza (1632–1677), Gottfried Leibniz (1646–1716), and Christian Wolff (1679–1754) are representative. Although Protestantism, with its spirit of individual freedom of conscience before God, had begun to gain wider acceptance in various quarters of Europe, the central tenets of Christian orthodoxy remained unquestioned. These philosophers planted seeds that later sprouted into the full bloom of Enlightenment philosophical trends in which the culturally dominant top-down teachings of Christianity were subjected to the scrutiny of rational analysis.[5]

Descartes is significant because he began the trend of questioning established traditions in philosophy and theology and emphasizing only that which could be understood through human reasoning. His famous quote, *Cogito, ergo sum*—"I think, therefore I am"—epitomizes this philosophical stance. Such notions were considered quite radical for their time but eventually gained popularity due to growing discontent with prevailing old-school (top-down) traditions and social ideas that were viewed as restricting personal freedom and thought. The works of others, such as the antiauthoritarian British philosopher John Locke (1632–1704), in his *Essay Concerning Human Understanding,* which dealt with what can and cannot be known about God, and his *Treatises on Government,* which greatly influenced political discourse, were attracting attention. This philosophical trend was also seen in the writing of Jean-Jacques Rousseau's (1712–1778) *The Social Contract,* emphasizing individual freedom, and in Johann Heinrich Pestalozzi (1746–1827) through his Rousseau-inspired individualistic ideas regarding pedagogy. Immanuel Kant's (1724–1804) *Critique of Pure Reason* emphasized that empiricism and mathematics were important along with understanding the limitations of metaphysics in discerning knowledge; and Wilhelm Friedrich Hegel (1770–1831) sought to explain universal and eternal truths logically through a process of dialectical reasoning. Although these philosophers viewed themselves as working within the Judeo-Christian tradition, their writings had the effect of giving much more importance to the place of human reason than had previously been customary in the culture of Western Europe up to that time.

Similar to this trend in philosophy, a nascent liberal theology began to emerge in Germany, the cradle of the Protestant Reformation, and its influence was felt throughout Europe. Primarily based in German universities, which enjoyed considerable license to explore concepts not widely shared in the wider culture, theologians began to advance ideas that were at variance with the old top-down theological teachings of former generations. Supported by philosophical approaches drawn from Kant and Hegel, a new sense of German idealism became intrinsic to the new top-down philosophical and theological discourse. These approaches gave new importance to individual thought, experience, and feeling in discerning divine revelation as opposed to exclusive reliance on tradition and dogma. One of the key exemplars of this trend was the German theologian Friedrich Schleiermacher (1768–1834), often referred to as the "father of liberal theology," who placed great emphasis on internal feelings as a means of understanding God. Unlike earlier theological Reformers, these later proponents of evolving liberal trends in Protestant theology did not feel constrained to subscribe to cardinal teachings of the Christian orthodoxy uncritically, but sought to bring a rational understanding to inherited doctrine. The German idealist Albrecht Ritschl (1822–1889) is representative of this later trend with his ethics-oriented efforts to interpret the gospel in a very practical manner, free of metaphysics or philosophy. He emphasized the idea of the "kingdom of God," arguing that history was in the process of being divinely guided toward a sense of perfection that, through good human labors borne of faith and love, could be achieved in society.[6] Following in this vein, German historian Adolf von Harnack (1851–1930), in his voluminous *History of Dogma* also sought to weed out the accumulated and extraneous metaphysics from Christian dogma, which he interpreted as including the doctrine of the Incarnation, so that the unencumbered essence of the gospel might be discovered free of Greek thought so as to better serve society.

It was against this philosophical and theological background that the discipline called sociology of religion was developed. Conceived as one of the subfields of sociology, the broader study of human social interactions, relationships, institutions, and behavior, the sociology of religion is often viewed as the intellectual cradle from which urban ministry springs. Auguste Comte (1798–1857), the nineteenth-century French philosopher, was one of the first to use the word *sociology* as part of his emphasis on Positivism, a new scientific system of human action that would replace outmoded theological dogmas and philosophical speculation.[7] Similarly, the writings of Émile Durkheim (1858–1917), Karl Marx (1818–1883), Max Weber (1864–1920), and Ernst Troeltsch (1865–1923)[8] are all understandably credited with providing critical analyses of the role of religion in society. Marx, for example, outraged by the squalid living conditions of the urban poor working in industrial cities, became notable for his dialectical materialism that interpreted religion as a negative factor in society ("the opiate of the masses"), contributing to the maintenance of systemic economic and social inequities. More commonplace were the positions taken by Durkheim, Weber, and Troeltsch in their collective heralding of religion (Christianity) as a catalyst for positive social change. These approaches sought to give scientific accounts of the influence and role of the church in society. As such, many scholars have attempted to view urban ministry's preoccupation with the functional outcomes of articulated faith beliefs as justification for their attempts to position it within the academy as a subcategory of sociology of religion. These views, however, ignore the issue of social location that separates learned scholars and academicians in universities from the uneducated poor, the unemployed, and the politically disenfranchised masses of people whose physical options and very existence tend to be perpetually precarious.

The Emerging Protestant Social Order

In this wide sweep of social, political, and philosophical events, the protest movement in Western Europe's Christianity emerged. In combination with increasing industrialism and its resultant growth in cities, the rise of a new bourgeoisie defined by capitalistic success, and the heightened authority of scientific methodology, the Protestant movement in the Christianity of Western Europe gained momentum. In areas in which Protestantism became numerically significant, the sociopolitical vulnerability of its adherents was reduced and its originally bottom-up posture became more widely affirmed. The prevailing Protestant ethos of independence gave rise to a variety of expressions in Christian faith originally identified as "sects," later to be known as denominations.[9] Differing Protestant groups, responding to the relative weakness of religious and educational life in the North American colonies, brought their own interpretation of orthodoxy, whether associated with the Church of England (Anglican), followers of Calvinist thought (Presbyterian), Wesleyan (Methodists), or independent Congregationalists and Baptists. These were critical factors in the religious and cultural formation of the United States, the first nation to be founded on essentially Protestant principles.[10]

Without question, the success of theological *protest-ism* in Christianity had reformed not only the faith, but the entire culture of Western Europe and North America in which it functioned. Adherents of the growing Protestant Reformation, in making their way from Europe across the Atlantic Ocean to a "new world" of relative isolation from past hassles and constraints, fashioned a new social context. The largest segments came from England, but during the eighteenth century, significant numbers of Protestants from France (Huguenots), Germany, Switzerland, Ireland, and Scotland also migrated to the colonies.[11] In this new geographic setting, the Protestant ethos in confident top-down fashion was evident in cities from Boston and Philadelphia to Savannah. It literally revolutionized itself into a social contract called the United States of America, whose governmental structure "disestablished" any particular religious dogma in favor of individual freedom of conscience in such matters.[12] In this context, Protestant thought now occupied a secure and top-down place in society, with its cultural ethos built on social advocacy for causes that were deemed to be morally upright and affirming of the human spirit.

Theological discourse in academic settings came to reflect the cultural and religiously affirmed top-down perspective. Under the influence of Enlightenment idealism and infatuation with scientific methodology, matters of faith and piety fused with scholarship into new and critical ways of interpreting scripture and doctrine so as to give a scientific twist to explaining appropriate religious activity in society. Protestant theology now took its place among the other intellectual disciplines of the academy dealing with human behavior: philosophy and the newly emerging sciences of psychology and sociology. Cultural leaders, whether or not they were overtly religious, began to function in concert with the new Protestant ethos. Although set forth as a political document, the lofty Jeffersonian ideals of the new American republic's founding document, the Declaration of Independence, articulated in near theological language beliefs that once energized previous generations of bottom-up Protestant theological activity in Europe against tyranny. Now these ideals became enshrined in the articulated credo of civil society in the new nation:

> We hold these truths to be self-evident, that all men are created equal, that they are endowed by their Creator with certain unalienable Rights, that among these are Life, Liberty, and the pursuit of Happiness.[13]

Religious historian Catherine Albanese identified what she called a "Protestant code" (expressed as clear conditions, institutions, and underlying patters for behavior) that fomented a social culture in the United States thoroughly enmeshed and influenced by Protestantism.[14] Sociologists Kevin Christiano, Peter Kivisto, and religious researcher William Swatos view Protestant principles of social action as a social underlay that influenced United States culture well before the majority of the country's population was formally affiliated with any Protestant church:

> Originating in Protestantism, a truly distinctive feature of religion in the United States is its informal system of *denominationalism*, an institutional pattern that both governs relations among the churches and organizes contact between them and the wider community. In its more theoretical form, denominationalism has been called "the ideology of pluralism." . . . The system derives its name from the ecclesiological term for the free churches that find themselves at home in a religiously pluralistic society.[15]

The individualist and freedom of conscience ethos embedded within the Protestant frame of reference was no longer confined to the realm of religious belief; it was now part of the cultural structure of the society as a whole, broadly affirmed in principle and very much founded on a top-down theological paradigm. Although these were some of the seminal events and thinkers shaping the top-down theological perspective in the United States, their contributions are only part of the heritage in Christian thought that informs the urban ministry context. Next, we shall turn to some of the seminal events and thinkers shaping the bottom-up theological perspective.

CHAPTER SEVEN

ANTECEDENTS OF A *BOTTOM-UP* THEOLOGICAL PERSPECTIVE

How long will you torment me,
*   and break me in pieces with words? . . .*
O that my words were written down!
*   O that they were inscribed in a book!*
Oh that with an iron pen and with lead
*   they were engraved on a rock forever!*
For I know that my Redeemer lives,
*   and that at the last he will stand upon the earth;*
and after my skin has been thus destroyed,
*   then in my flesh I shall see God,*
whom I shall see on my side,
*   and my eyes shall behold, and not another.*

—Job 19:2, 23-27

If there are any citizens within the state who by definition, stated or implied,
are denied freedom of access to the resources of community as established
within the state, such persons are assailed at the very foundation of their
sense of belonging. . . . The term "second class citizen" is often used to
describe such a status. This means that such persons are "outsiders"
living in the midst of "insiders," required to honor the same demands of
sovereignty but denied the basic rewards of sovereignty.

—Howard Thurman[1]

Conventional thought about urban ministry almost exclusively associates its roots with the old Social Gospel movement in the United States during the late nineteenth and early twentieth centuries. In this vein, the origins of urban ministry are seen as having been primarily influenced by German idealists in philosophy and liberal theology, interpreting the gospel primarily in response to social problems associated with industrial capitalism, its growth, and its influence on urbanization.[2] Although these elements were certainly involved, there is much more to the origins of the bottom-up theological frame of reference than this type of thinking suggests. The major limitation of this understanding of urban ministry's roots is that it tends to conceive of urban ministry from a sort of noblesse oblige perspective that views many of the negative situations or conditions found in the city as problems of the "less fortunate" or even the "morally reprobate" that "we, the privileged" are called to address as part of our Christian duty.

However well intended, this type of "us/them" religious approach tends to blur the spiritual unity of all people that is fundamental to appreciating the interrelatedness of all God's creation. This limited perspective can encourage a response to others as religious "clients" rather than as spiritual siblings. It sometimes forgets the Pauline reminder that "all have sinned and fall short of the glory of God" (Romans 3:23), which emphasizes our fundamental unity as human beings in needing the grace of God to survive and reach our full potential for good. The characterization, nonetheless, is understandable because the Social Gospel movement, as it came to be known in this country, did play a major role in forging a reassessment of how Christians interpreted theological doctrine in actual behavioral practice amid challenges presented by fast-growing industrial cities of the era.

Social Gospel Connections

During this period, the nation sought to surge ahead, putting the ravages of the Civil War behind and moving into the new century with unprecedented industrial growth and wealth. Ethicist J. Phillip Wogaman described the era as one of rapid change that revealed critical social problems:

> The Civil War . . . had quickened the pace of the Industrial Revolution in the North, as industries grew up overnight to supply the Union war machine. Unlike the South, which was devastated, the North was stimulated economically. The following years were a time of rapid expansion: new factories were developed to manufacture new products, railways were built spanning the continent, trade expanded. Wave after wave of new immigrants came to America to provide cheap labor. . . . It was a time of growing prosperity for many, and some became fabulously wealthy. . . . But many people—especially those concentrated in the working-class sections of the industrial cities—were caught in the backwash. For them, industrialization meant backbreaking toil, long working hours, child labor, exploitation of women, adulterated food, periods of unemployment, vulnerability to industrial accidents and disease, little educational opportunity, inadequate medical attention, and general impoverishment.[3]

One of the preeminent personalities calling attention to this situation was Walter Rauschenbusch (1861–1918), the nineteenth-century New York City urban-pastor-cum-seminary professor. With the publication of his *Christianity and the Social Crisis* in 1907, Rauschenbusch became one of the principal articulators of the Social Gospel movement of the early twentieth century, which is traditionally accepted as the precursor of urban ministry as we know it today. In this vein, the roots of urban-ministry theological analysis are broadly associated with liberal theology's socially progressive agenda, which sought to address these flagrant social injustices in the first half of the twentieth century. Although these approaches included individualistic and direct-service elements, such as soup kitchens and settlement houses such as Chicago's famous Hull House developed by Jane Addams, there were also more macro/systemic voices including the Congregationalist minister Washington Gladden (1836–1918). As an example of this more systemic critique of the social injustices of the era, Wogaman cites from Gladden's 1886 volume titled *Applied Christianity*, which decried the widening chasm between the wealth of employers and their workers:

> The hundreds of thousands of unemployed laborers, vainly asking for work; the rapid increase of pauperism, indicated by the fact that during the last Winter, in the chief cities of this rich commonwealth, nearly one tenth of the population sought charitable aid from the infirmary director or the benevolent societies; the strikes and lock-outs reported every day in the newspapers.[4]

This type of social-emphasis agenda was articulated by several urbane and influential preachers and academicians of the Protestant top-down theological establishment, including Harry Emerson Fosdick (1878–1969), Henry Sloane Coffin (1877–1954), and George A. Buttrick (1892–1979). Yet, there is another perspective that profoundly informed urban-ministry praxis of the era. We now turn our attention to consideration of the formative factors in its development.

Bottom-Up: The *Down and Out* Group Reality

In response to its own history of struggle against religious repression back in Europe, North American–style Protestantism reconfigured itself into a new sociopolitical and religious paradigm that welcomed victims of religious oppression. In forging its bottom-up sensibilities to social vulnerability, the now top-down Protestant theological culture nonetheless included in the new cultural matrix some practices from the old cultural setting that were quite exclusionary. Since the term *bottom-up* refers to discerning divine revelation from the perspective of the most sociopolitically and economically vulnerable persons in society, it is appropriate to consider those who were left "on the bottom" in the new cultural context as the spirit of Protestantism made its way to social, economic, and political acceptability and security. This brings us to a discussion of those who were excluded not only religiously and socially, but for economic, political, and ideological reasons as well. In the "new world" socioeconomic and political experiment in North America, two groups of people constituted the excluded: the indigenous ethnic groups that were native to the Americas and the enslaved Africans. In the former excluded group were such nations of people as the Choctaw, Hopi, Navaho, and Sioux, among others, and these were ultimately defined by the arriving settlers as hostile and dangerous. Within a relatively brief time, they were identified as the enemy to be overcome or contained. Tragically, through a continuing series of intervening negotiations, broken treaties, and wars, these people were nearly obliterated.

The latter group of excluded persons represented a huge variety of African nations: Akan, Bankongo, Ewe, Ga, Hausa, Ibo, Mandinka, Wolof, and Yoruba, among others, and they constituted the millions of people who were either prisoners of war or victims of overt abduction for profit and sold into slavery. These people became part of the socioeconomic and cultural context of the "new world," but they were defined as property rather than human beings through enslavement. In this process, their clothing, culture, language, and ethnic identity were systematically stripped away along with their status of being human. In slavery, they became things rather than people and were simply referred to by the color of their skin as compared to Europeans and became known primarily by the Spanish word for "black" or *negro*.

These Africans, simply referred to as "negro" slaves, constituted a new type of social "bottom": they were literally defined outside the human family. They developed overt and covert responses of resistance to their situation and began to incorporate in these responses the theological language of the top-down Protestant culture. All of this was done employing a theological praxis that sought to reclaim their humanity and freedom. It is this type of theological praxis that informs the bottom-up theological perspective found in urban ministry today. Of course, the chattel slavery of the "new world," so prevalent in the seventeenth through nineteenth centuries, no longer exists in the United States, and the urban reality of the twenty-first century is defined by an ethnic pluralism that is truly global. The fact remains, however, that the theological frame of reference that defines the theological milieu, both top-down and bottom-up, in which urban ministry takes place today, was significantly shaped by the events of this historical reality.

Before addressing the issue of African enslavement as part of the bottom-up religious framework, it must be recognized that hosts of ethnic and cultural groups constituting the mosaic of the United States' constituency have experienced cruel indignities throughout the story of the nation's history. Many people were socially and politically defined outside the new cultural environment. The Iroquois, Mohawk, Navajo, Seminole, and many other nations now commonly referred to as Native American peoples were not universally recognized by law as U.S. citizens until 1924. Also, there are tragic tales of xenophobic reactions by the dominant social, political, and religious culture as defined by "White Anglo-Saxon Protestant" to various other racial, cultural, and religious groups that have become, over time, part and parcel of today's multicultural society. Even today, many persons from Central and Latin America, the Caribbean, Arabian cultures, Asia, or from the Pacific Rim (whether Chinese, Korean, Filipino, Japanese, Indian, Vietnamese, or even those from the Hawaiian Islands) experience hostility in the U.S. much more openly than persons of European ethnic extraction. At the beginning of this century, even some southern European religious groups outside the mainline Protestant religious traditions (Catholics, Jews, Eastern Orthodox, or Muslims) were subject to many indignities in the process of carving out their niches in United States culture.

The significance of African enslavement, however, is uniquely insightful in understanding the resources of the bottom-up theological context because this was the only ethnic group denied legal recognition as part of the human family in courts of law because they were defined as property.[5]

For the first eighty-five years of the United States' 231-year existence, or roughly 37 percent of the nation's sovereign history, African people were legally defined by the Constitution as being subhuman or "three-fifths human." It took another ninety-three years, until 1954, for the nation's courts to begin the process of ending apartheid or forced racial segregation. Additionally, it was another eleven years, not until 1965, before the unequivocal right to vote for United States–born citizens of African descent was ensured by law. In all, full legal rights of citizenship for African Americans were not universally recognized in all states until 1965, with the passage of the Voting Rights Act, fully 189 years after the nation was founded. As a result, in the oldest nation to be founded on Protestant principles, it has been less than fifty years (less than 25 percent of U.S. history) that the full rights of citizenship, including freedom of movement and voting rights, have been universally acknowledged by law in all fifty states for African-descended persons. This is the best way to understand the bottom-up perspective in America.

The Influence of Slavery

The issue of slavery in the nineteenth century led to the Civil War, unprecedented loss of life including the assassination of the nation's president, disruption of society at all levels, and divided mainline denominations along sectional and ideological/theological lines for generations. Until the latter half of the twentieth century, relatively little attention was given to the theological perspectives of the victims of ethnic oppression in the West. Most analyses dealt with this issue as more of a sociological phenomenon than as a theological one.[6] Moreover, because the economic and social structure of slavery in the United States over time was framed as a regional (North/South) issue, with slavery in the antebellum South largely based in rural areas, the historical connection between this issue and urban reality has not been readily perceived.

Urban centers in the North and South were crucial in addressing the issue of slavery. Also, social justice efforts of the oppressed to alleviate their own oppression, regardless of urban or rural geographic locale, were a key resource in defining the bottom-up theological perspective of urban ministry. Thus, the roots of the bottom-up theological perspective, as drawn from the horrendous social location of enslaved Africans as well as that of their non-African sympathizers during this period, provide invaluable insight into urban-ministry praxis today for the socially and spiritually marginalized. What have we learned from the social, economic, political, and cultural context of those "on the bottom" during this period? What theological legacy was bequeathed as they addressed egalitarian ideas gleaned from interpretations of scriptural authority, divine grace, the Incarnation, or eternal salvation that, centuries before, had challenged socially and politically oppressive structures of religious authority, social privilege, and aristocracy? The answers to these questions lie in the responses of the disenfranchised of the emerging Protestant and top-down theological culture of the new nation, the United States of America.

The Nonhuman Status of Slavery

If personhood or humanity is defined theologically, in part, as being "created in the image of God" (Genesis 3), then being regarded as nonhuman by a society of people who believe in the God of scripture presents a special theological challenge. A part of understanding bottom-up theology, then, has to do with comprehending the reality of being regarded as somewhat less than human or, in fact, as a nonperson. Framers of the Constitution of the United States, operating from a religiously top-down perspective, decided the apportionment of congressional representation and taxation by excluding all the original population that was native to the North American continent and defined enslaved Africans as "three fifths" of a person.[7] This exclusion from membership in the human family defined huge numbers of individuals as theological nonpersons, more akin to beasts such as oxen or swine. How did this happen within the context of the formerly theologically bottom-up Protestant culture?

According to Cornel West, the cultural climate that produced chattel slavery in the West, including its invention of the idea of "race" and its doctrine of White supremacy, was intricately tied up with a number of complex factors in the early modern period in Europe that were especially dependent on supposedly "scientific" or empirical justifications as evidence:

> The authority of science, undergirded by a modern philosophical discourse guided by Greek ocular metaphors and Cartesian notions, promotes and encourages the activities of observing, comparing, measuring, and ordering the physical characteristics of human bodies. Given the renewed appreciation and

appropriation of classical antiquity, these activities are regulated by classical aesthetic and cultural norms. The creative fusion of scientific investigation, Cartesian epistemology, and classical ideals produced forms of rationality, scientificity, and objectivity which, though efficacious in the quest for truth and knowledge, prohibited the intelligibility and legitimacy of the idea of Black equality in beauty, culture, and intellectual capacity. In fact, to "think" such an idea was to be deemed irrational, barbaric, or mad.[8]

West argues that beginning with the Enlightenment period, the infatuation with classical aesthetics functioned to influence so-called scientific objectivity so as to produce hierarchical cultural assumptions regarding humanity that defined Blacks as intellectual and physical inferiors. He goes on to catalog a list of celebrated thinkers of this era whose racially pejorative ideas were so widely affirmed in the culture that their opinions on the matter were not thought to be an offense to human dignity:

> Montesquieu and Voltaire of the French Enlightenment, Hume and Jefferson of the Scotch and the American Enlightenment, and Kant of the German Enlightenment not merely held racist views; they also uncritically—during this age of criticism—believed that the *authority* for these views rested in the domain of naturalists, anthropologists, physiognomists, and phrenologists. . . . Voltaire's endorsement of the idea of white supremacy was unequivocal. In his essay "People of America," he claimed . . . "The Negro race is a species of men as different from ours as the breed of spaniels is from that of greyhounds." . . . [Hume] . . . "I am apt to suspect the negroes, and in general all the other species of men (for there are four or five different kinds) to be naturally inferior to the whites" [Jefferson] . . . "Comparing them by their faculties of memory, reason, and imagination, it appears to me, that in memory they are equal to the whites; in reason much inferior . . . and that in imagination they are dull, tasteless and anomalous . . ." [Kant, in reply to advice that a black person gave to Father Labat, wrote:] "And it might be that there was something in this which perhaps deserved to be considered; but in short, this fellow was quite black from head to foot, a clear proof that what he said was stupid."[9]

The overwhelmingly Protestant White slave owners in North America did not consider slavery an offense to human dignity, but perfectly normal and even divinely ordained. Eric McKitrick (1963) cited the writings of one cleric, Thornton Stringfellow, who wrote a treatise in 1856 entitled *A Scriptural View of Slavery* that is representative of the theological reasoning of the period. Fashioning a defense of slavery largely drawn from concepts extracted from Calvinist notions concerning the elect and the damned[10] as a justification for unequal status, Stringfellow argued that the relative social positions of individuals were ordained by God. Drawing on what became two of several standard slavery-justifying texts (specifically Genesis 9:25-27 and Ephesians 6:5-7), this theological premise justified the denial of civil rights to Blacks as follows:

The first recorded language which was ever uttered in relation to slavery is the inspired language of Noah. In God's stead he says "cursed be Canaan . . . God shall enlarge Japheth . . . and Canaan shall be his servant." Here language is used showing [how God] decreed Ham in a state of abject bondage. . . . The relative duties of each state [status of the individual] are pointed out [in scripture] . . . those between the servant and the master in these words: "Servants be obedient to them who are your masters, according to the flesh, with fear and trembling, in singleness of your heart as unto Christ"; . . . Here, by the Roman law, the servant was property, and the control of the master unlimited.[11]

Because the enslavers, the elect, viewed themselves as God-fearing people, they often interpreted their actions of aggression upon the enslaved as benevolent. Frequently, they were saving these "poor creatures" from even worse conditions of savagery and ignorance in their native environments of Africa. As religion professor Albert Raboteau noted:

From the very beginning of the Atlantic slave trade, conversion of the slaves to Christianity was viewed by the emerging nations of Western Christendom as a justification for enslavement of Africans. When Portuguese caravels returned from the coast of West Africa with human booty in the fifteenth century, Gomes Eannes De Azurara, a chronicler of their achievements, observed that "the greater benefit" belonged not to the Portuguese adventurers but to the captive Africans, "for though their bodies were now brought into some subjection, that was a small matter in comparison of their souls, which would not possess true freedom for evermore."[12]

It is against this social and theological backdrop that the bottom-up faith perspective of oppressed Africans evolved. Caring in an uncaring environment was a powerful ingredient in the conduct of the enslaved Africans and social life and the eventual cultural setting that developed around it. People were sensitized to the needs of others like themselves who were caught in the web of aggression based upon their status of being nonhuman. A tradition of caring values evolved that became part and parcel of the cultural values within this oppressed community. This sense of connectedness in the matrix of oppression was critical to understanding how and why these people reinterpreted for themselves a very different awareness of God, justice, and what "fellowship" meant than from their top-down oppressors.

African American Sacred Songs as Clue to Theology

Prior to the abolition of slavery, it was illegal to educate Black people in many areas (Herbert Aptheker, 1939; John Hope Franklin, 1980; Albert Raboteau, 1978), leaving the overwhelming majority of Blacks with no access to formal schooling. Except for a few scattered opportunities presented in the North by freedman status or sympathetic Whites, Blacks were not allowed to gain even the rudiments of education. Not surprisingly, historical accounts reveal that very few Blacks attended school in the eighteenth century and during the early part of the nineteenth century. In order to assess the theological reflections of oppressed Blacks during this period, researchers have largely turned to the songs they sang. Many writers have found a rich harvest of theological information within these songs.[13]

Benjamin E. Mays, in his monumental work entitled *The Negro's God* (1933), drew upon slave songs and narratives as source material for determining the theological perspective of American Blacks concerning God. James Cone, J. Rosamond Johnson, Wyatt Tee Walker, and others have also documented the divergent theological perspectives reflected in slave songs in noting differences from the theological views of the slave-condoning society.

> From the African Mother continent, African men and women, through the Middle Passage, through the Diaspora, to the Americas, carried the African gift and treasure of sacred song. To the Americas, African men and women brought sacred songs and chants that reminded them of their homelands and that sustained them in separation and in captivity, songs that respond to all the situations, and the ability to create new songs to answer new needs. African Americans in sacred song preserved the memory of African religious rites and symbols, of a holistic African spirituality, of rhythms and tones and harmonies that communicated their deepest feelings across barriers of region and language.[14]

The song "He's Got the Whole World in His Hands," for example, is an expression of confidence and security in divine *capacity*. Realities that are far beyond the ability of frail humanity to control, understand, or affect in any way cannot overwhelm the believer because of the sure knowledge that God is able. *"In God's hands"* is the capacity to safeguard the cosmos (*the world*), to protect the vulnerable (*the little bitty baby*), to control and contain wickedness at will (*lyin', crap-shootin', and gamblin' folk*), and to be a secure presence (for *everybody here*).

While African slaves in the U.S. may have been barred from engaging in academic debate on the merits of Kant's *Critique of Pure Reason*, slaves knew enough to know that "everybody talking 'bout heaven ain't going there." Although the language of ransom, sanctification, reconciliation, or atonement and other such concepts might not have made much sense, what was well known to slaves was that a very significant event took place on Calvary long ago: *"Were you there when they crucified my Lord?"* A grieving mother, sister, or wife could relate to Mary's pain: *"Were you there when they nailed him to the tree? Oh, sometimes it causes me to tremble, tremble, tremble."* A grieving father, brother, or cousin would want an answer to the question *"Were you there when they pierced him in the side?"* Even today, mothers whose innocent children are shot in schools, killed in drug-related cross fire, routinely harassed, falsely arrested or even killed unjustly by police, or whose daughters are raped and made to feel guilty about it understand this Jesus. Jesus was vulnerable to the pain and abuse of injustice. Homeless people can still relate to this Jesus whose life was so similar to their own lives.

Inside the *Outside* Group:
Bottom-Up Theological Approaches

Against this backdrop of slavery, the top-down *theological language* was reframed into a bottom-up *theological understanding* that found creative practical expression in a theology and daily behavior (praxis) that recognized not only survival, but also caring and compassion as its central hallmark and community as its means of expression. Although privileged people, who were free, safe, and socially secure in their "top-down" and socially affirmed status, talked about a caring God who loves all people, the absurdities of existence as enslaved people with no legal hope of freedom for them or their children presented a different reality to those who were socially "on the bottom."

The social location of enslavement gave concrete meaning to the reality of evil, meanness, and unrelieved suffering. Identification as a slave placed one outside the regular norms for membership in the human family, rendering the individual in absolute social and political *alienation. Fear* was a daily companion: fear of forced separation from family, of deprivation of food and clothing, of perpetual unpaid labor, and of inadequate shelter, sickness, or even loss of life. Violence was intrinsic to this type of existence, with endless days of terror involving wanton brutality of the lash, physical maiming, rape, and all the enforced mental and spiritual anguish that was needed to maintain the institution of slavery. Historian John Hope Franklin interpreted the antislavery movement in the United States as a cause that drew together, in religious fashion, various social and spiritual injustice issues that characterized the young Republic:

> The militant antislavery movement that had developed by 1831 was, itself, a powerful religious crusade. . . . It stemmed from the growing popular concern for the welfare of underprivileged persons, which manifested itself in the antislavery movement, the crusade for better working conditions in England, and the search for a better life in America. It was closely connected, in many respects, with movements for peace, women's rights, temperance, and other reform programs that developed simultaneously. In the West, it was connected with the Great Revival, of which Charles G. Finney was the dominant figure, emphasizing the importance of being useful and thus releasing a powerful impulse toward social reform. The young converts joined Finney's Holy Band, and if the abolition of slavery was a way of serving God, they were anxious to enter into the movement wholeheartedly.[15]

The bottom-up theological perspective in the United States, then, finds some of its clearest models of early expression in the resistance to slavery ministries that formed among the enslaved themselves as well as among the anti-slavery advocacy of the abolitionists. Richard Allen (1760–1831), who was born in slavery and purchased his own freedom, is an example of the principle. In 1787, he led a group of Blacks from Philadelphia's St. George Methodist Church in protest of its practice of racially segregated seating during worship. His action eventually led to the founding of the African Methodist Episcopal Church and represented the same type of bottom-up theological rejection of injustice and oppression tolerated by the top-down prevailing social order that led the German priest Martin Luther to post his Ninety-five Theses in Wittenberg, Germany, centuries before. He was twenty-seven years old.

Ten years after Allen's bold step in Philadelphia, a female slave named Isabella Baumfree was born in New York. She would eventually be known throughout the United States as Sojourner Truth because of her religious advocacy against slavery and for women's rights. As a slave, Isabella was sold several times, and while owned by the John Dumont family in Ulster County, she married another slave owned by Dumont, named Thomas, and gave birth to five children. In 1827, New York law emancipated all slaves, but Isabella had already left her husband and run away with her youngest child.[16] Following her religious conversion, she traveled through New England and the West, moving audiences by her powerful and quaint speech patterns framed in the context of her religious faith and experience that articulated her hatred for slavery and advocacy for women's rights.[17] At an 1851 women's convention in Akron, Ohio, responding to derogatory comments by a White clergyman regarding women, Sojourner Truth uttered what immediately became a classic example of gender and racial justice advocacy from the bottom-up theological perspective:

That man over there says that women need to be helped into carriages, and lifted over ditches, and to have the best place everywhere. Nobody ever helps me into carriages, or over mud-puddles, or gives me any best place! And ain't I a woman? Look at me! Look at my arm! I have ploughed and planted, and gathered into barns, and no man could head me! And ain't I a woman? I could work as much and eat as much as a man—when I could get it—and bear the lash as well! And ain't I a woman? I have borned thirteen children, and seen them most all sold off to slavery, and when I cried out with my mother's grief, none but Jesus heard me! And ain't I a woman? . . . Then that little man in black there, he says women can't have as much rights as men, 'cause Christ wasn't a woman! Where did your Christ come from? . . . From God and a woman! Man had nothing to do with Him. If the first woman God ever made was strong enough to turn the world upside down all alone, these women together ought to be able to turn it back, and get it right side up again! And now they is asking to do it, the men better let them.[18]

The varied approaches of leaders such as Bishop Allen and of public advocates such as Sojourner Truth were part of a host of other clergy and other public leaders serving African American communities in Northern cities during the antebellum period when the social context of Africans, while not enslaved, was still economically, educationally, and politically precarious. This social vulnerability shaped a bottom-up approach to their theological reflection that challenged religiously top-down assumptions that tolerated racial and gender discrimination and economic injustice. Nonclergy leaders, notably Frederick Douglass, an ex-slave who became the nation's most well-known antislavery orator, and Harriet Tubman, the diminutive personality who clandestinely cheated death countless times to bring literally hundreds of enslaved persons from slavery to freedom on the Underground Railroad, embraced their opposition to slavery as a religious crusade for righteousness.

Samuel Cornish, a Presbyterian minister and a protégé of the Reverend John Gloucester, a freed slave from Tennessee, who in 1807 had founded in Philadelphia the first African American Presbyterian congregation in the nation, shortly thereafter started a church in New York City. After laboring for two years as a missionary to indigent Blacks in the slums of lower Manhattan, Cornish founded the First Colored Presbyterian Church of New York City and became known for his antislavery advocacy.[19] During this time, African Americans in New York City, though generally poor and few in number, nonetheless founded and supported their own institutions, organized an antislavery society, and ran charities for orphans.[20] With much of this being clergy-led, it was not surprising that Reverend Cornish served for twenty years on the executive committee of the American Anti-Slavery Society in New York and eventually become the founding editor of the first Black newspaper in the United States, *Freedom's Journal*.[21] Reverend Henry Highland Garnet viewed slavery as such a blatant social injustice that he declared:

> God would smile on every effort the injured might make to disenthrall themselves. . . . The humblest peasant is as free in the sight of God as the proudest monarch that ever swayed a scepter. Liberty is a spirit sent from God and, like its great Author, is no respecter of persons.[22]

Post-Slavery Bottom-Up Theological Challenges

The many opportunities for growth and healing that became apparent after the Civil War also revealed social challenges that would affect Christian mission and refine the bottom-up theological approach in the near future. Concurrent with new opportunities of burgeoning and industrial expansion came the social and economic devastation of the Southern region left in the wake of the war along with its huge population of newly emancipated and poorly educated ex-slaves. Reconstruction efforts in this region were met with hostility by former Confederate loyalists. Industrial growth of Northern cities and westward expansion also drew rising numbers of immigrants from Europe, and living and working conditions in the Northern cities continued to deteriorate under the stress of overcrowding and rising crime. During this period, the dominant top-down theological perspectives of Northern and Southern missionary approaches would come to view education for former slaves in similar fashion, but from the different orientations they had prior to the Civil War:

> The nineteenth-century origins of the social gospel (movement) are found in domestic missions. . . . Northern missions to the South feared that the races might degenerate to barbaric conditions in the postwar years and sought to sustain, regenerate, and redeem them by replicating Northern social Christianity in the South. As Southern churches recovered their footing, some of their leaders, drawing on the memory of missions to slaves, joined in the missions to freedmen. They rejected Northern missionary assumptions of Yankee superiority, but they too defined the problem largely in moral terms and saw its solution in the extension of white social and cultural norms to their brothers in black.[23]

Unabated racial hostilities between former slave owners and former slaves continued to fester and eventually forced the federal government to abandon its reconstruction efforts, giving rise to terrorist tactics that circumvented the political gains of newly emancipated citizens. The rise of the Ku Klux Klan and the widespread use of lynching to disenfranchise African Americans politically, economically, and educationally transformed emancipation into little more than a slightly modified form of slavery in which racial segregation, sharecropping, and subservience became the norm in rural and urban contexts. By 1884, affairs had reached such a dismal state that when a former schoolteacher-turned-journalist-and-civil-rights-advocate in Memphis, Tennessee, Ida Barnett Wells, used the small newspaper she edited, *Free Speech and Headlight,* to denounce the lynching of three Black businessmen and the flimsy public investigation into the matter and called for the prosecution of the killers, her printing press was destroyed by a mob of White men. Wells, who was on her way to a church convention at the time of the attack on her establishment, was threatened with murder if she returned to the city.[24] Although slavery was officially dead, socially condoned violence and oppression were not. Ida B. Wells moved to New York where she continued her vigilance against lynching, documenting hundreds of such incidents and joining with other social justice advocates such as Jane Addams, the Reverend Harlan Douglas, and educators Booker T. Washington and William E. B. DuBois leading the crusade in calling public attention to this deplorable situation. The sad fact is that in the last sixteen years of the nineteenth century, there were more than twenty-five hundred lynching victims documented in the United States, the great majority of these having been Negroes, and the states of Mississippi, Alabama, Georgia, and Louisiana prominently figuring in these statistics.[25]

These ugly realities fomented the impetus for an unprecedented migration of African Americans from rural areas into urban centers and especially from the Southern states to Northern cities in search of better living conditions. They also constituted one of the central social-justice realities framing the bottom-up theological perspective giving rise to that which would later be described as urban ministry. In 1900, 90 percent of all African Americans lived in the South.[26] Although racial segregation and limited opportunities also characterized Northern cities, Southern Blacks were nonetheless drawn to them in unprecedented numbers as the United States became preoccupied with events leading up to World War I. The supply of immigrant labor from Europe rapidly declined from more than a million new arrivals in 1914 to only 110,618 in 1918.[27] Railroads, steel mills, and a wide assortment of eastern industries, many of them war-related, began recruiting in the South, using Black as well as White agents.[28] Historian Carter G. Woodson, in 1918, asserted that "within the last two years there has been a steady stream of Negroes into the North in such large numbers as to overshadow in its results all other movements of the kind in the United States."[29] During this period, the work of the Young Men's Christian Associations, active in the United States since the 1850s and represented in many of the larger cities, began to reach out to members of the Black community, although by means of establishing racially segregated facilities in these urban centers.[30]

Cities across the North including Chicago, Illinois; St. Louis, Missouri; Detroit, Michigan; Cleveland, Ohio; New York City; and Philadelphia, Pennsylvania, witnessed the arrival of wave after wave of African Americans entering formerly all-White neighborhoods. Between 1890 and 1910, New York's African American population grew from 1.4 to 2.0 percent; Chicago's African American population increased from 1.3 to 2.0 percent of total residents, and the African American population of Philadelphia went from 3.8 to 5.5 percent.[31] Cities bordering the South had more substantial African American population figures: Indianapolis, Indiana, 9.3 percent; Wilmington, Delaware, 10.4 percent; Baltimore, Maryland, 15.2 percent; and Washington, D.C., 28.5 percent.[32] In the South, where most African Americans still lived, more than 80 percent of these were in rural areas, but several Southern cities also experienced substantial growth, including Atlanta, Georgia; and Chattanooga and Memphis, Tennessee, where the African American population tripled in twenty years.[33] Although widely criticized for undercounting the nation's African American population, the U.S. Census of 1920 still reported that the Black population of the North had increased by approximately 450,000 since 1910, while the South's grew by only about 150,000.[34]

The perception of the North as the "Promised Land,"[35] however, in reality left much to be desired and, in many ways, the North proved little different from the hostile environments from which Blacks left. The new arrivals from the South often found themselves the victims of economic and social exploitation and forced into squalid living conditions. Hostile Whites, often socially acculturated in the wider society to view Blacks as intellectually and morally inferior, occasionally resorted to physical violence against Blacks, whom they saw as competing for their jobs. Urban race riots in cities across America, North and South, broke out with dismaying regularity. New York (August 1901); Springfield, Ohio (August 1904); Greensburg, Indiana (1906); Atlanta, Georgia (September 1906); Brownsville, Texas (August 1906), East St. Louis, Illinois (July 1917), and Tulsa, Oklahoma (May 1921) were some of the more notorious incidents involving both loss of life and extensive property damage. In January 1917, the entire Florida town of Rosewood, mostly populated by African Americans, was completely destroyed by frenzied mob racial violence, lynching, and general lawlessness prompted by unfounded accusations that a Negro male had assaulted a White woman. In both the North and the South, social, economic, and physical vulnerability and blatant injustice were obvious characteristics that informed the African American bottom-up theological perspective during this period.

Evangelism, Education, and Social Uplift Goals

Like Christian churches through the ages, Black churches in the United States always understood the classic scriptural reference of the Great Commission found in Matthew 28:19-20 to include the twin mandates of evangelism and education: "Go therefore and make disciples of all nations [that is, *evangelize*] . . . teaching them to obey everything that I have commanded you [that is, *educate*]." As such, education was always a high priority in the Black church's efforts at disciple making and enhancing the spiritual formation of society. Education was seen as the means for enabling disciples to live harmoniously as members of the covenant community within the church family as well as members of and positive contributors to the wider society. This is one of the main reasons that Black churches, urban and rural, were interested in the establishment of schools at all levels insofar as their resources enabled them: elementary, secondary, and college. Education was and continues to be an inseparable motivation in the church's missionary focus. In urban ministry, this twin focus (evangelism and education) remained consistent with the church's historic understanding of its role in the wider society as churches sought to respond to the urban challenges of this period.

Born in the crucible of slavery and, after emancipation, nurtured in the context of racial segregation, conversion to faith in Jesus Christ in the Black church was always understood to carry with it certain expectations of moral uplifting and improved social responsibility. Part of the bottom-up theological perspective, therefore, involved recognition of the Christian duty to equip victims of injustice and oppression with both the spiritual and social skills needed to live their lives as persons truly seeking to respond affirmatively to the charge given in Romans 12:1-2. They were attempting to become "a living sacrifice, holy and acceptable to God" as their spiritual worship, not "conformed to this world, but . . . transformed by the renewing of [their] minds, [in order to] discern what is the will of God" for themselves. The spiritual blessings of conversion to faith in Jesus Christ were inseparable from the social responsibilities to live a holy life that took into account the welfare of the neighbor. Education was not merely an academic exercise; rather, it involved social uplifting and communal responsibility. Christian educator Fred Smith describes this phenomenon as one of inspiring African-descended victims of oppression toward a focus on human dignity:

> A goal of Africentric Christian education is to awaken in oppressed people a sense of transcendence that corrects the tendency of demeaning social and political structures to limit their attention to the dynamics of oppression rather than to draw attention to sources of human dignity. The function of religious education as a response to oppression is to present persons with appropriate metaphors through which they may come to see and understand their condition differently. These metaphors provide a vision by which persons begin to see what should be what they can hope for, and how they ought to act.[36]

Learning a skill or trade, or mastering a newly acquired discipline, was not merely used as a means of individual economic survival, but as a step toward the personal realization of God-given purpose and potential in order to be of service to others. "Lifting as we climb" became the motto of this unified spiritual and social conversion to faith in Jesus Christ as was symbolized in the old African American spiritual "We Are Climbing Jacob's Ladder."

In partnership with Northern and Southern missionaries, the federal government's Freedman's Bureau during Reconstruction, and a host of private philanthropists, the establishment of schools for Africans during the colonial period as well as for newly emancipated Blacks following the Civil War was embraced by African Americans and European Americans throughout the South with a religious zeal that betrayed the bottom-up determination to present workers worthy of "approval by God without the need to be ashamed and rightly explaining the word of truth" (2 Timothy 2:15, paraphrased from the NRSV). Many "normal" schools or teachers colleges were established to assist in educationally preparing the descendants of Africa in the United States to better themselves. Its purpose was to establish teaching standards or norms, hence its name. These norms often also included social skills and moral demeanor that teachers were to exemplify and pass on to their students. With this focus in mind, a host of schools serving children of all ages through the college level were established to help in the social uplifting of Blacks. Some of the more nationally known of these historic institutions of higher learning are Pennsylvania's Lincoln University (1854); Washington, D.C.'s Howard University (1867); Virginia's Hampton Institute (1868); Alabama's Tuskegee Institute (1881); Nashville's Fisk University (1866); Georgia's Atlanta University (1965); Morehouse College (1867); Clark College (1869); Spelman College (1881); and South Carolina's Bennett College (1873).

Early Models of Bottom-Up Theological Praxis

Four persons whose ministries typified the bottom-up theological perspective are illustrative of how this approach sought to address the painful realities of social, political, and racial disenfranchisement in urban ministry during the first half of the twentieth century. These include the ministries of the African Methodist Episcopal bishop Reverdy Ransom of Chicago, Illinois; the Reverend Adam Clayton Powell, Sr., of New York City; Dr. Mary McLeod Bethune of Daytona Beach, Florida; and the Reverend Matthew Anderson of Philadelphia, Pennsylvania.

Bishop Reverdy Ransom

In response to the rising social problems of these cities, movements to address the deplorable situation of the incoming masses of Negroes and system abuse gave rise to organizations such as the National Association for the Advancement of Colored People, founded in 1909, and the Urban League movement, founded in New York City in 1911. Several churches in the Northern cities in predominantly Negro communities recognized that they could not ignore the physical plight of the newcomers moving into their neighborhoods. Because racism defined the economic, political, and educational vulnerability that limited the social context of these burgeoning numbers of newly arriving inner-city residents, the theological approach to addressing their situation was defined by their status as "outside" society's mainstream. These new urban immigrants addressed the reality of their socially marginal situation and the theodicy issues it posed from the insecurity of the "bottom-up" perspective.

Addressing the practical issues of physical survival was inseparable from fidelity to faith in Jesus Christ. Indeed, the bottom-up perspective forged by racial oppression has always interpreted efforts to address social injustice as an extension of Christian ministry by church leaders throughout the history of the Black church and explains the close relationship between civil rights organizations and other civic social-uplift efforts that have operated in inner-city communities. Although the eternal goal was heaven, the temporal goal was survival in society on earth as explained in a sermon by African Methodist Episcopal bishop Reverdy Ransom:

> While Heaven is our final goal, our chief present concern is with the life on this planet and human relations in our present society, to the end that the Kingdom of God may be established among men. I see little hope for the survival of the A.M.E. Church, or any other distinctly religious Negro denomination, if we do not so apply the Gospel of Christ as to make it a vital force in the life of society. While the National Association for the Advancement of Colored People and the Urban League may argue, petition, protest, and appeal, we are clothed with authority to declare, "Thus saith the Lord."[37]

Bishop Ransom's declaration was very much in line with the model of ministry embraced by congregations under his leadership. Ordained in 1886, then pastor Ransom served congregations in Pennsylvania, Ohio, and Illinois. He also had experiences in Allegheny City, Pennsylvania, where he walked "through the alleys and climbed the dark stairways of the wretched tenements or walked out on the planks to the shanty boats where people lived on the river," which convinced him of the need for a type of ministry that addressed both spiritual and physical need. Bishop Ransom's ministry, according to Ralph Luker, represented one of the foremost examples of social outreach ministries in his day:

> At Chicago's Bethel AME Church in 1896, he organized a "Men's Sunday Club" of five hundred men who met weekly to discuss moral, social, and cultural issues, supported Ida B. Wells in establishing a kindergarten at Bethel Church, and opened a church to the Manassa Society, an organization of seven hundred men and women in biracial marriages. . . . [In 1900] Ransom founded Chicago's Institutional Church and Social Settlement . . . to serve both new migrants and middle-class black Chicagoans. It opened in a building with an auditorium seating twelve hundred, a dining room, a kitchen, a gymnasium, and eight other large rooms. Its activities included a Men's Forum, a Women's Club, and a nursery, a kindergarten, clubs for boys and girls, a print shop, and an employment bureau. It offered concerts, classes in sewing, cooking, and music, and lectures by leading black and white speakers. Ransom hired two University of Chicago seminarians to assist him with the boys' club.[38]

During this era, the term *institutional church* began to be used by congregations that specifically defined their Christian mission as being more inclusive in addressing the needs of the community it saw itself as called to serve. Frequently, the ministries of these churches sought to positively address a variety of debilitating social, cultural, educational, economic, and political challenges faced by their congregants and surrounding communities. In addition to the usual schedule of church activities including worship and preaching, prayer meetings, Bible study groups, and pastoral visitation, institutional churches also sought to incorporate service-oriented ministries as part of their regular schedule of weekly activities. Some of the activities included recreational opportunities, various types of work skills, economic or social instruction, and intellectual or cultural events. The larger institutional churches often started schools in the basements and acquired houses or other property to provide shelter and meals for displaced or indigent persons. "Settlement house" ministries came to be associated with the process of providing not only shelter, but also the needed protective care, domestic and manual skills, and training of new immigrants from the South or elsewhere who might need to become acclimated for survival in the often hostile and harsh living environment of the industrial city.

The Reverend Adam Clayton Powell, Sr.

Institutional church–type ministries began to surface in a variety of cities, North and South, and were represented among all denominational traditions, including African Methodist Episcopal and African Methodist Episcopal Zion, Baptist, Congregationalist, and Roman Catholic. One of the more famous examples of this type of ministry was represented by New York City's Adam Clayton Powell, Sr. A Virginia Union University graduate, Powell had served churches in St. Paul, Philadelphia, and New Haven before accepting a call as pastor of the Abyssinian Baptist Church in New York City in December of 1908. Under the influence of his outstanding preaching skill and administrative acumen, the congregation grew substantially. Worship services epitomized the joyful celebration of God's presence among the masses of people flocking into Harlem at the turn of the century. Emotionalism, Powell explained, "was the heart of religious experience. It is the electric current in the organized Christian Church. Confine it to batteries, and this wild and frightful something could run our trains, drive our automobiles, and bring New York and South Africa within whispering distance of each other."[39]

Clearly, Adam Clayton Powell, Sr.'s approach to urban ministry was consistent with the bottom-up theological perspective of ministry that lodged itself squarely in the center of the socially and politically disenfranchised and sought to address social vulnerability in tandem with their spiritual needs. As such, Powell's approach to ministry embodied the "institutional church" model of ministry. His public ministry was characterized by his activism in the struggle for racial justice; he served as one of the cofounders of the National Urban League, was an early leader in the National Association for the Advancement of Colored People, and lectured on race relations at Colgate University, City College of New York, and Union Theological Seminary.

In 1920, Reverend Powell led the congregation in the purchase of land in

Harlem on West 138th Street for construction of a new edifice, Abyssinian's present site. He also led the congregation in building one of the first community recreation centers in Harlem, the establishment of a social/religious education program, and during the Great Depression, he campaigned to feed the poor, for better jobs, and for city services. By the mid-1930s, Abyssinian Baptist Church had become one of the largest Protestant congregations in the nation, with membership numbering fourteen thousand. Powell's public ministry was such a vital part of the Harlem community in addition to his service within the congregation that it was only on his third attempt that the church agreed to let him retire after twenty-nine years of leadership.

Dr. Mary McLeod Bethune

Another example of the bottom-up theological perspective is reflected in the life and ministry of Dr. Mary McLeod Bethune. At the turn of the twentieth century, clergy roles for women did not exist. Many women who felt called to service as a Christian leader turned to the field of education; Mary McLeod Bethune proved to be one of the most outstanding examples of this reality. Born to former slaves in 1875, scarcely more than a decade after the Civil War, Mary Jane McLeod originally desired to become a Christian missionary to Africa. Her efforts to fulfill this dream rebuffed by White mission sponsors, McLeod's call to Christian service was more than ably fulfilled through her efforts in education. She taught at schools in Georgia, South Carolina, Florida, and Illinois.

As a young teacher in Chicago, she visited prisoners in jail, giving them inspiration through song. After marriage, she opened the Daytona Normal and Industrial Institute for Negro Girls in 1904. Bethune believed that through education, Blacks could improve their social and economic status even in a culture that still opposed racial equality. Her school fees were modest, fifty cents per week, and no child was ever refused an education for lack of fees. In Florida, she also organized a Sunday school and continued her work among the prison population. In spite of the initial resistance to her educational efforts due to the intense racial hostilities of the era, Bethune persisted, and eventually communal opposition by the dominant White power structure was dismantled.

In 1923, Dr. Bethune oversaw the merger of her school with another institution, the Cookman Institute, with the result that she then became president of the newly established Bethune-Cookman College. Because of her effectiveness in education and reconciliation and with her school's success well established, Dr. Bethune gave more attention to public ministry in opposition to racial injustice and bigotry. Her vigilance for racial justice based upon her strong faith convictions brought her national respect and acclaim, and she eventually became counsel to presidents Calvin Coolidge, Herbert Hoover, Theodore Roosevelt, and Franklin D. Roosevelt.

In 1917, she became president of the Florida Federation of Colored Women. In 1924, Bethune became president of the National Association of Colored Women, at that time the highest national office to which a Black woman could aspire. In 1935, she formed the National Council of Negro Women to take on the major national issues affecting Blacks.

Bethune served as director of the National Youth Administration's Division of Negro Affairs (1936), as vice president of the NAACP (1940), and on President Truman's Committee of Twelve for National Defense (1951). She also continued working with many organizations, such as the National Urban League, the Association of American Colleges, and the League of Women Voters. Her legacy of faith stands as one of the most effective examples of what the bottom-up theological perspective has achieved in enhancing the quality of life in society from a faith-centered position.

The Reverend Matthew Anderson

In 1879, the Reverend Matthew Anderson became pastor of the Gloucester Presbyterian Mission in Philadelphia. A year later, his mission was reorganized as the Berean Presbyterian Church, and by 1884, it had built a substantial blue-marble building on South College Avenue. Twelve years later, Anderson noted that the church had less than a hundred official members but had a constituency of 300, with 150 persons in Sunday school. The Berean Church had a Woman's Christian Temperance Union of sixty members, a Christian Endeavor Society of forty, a kindergarten, a boys' cadet corps, two literary societies, an employment bureau, and a medical dispensary. The Berean Young Woman's Parlor offered literary classes, a light supper, and weekly socials for young women employed as domestics. The Berean Building and Loan Association, established in 1888, enabled Black families in its vicinity to buy 150 homes in its first twenty years. In 1899, Anderson founded the Berean Manual Training and Industrial School, which offered classes in carpentry, upholstery, millinery, electricity, sewing, dressmaking, stenography, cooking, and tailoring to a thousand students in its first ten years.

Conclusion

It is important to understand that the oppression experienced by Africans during legalized enslavement in this period of United States history as well as by the sons and daughters of former slaves after political emancipation came from a warped perspective of humanity. This perspective did not view the interrelatedness and equality of all people as something of divine origin. Such a perspective inevitably gives rise to behavioral realities of alienation, fear, and violence. As such, African slavery in the United States grew out of the same factors then that oppress people today, people who have never been politically enslaved, but are experientially enslaved, nonetheless, by economic, ethnic, cultural, religious, or political oppression.

Factors that motivate oppression today manifest themselves in the debilitating behaviors that characterize Middle Eastern politics, Pakistani-India border tensions, or conflicts in places as varied as Ireland, Indonesia, Sudan, or Venezuela. These are the oppressive factors of alienation, fear, and violence. Howard Thurman, in his classic work *Jesus and the Disinherited,* expressed well the theological challenge that Christianity has of defining "what the teachings and the life of Jesus have to say to those who stand, at a moment in human history, with their backs against the wall."[40] It is the response to this question that gives substance to urban theology as holistic God-talk.

PART 3
PERSPECTIVES

CHAPTER EIGHT

CORE VALUES IN URBAN MINISTRY

Finally, beloved, whatever is true, whatever is honorable, whatever is just, whatever is pure, whatever is pleasing, whatever is commendable, if there is any excellence and if there is anything worthy of praise, think about these things.

—Philippians 4:8

As pastor of a church in a poor inner-city neighborhood for fourteen years, over time I learned about the power of core values to influence systemic change, even among people of very limited means. One example of this power is revealed in the story of a single mom, a divorced African American woman of very modest means whom I shall call Anabelle. She had seven children and worked mornings for a meager salary by cleaning dorm rooms for mostly White and privileged students at a nearby college. Often shocked by the behavior of what she called the "spoiled brats" at the college, she frequently gave them "motherly advice" in an effort to keep them out of trouble. But Anabelle determined that her own children's moral and academic values would exceed those of the "spoiled brats" whose rooms she cleaned.

Although she was poor, Anabelle's core values kept her from sinking into depression or viewing herself as a person of limited resources. She was a frequent volunteer at church, singing in the choir or helping cook and serve meals on special occasions. In her community, she regularly used her old car to help transport the elderly to the doctor's office or to polling sites after work on Election Day. As a single parent who took her children's education seriously, Anabelle regularly visited the schools her children attended, and her home was a veritable drop-in center for neighborhood children after school. Anabelle was not a college graduate, but over the years, all seven of her children accomplished that goal. Her five daughters include a university professor, a lawyer, two social workers, and a physicist. One son is a high school teacher, and the other is a minister of the gospel. While a host of other factors clearly were involved, it cannot be denied that Anabelle's moral and academic values made an impression on her children.

As we have seen earlier, *value* is the word we use to refer to the importance attached to something: an object, a service, a concept, or even our opinion of an individual. The esteem in which something, someone, or some ideal is held qualifies as its value, its worth, or significance to us. The word *core* refers to that which is at the center of something: its essence. The phrase "core values" generally refers to those ideals or principles that are fundamental to any enterprise. In our discussion of urban ministry, *core values* are those ideals or principles that form the center or essence of Christian ministry in the city and are fundamental to its effectiveness. They are the basic, central, and nonnegotiable beliefs that motivate and energize ministry. As such, core values in urban ministry are to be distinguished from objectives, strategies, and methodologies that refer to the implementation and execution of activities.

Frequently, so much emphasis is placed on the processes of implementation, such as the tools and strategies that support effective city ministry, that core values in urban ministry are given short shrift. Implementation and planning tools such as the research and information-gathering resources of sociology (surveys, ethnographic studies, and so on) or some of its operational methodologies (urban planning, neighborhood mapping, community organizing, to name a few) are championed as if they are core values. While these tools are important resources in the practice of urban ministry, a clear distinction must be made between these tools and the foundational principles or core values that motivate their use. Otherwise, these vital tools of urban ministry can become quite ineffective in enabling successful Christian ministry in the city. It must be stressed, however, that these core values cannot be implemented without careful attention to the sociological resources of data gathering that can set the context for positive systemic change in urban realities.

All core values of urban ministry listed below are based on the gospel of Jesus Christ. It would be presumptuous to suggest that these particular core values are all-inclusive, for they certainly make no claim as such. Based on my observation of urban ministry in a variety of contexts, these are some of the more common guiding principles that seem to be operant regardless of location, whether in Los Angeles, Shanghai, Philadelphia, Paris, Bangkok, Johannesburg, or Abuja. The significance of these core values, however, is not simply that they characterize urban-ministry efforts; they are often the distinguishing features between productive and unproductive urban ministries. Cities attempt many well-intended endeavors that come to naught insofar as truly empowering and enabling socially, economically, politically, and spiritually challenged inner-city residents to improve their lot. Worse still, some religiously motivated ministries in the city have the effect of persuading disenfranchised people to become better accommodated to their plight. The importance of the values discussed herein is that they constitute critical ingredients of the type of urban ministry that ultimately produces positive and systemic behavioral change in the urban environment, *enhancing the quality of life-affirming realities in the metropolitan context*. There is no mystery to them, for

110

they are seven broad characteristics that appear to motivate behaviors in urban ministry that are clearly rooted in the gospel of Jesus Christ as reflected in scripture. They are the core values of *theism, love, justice, community, creativity, reconciliation,* and *hope.*

On the surface, these seven concepts represent ideals that would seem to be so universally accepted in principle within most contexts and cultures that their identification as core values in urban ministry hardly seems worth mentioning. Yet, focus on these core values is important for at least two reasons. First, it gives the urban-ministry practitioner an ethical framework for translating lofty ideals that are part of the gospel message into concrete behaviors aimed at improving the quality of city life. In chapter 3, we mentioned that one of the challenges in urban ministry involves *bridging the artificial chasm between urban ministry's roots in justice advocacy (ethical agency) and evangelistic mission.* Attention to the core values in urban ministry addresses this challenge and helps close this chasm. When the utopian ideals are applied to the rigors of analyzing massive slums that spread across inner-city landscapes, pervasive joblessness, or public health issues that disproportionately characterize certain urban racial groups, the significance of affirming these core values as guiding principles for ecclesiastical activity in the city takes on new meaning. As urban activist Jim Wallis asserts:

> The world isn't working. Things are unraveling, and most of us know it. Tonight, the urban children of the world's only remaining superpower will go to bed to the sound of gunfire. Bonds of family and community are fraying. Our most basic virtues of civility, responsibility, justice, and integrity seem to be collapsing. We appear to be losing the ethics derived from personal commitment, social purpose, and spiritual meaning. The triumph of materialism is hardly questioned now, in any part of our society.[1]

Emphasis on the core values of urban ministry gives clarity not only to its missional focus of preaching the gospel in the city, but also to its ethical essence that is drawn from the gospel and works to enhance the quality of human life in the city and encourages an environmental context that is life-affirming.

The second reason attention to these core values is important is that so much of urban society is considered negatively, especially by persons living outside that context (whether on its fringes or far away). Much of the analysis of urban realities, therefore, is approached pejoratively, emphasizing problems, dysfunction, and hopelessness. Affirmation of these seven core values as starting points for analysis of urban ministry provides a much healthier means of organizing for effective Christian ministry in the city. Let us now consider these core values in the setting in which urban ministry takes place.

Chart of Core Values, Strategies, and Action-Steps

Chart 5, "Core Values, Strategies, and Action Steps," located at the end of this chapter (pages 135-41), identifies each value and includes a summary of related urban strategies and action steps that typically may be associated with the core value indicated. It should be noted that various strategies and action steps may correspond to more than one of the core values indicated in the chart. As such, these associations are intended only to help clarify how these values motivate various types of activity intended to make real the ideals of the gospel as applied to the praxis of ministry in the city.

Core Value 1: THEISM

The theist is one who believes in God. Of course, the opposite of the *theist* is the *atheist*—one who does not believe in God. In urban ministry, *theism* refers to a God-consciousness based upon *faith* rather than on the exclusive use of scientifically objective or observable data. It reflects an *affirmation of divine involvement in life* as well as in all aspects of existence that gives the believer a unique perspective on reality, encompassing both the physical and the metaphysical. In scripture, this God-consciousness is affirmed with the very opening sentence (Genesis 1:1 RSV): *"In the beginning God . . . ,"* and thus is understood as the explanation or causative reality for everything that follows. For the urban ministry practitioner, this affirmation of the reality of God in all spheres of existence is the first core value that inspires life-enhancing activity in the metropolitan context. Theism involves "God-talk," a God-consciousness that inspires a "God-walk" (behavior that reflects faith in God). Three distinguishing features of theism as a core value in urban ministry are: (a) *Theism and Urban Variety*, (b) *Theism and Ethical Challenges*, and (c) *Theism and Social Science*.

Theism and Urban Variety

The Greek word for that which, in English, is rendered as "God" is *theos*. In Arabic, the word for God is *Allah*. In Swahili, one of several words for God is *Mongu*. Depending on the continent, the region of the continent, the ethnic group in that region of the continent, and the religious traditions affirmed within the particular ethnic group of that region, the word for "God" may be represented in an infinite variety of ways. Accordingly, urban ministry is characterized by the interface of a plethora of beliefs and terminologies that refer to the phenomenon humans recognize as divine and, in various ways, call God. This is one of the unique features of urban life: it draws together a huge variety of differing groups of people in comparatively close space, along with their varying traditions, languages, and beliefs.[2] Theism as a core value in urban ministry, therefore, recognizes in a respectful way the variety in urban "God-talk" from differing religious perspectives in addition to those that are

Christian. As such, theism includes reference to all people who genuinely believe in God as the motivating factor in their lives. The urban Christian, therefore, is the type of *theist* who gladly embraces the cultural and religious variety of the city, but whose theological understanding of life is defined by her or his faith in God as revealed in Jesus Christ of the Holy Scriptures.

Theism, in this sense, refers not to an academic or philosophical acknowledgment of the "idea of God" that implies rational or cognitive recognition on the part of an individual, but to a visceral belief that governs the person's life and actions. Theism also is to be distinguished from the casual but overt adoption of or ascription to religious ritual and creedal orthodoxy that seems to represent external social conformity more than intrinsic belief.

Central to any understanding of Christian urban ministry is subscription to the profound reality summarized by the brief sentence recorded in the Gospel of John (1:14): "And the Word became flesh and lived among us, and we have seen his glory, the glory as of a father's only son, full of grace and truth." This is the critical uniqueness of Christian theology's claims about God that inform urban ministry from the particularly *Christocentric* perspective and distinguishes its God-talk from other forms of *theism* reflected in the city. The inescapable fact of Christian faith is that, somehow, ethereal and metaphysical realities historically identified in human thought as God were evident in the life of Jesus of Nazareth. Moreover, these qualities were evident with such clarity that Jesus' peculiar personality continues to inform our understanding of God.

Theism and Ethical Challenges

Although theism from the Christian perspective refers to faith in God as revealed in Jesus Christ, such a short definition tells us little about the nature of urban ministry that produces positive systemic change in society. Statistics indicate that 85 percent of the United States population claim to be Christian and 11 percent identify with a faith other than Christianity.[3] Such statistics appear to reflect a high degree of faith in God within the nation. Sadly, however, the United States has some of the worst crime statistics and the highest percentage of its citizens incarcerated among developed Western nations. The gap between its wealthiest and poorest citizens is growing rather than abating. Obviously, while *evangelistic* activity in the nation has been effective in promoting an articulation of faith, more work needs to be done regarding implementation of the *ethical* dimensions of the gospel. Claims of belief in God are just a starting point for encouraging behavior that actually produces positive change in society. According to Matthew 7:15-23, among other places, Jesus was clear that more than talk about faith in God was needed to effect positive behavioral results:

Beware of false prophets, who come to you in sheep's clothing but inwardly are ravenous wolves. You will know them by their fruits. . . . Not everyone who says to me, "Lord, Lord," will enter the kingdom of heaven, but only the one who does the will of my Father in heaven. On that day many will say to me, "Lord, Lord, did we not prophesy in your name, and cast out demons in your name, and do many deeds of power in your name?" Then will I declare to them, "I never knew you; go away from me, you evildoers."

The urban Christian, however, cannot be deterred by the reality that the behavior of many Christians is sometimes difficult to distinguish ethically from that of nonbelievers. Theism as a core value in urban ministry refers to the fidelity of the urban-ministry practitioner's faith in God as revealed in Jesus Christ to bring about positive systemic change in society and the ethical decisions he or she makes based upon that faith, regardless of the belief or non-belief of others.

Theism and Social Science

Theism is the singular characteristic of urban ministry that distinguishes it from scientific inquiry and practice and separates it from "social science" because urban ministry is inherently *faith-based*. In essence *theism*, as a core value in urban ministry, refers to the fundamental God-consciousness of ministry practitioners based upon their cognitive decision to embrace an awareness of God's involvement in life as well as all reality purely on the basis of faith rather than on the basis of strictly empirical data. Theism is belief in the existence of a divine and almighty Creator of all existence and the ground of all reality. It is an approach to life that views God as the creative source of everything that exists in the world, including the human race, and everything that exists anywhere beyond the world and that transcends human understanding; this God is nonetheless present in the created order of existence despite these apparent contradictions. While *scientific* social work and *faith-based* urban ministry may both analyze data related to a given social challenge and attempt to craft a response to correct the situation, the urban-ministry practitioner additionally recognizes the proverbial "hand of God" working in both the assessment of the challenge and the proposed response to it.

More than twenty years ago, Bill (not his real name) was convicted in connection with his involvement in drug trafficking and was incarcerated. He maintains that his arrest and conviction was the best thing that happened to him because through this ordeal, he was converted to genuine faith in Jesus Christ. As a youth, he had been reared by Christian parents and went to church, but admits that at the time he never had a real relationship with Christ. As soon as he was old enough, Bill abandoned all pretenses at religion. As he drifted into illegal activities, he never forgot the faith values his parents

114

taught him as a boy, he just ignored them. According to Bill, his conviction and the unpleasantness of incarceration were God's way of "getting his attention." Once Bill was behind bars, Christ showed him his real purpose in life: to help redirect other "wild guys" toward life-affirming behaviors rather than destructive ones. While imprisoned, Bill became a "model citizen" and over time following his release he reconnected with family, managed to get a job, married, and enrolled in school. Bill currently volunteers as a counselor, a task in which he has himself engaged for more than a decade. Bill's interpretation of his life's transformation cannot be explained without considering his theistic outlook. While the positive outcomes of his profound behavioral changes can be empirically documented, his understanding and interpretation of the motivational factors prompting them go beyond the ordinary parameters of social science.

As discussed earlier, overwhelmingly the first Christians were urban people. Christianity was born amid the economic, ideological, social, political, and religious struggles that defined the urbanized, global, and non-Christian culture of the Roman Empire. For the first three centuries of the church's existence, its urban context was culturally and politically hostile. Divine revelation, as uniquely revealed in Jesus of Nazareth and interpreted through the post-Resurrection faith of the early church, shaped the theistic character of urban ministry in a manner that inspired the action and the rearrangement of the believer's life. Faith in Christ was not a matter of glib social affirmation or academic or philosophical intellectualizing.

It was in this context that the God-consciousness of the first witnesses to the Resurrection and later believers across the early centuries of the church set the context whereby a profound systemic change in the social and political reality of their day was achieved. These people did not just talk about God, they believed in God. It is against this background of theism that, first and foremost, one of the intrinsic characteristics or core values of urban ministry aimed at producing positive and systemic change enhancing the quality of city life. It is a theism that reflects a God-consciousness borne of the type of belief in God as reflected in Jesus Christ of scripture and views God as the ground of all existence and primary motivator of one's life.

Core Value 2: LOVE

A second core value in urban ministry is *love*. It almost seems trite or superfluous to include something so obvious as *love* as one of the core values in urban ministry or as being foundational to any form of ministry. Yet, the term is so ubiquitous in the popular culture of our society and has such a wide range of interpretations attached to it that some explanation of what is meant by "love" in the context of urban ministry is warranted. The term *love* is applied to everything from the more traditional meanings like a "strong affection" based on kinship or family ties, as in parental love, to amorous attraction and even as a reference to sexual intercourse. In the game of tennis, the word *love* refers to a score of zero, but at a hip-hop concert, the phrase "show 'em some love" merely refers to expressing appreciation or applause.

People whose relative privilege in society encourages them to be satisfied with social and economic status quo realities tend to emphasize the sentimental aspects of Christian love, often spiritualizing away its practical implications regarding equity and justice concerns. Flowery and spiritualized approaches to love may sound nice, but by themselves they can do little to alter the power-dynamics that produce and maintain systemic injustices, oppression, and inequity. The complaints of the disadvantaged are frequently viewed as being without merit and contemptible. Those whose social position is less fortunate, however, have tended toward understandings of Christian love and embrace it as a force that motivates and energizes activity ceaselessly devoted to the opposition of injustice, oppression, and inequity, with a view toward the potential conversion of enemies into friends.

Long ago, Howard Thurman identified love as the central element in any understanding of Jesus:

> The religion of Jesus makes the love-ethic central. This is no ordinary achievement. It seems clear that Jesus started out with the simple teaching concerning love embodied in the timeless words of Israel: "Hear, O Israel: The Lord our God is one Lord: and thou shalt love the Lord thy God with all thy heart, and with all thy soul, and with all thy might," and "thy neighbor as thyself." Once the neighbor is defined, then one's moral obligation is clear.[4]

For Thurman, the value of the love-ethic is its ability to enable a "fundamental attack on the enemy status"[5] that does not overlook the presence of social, economic, cultural, or political realities governing relationships between the privileged and the underprivileged, but affirms the potential for recognition of the humanity of all involved.

Love in action also dissolves the "stranger" status so as to create behavioral bonds of unity where none previously existed, as the example of Beverly (not her real name) demonstrates. She and her husband, Jim, are foster parents who take care of abused or abandoned children. They have had as many as nine children in their home at one time in addition to their two biological children. Beverly completed nursing school more than thirty years ago, and twelve years later she began keeping "her special children" full-time. Many of the children she cares for are too sick for their parents to handle, but Beverly prays a lot as she seeks to return these children to health. "My babies all have special needs and most need medical procedures. But we're a family," she says. "My teens learn to have responsibility for a younger brother or sister because teens become self-centered if they only have themselves to think of. They need to understand that you have to be helpful to others. That's how you learn what love is, by helping others." She refers to their home as "God's Little Helping Hand." Over the years, Beverly and Jim have reared fifty-five children until they were eighteen. She proudly says, "They are all over the world now, but they keep in touch because they know they are loved here at home."

Drawing upon this same concept, Martin Luther King, Jr., based his leadership of civil rights efforts from 1955 until his death in 1968 squarely on the scriptural concept of love he drew from the Greek word *agape*, meaning a type of altruistic and unselfish love. For King, the significance of love was its capacity not just to effect change within the individual, but also to serve as a resource to implement systemic change in society and even as a catalyst for public policy change. Early in his public ministry leadership, when discussing the 1955–56 Montgomery, Alabama, bus boycott to end racial segregation on that city's public transit bus system, Martin King noted the effort's dependence on the concept of love as its basis. Years later, less than nine months before his assassination, King was still clearly articulating his position on the role and significance of love as a basis and motivation for systemic change. Martin King was careful to distinguish his notion of love from shallow emotionalism that he viewed as "anemic" and devoid of the power to bring about good results as an antidote to debilitating social realities. In a 1958 article entitled "An Experiment in Love," King outlined six major points of the "basic philosophy" that guided the implementation of the Montgomery bus boycott. While the boycott's strategies involved what had been called nonviolent resistance, non-cooperation, and passive resistance, King's aim was to clarify the fact that the movement's basic inspiration had been drawn from the ideal of Christian love as expressed at various points in scripture:

> In speaking of love . . . we are not referring to some sentimental or affectionate emotion. . . . Love in this connection means understanding, redemptive good will. . . . We refer to neither *eros* nor *philia*; we speak of a love which is expressed in the Greek word *agape*. *Agape* means understanding, redeeming good will for all men. It is an overflowing love which is purely spontaneous, unmotivated, groundless, and creative. It is not set in motion by any quality or function of its object. . . . It is a love in which the individual seeks not his own good, but the good of his neighbor. . . . *Agape* is not a weak, passive love. It is love in action. *Agape* is love seeking to preserve and create community. It is insistence on community even when one seeks to break it. *Agape* is a willingness to go to any length to restore community. It doesn't stop at the first mile, but it goes the second mile to restore community.[6]

Nearly a decade later, King addressed the Tenth Southern Christian Leadership Conference (SCLC) in August 1967, and again reiterated his convictions concerning the significance of love as a resource to bring about good ends in society. Addressing the growing perception at the time that love was impotent to enable oppressed people to gain the economic and political power needed to improve their lot, King reaffirmed his commitment to love as a strategy for creative, positive, and systemic change in society. King maintained, as he had consistently done over the intervening years, that love was not merely sentimental emotionalism and was often misunderstood as the polar opposite of power. He argued that correctly understood, love was, in fact, a powerful force that led toward the implementation of justice:

> One of the great problems of history is that the concepts of love and power have usually been contrasted as opposites—polar opposites—so that love is identified with a resignation of power, and power with a denial of love. . . . What is needed is a realization that power without love is reckless and abusive, and love without power is sentimental and anemic. Power at its best is love implementing the demands of justice, and justice at its best is power correcting everything that stands against love. And this is what we must see as we move on.[7]

Desmond Tutu provided a similar example concerning the usefulness of the love-ethic as a resource for change with the creation of the Truth and Reconciliation Commission of South Africa. Without genuine compassion for those with whom one is engaged in urban ministry, efforts to improve the quality of life in the city will meet with little success. One of the major problems with the classic mission approaches of the past is that the devotion of the missionaries was directed, first and foremost, to God with such zeal that the corollary requirement of "love of neighbor" was often left out. Love of God is not enough to foster change in the city. Love of city residents is required.

Core Value 3: JUSTICE

A third core value in urban ministry for enhancing the quality of life-affirming realities in the metropolitan context is *justice*. Frequently among the poor in urban settings and specifically among people of color in such contexts, the word *justice* is commonly replaced with the phrase *"just-us."* This is a colloquial reference to the expectation of many people who live in such areas that they need only expect condemnation and punishment from the legal codes of society and not fair treatment. Sadly, this rather jaundiced perspective is not without significant foundation in the experience of many urban dwellers who have come to realize that, at best, justice is an ephemeral concept in their neighborhoods. The fact is that much of society's God-talk, while full of rhetoric and platitude-laden resolutions that bespeak compassion, justice, and reconciliation, fails to produce these values in its behavioral outcomes socially. Consequently, the idea of justice in society can be confusing. With regard to the plethora of communal contexts that constitute the urban arena, including its varieties of cultural, political, economic, ideological, ethnic, or religious constituencies, discerning that which constitutes the core value of justice in urban ministry poses formidable challenges. Public policies that take virtually no action against wealthy thieves who defraud investors and bankrupt retirement plans yet incarcerate the poor in record numbers and ignore the withering misery and survival hazards that define ghetto life, are behavioral evidence of this flawed type of theological talk with its ethical deficiencies that warps justice and creates cynicism among the poor. In our society, where the virtual idolization of wealth and materialism is so widely accepted, there is a growing realization that people can only have the best "justice" that money can buy.

For poor and other socially vulnerable people, the idea of justice is central to any understanding of urban ministry no matter how tattered its popular image may be. Yet there are at least two major factors that have contributed to the confusion that now surrounds almost any discussion of justice. First, in today's society the notion of justice seems to have become almost exclusively associated with jurisprudence and the enforcement of applicable laws of the land, whether in cases of civil or criminal law. In this context, matters of ethics or moral virtue are limited to the prescribed codes adopted in legislation and the arena of civics. As such, the term *justice* seems to have lost its religious connection with the biblical concept of righteousness or spiritual holiness that it may have had in previous generations.[8]

In our society, righteousness, holiness and piety, are all matters of faith and relate to religious laws that are a separate matter from civil law. That which may constitute righteousness according to ecclesiastical canons may not square with the technical provisions of civil law and, as such, may not prove to be legally correct or just. The converse also applies. The result is that in society today, a distinction can be made between that which can be defined as spiritually virtuous or righteous and that which technically meets the requirements of civil and/or criminal laws used by the state to determine justice. An example of this was seen in the controversy surrounding whether it was appropriate (just/righteous) for the Salvation Army to decide, on the basis of its religious beliefs, not to hire persons who were openly gay/lesbian while accepting public funds for some of their social programs. Such action prompted a civil suit filed in federal court.[9]

Second, the problem of discussing justice is further complicated in the United States by the involvement of the entertainment industry, which has made various judicial proceedings in the nation a matter of public amusement. As with most recreational activity, the attraction of the amusement or sport is in its ability to excite and engage participants or observers. The commingling of judicial proceedings with entertainment (such as popular court television personalities, e.g., Judge Judy, Judge Hackett, or any of a number of actual courtroom proceedings on television) further confuses any discussion of justice because these two very important functions of society, jurisprudence and entertainment, have very different purposes. In judicial proceedings, at some basic level, the goal is the discernment of fact or truth regarding reality in order to benefit society. The goal of amusement or entertainment in society, however, is essentially to provide some level of diversion from reality. It is hard enough to discern fact or seek truth when focusing as best we can on reality. It is all but impossible to discern fact or seek truth when the goal is overtly some form of diversion from reality.

Cain Hope Felder's analysis of justice in scripture is quite helpful in understanding the importance this concept has in urban ministry.[10] In his book *Troubling Biblical Waters*, Felder notes that the term *justice* in Greek antiquity included more than is associated with the term today, citing that the notion involved ideas about "observing the law, doing the right thing, honesty, respect for the other person's property and rights and fair play [equity]."[11] He stresses, however, that ideas about justice in Hellenistic culture were grounded not in religion, but in politics and philosophy:

> Greco-Roman religion did not give rise to notions of social justice. This explains why matters of social justice in these societies were handled by politicians and philosophers rather than by priests, diviners, or "prophets." The matter is very different when one turns to ideas about justice in [scripture]. . . . The earliest traditions of Hebraic thought or ancient Judaism do not separate social ethical obligations and religious observances. . . . The element of a divinely ordained law that provides both moral and ceremonial obligations was one of the key features that distinguished Judaism from the indigenous religions of the Greco-Roman world.[12]

Like Martin Luther King, Jr., Cain Felder argues that in the New Testament, the notions about agape/love cannot be separated from the idea of social justice that finds its roots in the Old Testament. In the New Testament, there exists "a rich variety of terms relating to justice. These include freedom (*eleutheria*), love (*agapē*), mercy (*eleos*), equality (*isotēs*), integrity (*aphthoria*), commandment (*entolē*), and law (*nomos*)."[13] New Testament writers clearly defined their ideas about justice from the Hebrew Scriptures. In the Old Testament, justice meant being not only socially fair and unbiased in dealing with other members of the covenant community (the horizontal or communal dimension), but it also involved correct relationship with God (the vertical or spiritual dimension). Concepts about justice in the legal sense, therefore, were inextricably involved with the idea of moral virtue or righteousness before God.

Although these Old Testament prescriptions regarding justice generally applied to relationships within the covenant community and especially among its free male members, it is important to note that there were also laws pro-tecting the rights of the socially vulnerable within the community. While their status was subordinate to the privileges enjoyed by the free men, certain laws specifically addressed the communal responsibility to protect the welfare of the poor, widows, orphans, women, sojourners, strangers, and slaves within its midst (Exodus 22:21-22; Leviticus 19:10, 33; Deuteronomy 24:17; 26:12-13).[14] In essence, even though social status involved unequal hierarchical arrange-ments (free males, women, children, strangers, slaves, et al.), there was a fun-damental recognition of certain intrinsic human value before God. As such in the Old Testament, justice was based on the concept of equity (each person in society having assigned social responsibilities in proportion to their expected capacities) rather than equality (all having the same or being equal). For example, the responsibilities of judges, kings, or other rulers differed from those of Levitical priests, and their respective roles were fixed socially. Circumstances that placed some members of the community at additional risk, thereby making them socially vulnerable beyond the expected customs of social location (for example, the poor, the orphaned, the widowed, or the wrongfully abused), were to be taken into consideration by the more socially favored members of the community.

As in the Old Testament, New Testament writers recognized the notion of love of God and love of neighbor as the basis governing all social arrangements (Lev. 19:18; Mark 12:29-30). In the New Testament, however, application of the idea of who is the neighbor clearly has been extended to include those out-side Judaism, as is exemplified in Jesus' parable of the good Samaritan (Luke 10:29-37). Likewise, the apostle Paul's insistence on preaching the gospel to the Gentiles and Peter's conversion and subsequent visit to Cornelius (Acts 10) are evidence of this broadened and broadening perspective regarding who is to be understood as neighbor. It is against this backdrop that scriptural teachings regarding justice must be understood and applied to urban ministry.

Felder rightly cautions that "in our modern world of selfishness, greed, indi-vidual competing self-interests, and human exploitation, the New Testament teaching [on justice] is alien (frequently even in the Church)."[15] The post-resurrection faith of the early church so anticipated the quick return of Christ that some biblical scholars have argued that the "apocalyptic hope of the first Christians tended to discourage any quest for social reforms or revolutionary jus-tice."[16] This has often allowed for an overly otherworldly view of New Testament teachings about love, which sometimes leaves the ethical dimensions of justice omitted. For this reason, Felder identifies five scriptural understandings concerning justice that inform the urban context of ministry's focus on ensuring that those most vulnerable in society are treated with respect and dignity. These include: (1) *reciprocal justice* (which emphasizes the "Golden Rule" approach to justice, treating others as you want to be treated; see Matthew 7:12); (2) *eschatological justice* (the affirmation of belief that even when injustice prevails in the short term, God's accounting of fairness will ultimately prevail over time and/or, finally, in the eternal reality; see Matthew 25:31-46; 2 Thessalonians 1:6-10; and the Revelation); (3) *compensatory justice* (involves redressing past injury and remedying hurt with restitution or reparations; see the aspirations revealed in Leviticus 25:10; Luke 1:46-55; or the example found in the story of Zacchaeus, Luke 19:1-10); (4) *commutative justice* (the strategic disavowal of one's own rights in order to reduce the possibility of greater future harm or to bring about an improved reality, such as the apostle Paul's declining to claim his right to be paid for his work as an apostle in 1 Corinthians 9:15, 19); and (5) *charismatic distributive justice* (refers to the unique and divinely given characteristics or abilities possessed by different persons as represented in 1 Corinthians 12:11, 14-20, 28; and Romans 12:6-8).[17] In a cultural setting where violence and sociopolitical, educational, and economic harm are often accompanied by injustices that fail to provide either relief from vulnerability or redress for incurred harm, all five of the above types of justice are helpful in understanding the broad scope of this particular core value in urban ministry.

Core Value 4: COMMUNITY

A fourth core value in urban ministry for enhancing the quality of life-affirming realities in the metropolitan context is *community*. In this context *community* refers to a sense of *community awareness* that involves the experience of being together in an environment or a group where common interests, concerns, values, and beliefs shape the context of the shared social vision and expression of common life and well-being. In urban ministry, the high value placed on community awareness actually has two foci: the *internal community* and the *external community*. The *internal* focus of community awareness has to do with the well-being of the "covenant community of faith," while the *external* community awareness is concerned with the covenant community's responsibility for the well-being of the wider society.

Internal community awareness is revealed in the demonstrated concern for the welfare of the individual and collective participants within the covenant community or congregation of believers. This concern is understood as evidence of actually doing as God would have believers to do. The Gospels (Matthew 12:46-50; Mark 3:31-35; Luke 8:19-21) record an incident that took place after Jesus had begun his public ministry in which Jesus' mother and siblings were seeking him. While deeply engaged in ministry, Jesus learned of his family's interest in seeing him, and his initial response to the situation is recorded as being *whoever does what God wants him to do is my brother, my sister, my mother* (Matthew 12:50; Mark 3:35; Luke 8:21). Rather than a rebuff of his blood relatives, Jesus' response is more appropriately understood as affirming a type of extended family bond or relationship that characterizes people who believe in God and, thereby, care about one another's welfare.

In this sense, the defining characteristic of people who are defined as part of God's extended family (the covenant community) is their commitment to doing the will of God by exemplifying compassionate concern for the welfare of others. In New Testament writings, this type of connectionalism was often referred to as the *koinonia* (communion, fellowship, participation) experienced among members of the early church.

Considerable attention is given today to organizational analysis of congregational functioning as one of the most important institutions in society.[18] This is both understandable and appropriate since effective church functioning (organizational administration) is a key factor in the spiritual and physical well-being of individuals, families, and communities. The church, however, is essentially a relational construct (Jesus never claimed to establish any organization). In order to understand more fully how urban congregations, as covenant communities of faith, can be of support to individuals and families in the wider urban context, we cannot lose sight of this sense of relationship that defines the community of believers in Christ. Although the significance of the covenant-community relationship certainly is not unique to the urban context of ministry, it is an important value, the importance of which cannot be overstated for effectiveness in urban ministry. Within this focus, the scriptural norm of *koinonia* grounded in the notion of divine love (*agape:* selfless, altruistic affection), provides the context for relational understanding of internal community as the *extended family* of faith.

External community awareness is a core value that focuses on the role of the covenant community as a "model of community" within the wider society of the urban context. This is a notion that clearly emerges in a variety of scriptural settings. Representative examples are found in the hopeful writings in Isaiah 40:3-5 and in Matthew 5:13-16, a teaching from the Sermon on the Mount. In the Isaiah passages, the model of the covenant community is to be an example of divine blessing for the whole world (verse 5, "all flesh . . .") to be able to see:

> A voice cries out: "In the wilderness prepare the way of the LORD, make straight in the desert a highway for our God. Every valley shall be lifted up, and every mountain and hill be made low; the uneven ground shall become level, and the rough places a plain. And the glory of the LORD shall be revealed, and all flesh shall see it together, for the mouth of the LORD has spoken." (RSV)

In Jesus' Sermon on the Mount (Matthew 5:13-16), the idea of the model community is lifted as a demonstration for "the earth" (verse 13) and a model that is boldly set "before others" (verse 16) (all humankind):

You are the salt of the earth; but if salt has lost its taste, how can its saltiness be restored? It is no longer good for anything, but is thrown out and trampled under foot. You are the light of the world. A city built on a hill cannot be hid. No one after lighting a lamp puts it under a bushel basket, but on the lampstand, and it gives light to all in the house. In the same way, let your light shine before others, that they may see your good works and give glory to your Father in heaven.

In urban ministry, this concern for the welfare of the wider community includes far more than moral or spiritualized role-modeling alone, but involves active participation in practical endeavors to improve the physical, economic, social, educational, environmental, and civic quality of life in the neighborhood. In response to the civic injustices experienced by large numbers of African Americans migrating to Northern cities from the South in the early years of the last century, urban churches in predominantly African American communities played key roles in the establishment of civil rights organizations like the National Association for the Advancement of Colored People (NAACP, 1909) and the National Urban League movement (1911) as a response to this situation.[19] Today, urban congregations of varying membership sizes continue to model what healthy community or civic responsibility involves by engaging in ministries targeted to strengthen the well-being of the wider community.

The story of the Grace Memorial Presbyterian Church of Pittsburgh is one example of this core value in practice. Grace Memorial Church is located in Pittsburgh's Hill District community, the oldest African American neighborhood in the city. Like many inner-city churches, this congregation copes with the reality of drive-by shootings in its neighborhood and conducting funerals for youth killed on neighborhood streets by gunfire. The church was founded in 1867 by the abolitionist preacher Henry Highland Garnet to help improve the lot of recently freed slaves and other free Blacks living in Pittsburgh. As of 2005, the congregation's membership was recorded at 383 with an average Sunday attendance of about 200 persons. Its community outreach ministry to community youth, however, serves about 250 youngsters a week and has been nationally recognized for its excellence in improving the academic performance of children in the local public schools. The congregation established a separate nonprofit organization corporation for the purpose of supporting its after-school ministry, which includes academic tutoring, cultural enrichment, and recreational ministries serving children in grades K-6. The ministry also includes a full-day summer program of academic and recreational activities when local public schools are not in session. Here the core value of community awareness engages the congregation's ministry in modeling the type of community concern for the welfare and safety of children that should be reflected throughout the city. Whether *internal* or *external* to the covenant community, the sense of *community* is a core value in urban ministry that interprets faith in God as a motivational factor that encourages the believer to engage in behaviors that seek to enhance the quality of city life.

Core Value 5: CREATIVITY

Another core value in urban ministry for enhancing the quality of life-affirming realities in the metropolitan context is *creativity*. An old adage suggests that "necessity is the mother of invention." In brief, this adage explains the source and vigor of the creative spirit that inspires a lot of talent found in effective urban ministries. In this context, creativity is shaped by three elements: capacity, will, and determination. First, the word *creativity* ordinarily refers to the ability to create or the characteristic of being creative. This generic usage of the term appropriately implies the functional *capacity* to create. In urban ministry, however, this core value reflects not only capacity, but perhaps more importantlt, it also implies a second element: *the will to be resourceful in problem solving.* More than mere capacity is involved; in urban ministry, creativity also has reference to *volition* and *desire*. This core value speaks to the passionate quest to help fashion positive solutions to the negative situations that impede the realization of healthy communities that display spiritual wholeness and egalitarian social outcomes. Finally, *determination* is required. In our "microwave" culture, which is so accustomed to fifteen- or thirty-second commercials, patience is practically a lost art. Yet, in urban ministry, positive and systemic change does not and cannot happen instantly.

The element of *capacity* in the core value of creativity is exposed by the sheer constancy of motion and change inherent in all life, but in urban ministry is magnified many times over in the matrix of the metropolitan context. This reality alone explains why the need for creativity is so vital to success in urban ministry. Because the paucity of adequate resources is endemic to distressed communities frequently found in the cities, resourcefulness is required in order to fashion new opportunities and solutions when old ones fade. Being flexible enough to attempt new ways of doing things is required. This is where the element of capacity in creativity plays such a vital role—in the need of the urban community for persons who bring the technical skills and expertise needed to help core-city communities toward self-improvement.

The strategic importance of the behavioral and empirical sciences and how they contribute to the processes of adequate research, assessment, planning, and organizing cannot be overestimated in urban ministry. Without bringing to bear the skilled resources of sociology, medicine, economic theory, civil and criminal law, community organizing, education, math, physics, and urban planning as well as Bible, theology, homiletics, church administration, and pastoral care, core-city areas will remain blighted political colonies variously exploited and ignored by other communities whose relative affluence is shaped, in part, by the degradation of the inner city. Creativity to change ugly realities requires skilled capacity and the very best intellectual and academic resources available. The apostle Paul's poignant words in Romans 10:1-3 summarize the tragedy that often befalls urban ministry not only with regard to misplaced spiritual emphasis, but also unfortunate approaches to technical skill needs:

> Brothers and sisters, my heart's desire and prayer to God for them is that they may be saved. I can testify that they have a zeal for God, but it is not enlightened. For, being ignorant of the righteousness that comes from God, and seeking to establish their own, they have not submitted to God's righteousness.

Too frequently, urban-ministry efforts attempt to make up for an absence of competence in dealing with pressing urban challenges with a misguided overemphasis on commitment. As my dad used to say, "consecrated ignorance and dedicated incompetence" are found in many churches.

Competence alone is not enough, however. The core value of creativity in urban ministry also involves the *will* or the desire to be involved in seeking to fashion more life-enhancing realities. When I was a pastor in Miami, Florida, the elementary school two blocks from my church was populated by many Hispanic children from families that were, in fact, homeless. The children, therefore, often did not attend the school longer than one or two months on average. The school principal, a member of my congregation, told me that some of those children might attend as many as three or four different schools in one academic year, not to mention the challenges of truancy that homelessness produced. Moreover, enrollment in or withdrawal from school clearly was managed outside normal processes—children just disappeared from the school only to show up at another some weeks later, if then. Tracking down children and being realistic about homework expectations among this population were problematic concerns.

The hurdle this school's principal and teachers obviously had to clear was finding a means to create an educationally wholesome environment for these children, as well as for those who attended more consistently, although the student population was in perpetual flux throughout the school year. Instructional approaches and methodologies, lesson plans, or learning objectives designed for schools with more stable enrollments could not work in this school. The intellectual giftedness and vast levels of experience present among the faculty, the administrative expertise, and efficiency of the staff (the capacity represented in the school) were insufficient to address this daily challenge without the requisite inner motivation of all those persons (the will) to remain involved in this context. It took both capacity and *will* to inspire the creativity necessary to make a positive impact upon the children's lives while they were enrolled. It was the capacity and the will of these teachers, administrators, and staff that creatively rendered a near-impossible educational situation a minimally viable one. Flexibility, ingenuity, and a desire to help were characteristics that combined to produce what we collectively describe as creativity.

Determination as a major element in the core value of creativity refers to the commitment needed to remain involved in ministry until the goal is completed. Positive systemic change takes time. In our microwave culture that looks for significant change in a matter of seconds, the urban practitioner must understand that undoing the long-term effects of multigenerational poverty and educational underachievement cannot be accomplished overnight. Problems that took years to compound their negative effects will also take a long time to correct.

In all areas of life, but particularly in megastructures and systems operant in urban society (including its ecclesiastical institutions), change comes slowly and is often resisted as a threat to the status quo. The most familiar household names from scripture and extrabiblical history were all challenged at some point by both internal and external resistance to change. Moses, Esther, Socrates, John the Baptist, Galileo, Harriett Tubman, Mohandas Gandhi, Rosa Parks, or Nelson Mandela—the list is long of heroic figures whose lives were shaped by their *capacity* and *will* to be resourceful in problem-solving to enhance the quality of life-affirming realities. In short, these two characteristics combined to reveal an inner creative spirit that could not rest until some measure of relief had been fashioned to resist negative and debilitating realities, no matter how powerful they might have seemed. This is the essence of the core value we refer to as creativity: that *capacity* and *will* (motivation, volition) combine with *determination* to produce responses borne of problem-solving activities to produce systemic change that enhances life-affirming realities in the city.

Core Value 6: RECONCILIATION

In June 2006, I visited the city of Takum in the Taraba State of Nigeria and saw the charred structures of burned schools, medical clinics, churches, and entire neighborhoods, stark evidence of remaining physical scars from the 1997–2001 fighting that raged between the Jukun and Kuteb ethnic groups as well as the Chamba and Tiv. All around the globe, cities are often the central points where ethnic, ideological, or territorial violence is focused: Baghdad, Beirut, New York City, Jerusalem, Madrid, Los Angeles, or London. Across the United States, students are increasingly subject to searches before entering school buildings as a precaution against gun violence in school. Gang-related violence nationwide increased by 50 percent between 1999 and 2006.[20] With tension and violence playing so profound a part in the global experience, especially in cities, it should not surprise anyone that *reconciliation* is a core value in urban ministry. Only through reconciliation can there be any real hope for enhancing the quality of life-affirming realities in the city or in any other context.

Although the interface of a great variety of participating constituencies in relatively close spatial contexts is one of the most obvious characteristics defining urban society, this feature, for many, is also among the most challenging characteristics of urban life. The various differences in ethnicity, culture, politics, religious beliefs, education, lifestyle, ideology, neighboring environments, economic status, and architectural styles are what make city life *urban*. As we noted in chapter 3, the word *urban* is frequently a code word for *difference* because its juxtaposed and often competing communities, networks, and cultures are seen as being in various states of irreconcilable tension with one another.[21] Yet, in urban ministry, it is the plural nature of the metropolis that is perhaps its most valuable asset, and the core value of *reconciliation* is understood as the means of helping society, through faith, to take advantage of this strength.

Numerous scriptural passages in the Old and New Testaments, drawn from several contexts and time frames, recognize the notion of difference in God's creation as essentially a positive reality divinely ordained from the foundation of the world. Scripture views the variety in creation as a blessing from God, evidence of divine majesty and power, and as a symbol for right living among believers (Genesis 1:20-31; Ruth; Psalms 8; 24:1-2; Isaiah 45:9-12; Acts 10; 1 Corinthians 12:14-20; Galatians 3:28; Revelation 7:9-12). Yet, the ecologically complementary implications of scriptural teachings concerning variety and difference in creation are often overshadowed by the confrontational postures that are also quite obvious as characteristics of urban society.

Earlier, I also identified (in chapter 2) *alienation, fear,* and *violence* as three of the defining characteristics of the human condition affecting the urban context. The profound sense of alienation is evident in competitive and confrontational patterns of interpersonal and intergroup dynamics. People are acculturated to recognize and affirm their own uniqueness in distinction from others. This is a part of the socialization process of self-preservation. Understandably, children are taught not to talk to strangers; and in public places and gatherings, it is customary for adults to avoid eye contact. In this manner, a pervasive strain of fear has become part of the cultural fabric of society. Heightened personal and public safety concerns (fears) are fed by a habitual diet of crime, death, and savagery in the news, ranging from the daily fare of drive-by shootings in local media reports to the sensationalized national coverage of trials like that of O. J. Simpson during the 1990s, and widely publicized terror-laden events like pathological murders that crowd national television coverage (e.g., the 1991 macabre killings by Jeffrey Dahmer committed in Milwaukee; the murder of James Byrd, Jr. in Jasper, Texas, in 1998; or 1999's Columbine High School shootings in Colorado).[22] Additionally, news reports are regularly filled with news of international issues tied to bizarre individuals or conspiracy-related mass destruction (e.g., Oklahoma City Federal Building, World Trade Center, and the Pentagon).[23] Compounding this tension is the now common practice of public terror alerts of various kinds from the federal government and Amber alerts concerning endangered children in our local neighborhoods.

In this cultural atmosphere, the "in your face" culture of urban life produces tension and sets the context for overt conflict in families, neighborhoods, on the job, during recreational events, at church, and just about everywhere people gather. Instead of a culturally neutral posture toward other human beings we do not know in society, historically recognized as strangers, sadly we now view persons unknown to us with distrust or even hostility. Instead of everyone being a potential "brother or sister" member of the human family, everyone is now a potential enemy! Thus, the cultural assignment of "enemy-status" to all strangers in society has set the environmental stage for confrontation; increasingly, opportunities for finding a "middle ground" disappear. Typically, the enemy-status mind-set, whether in school, business, politics, recreational events, or even in religious organizations, results in behaviors that seem focused on emotionally, spiritually, or even physically destroying the opposition by whatever means necessary. Conflict resolution activities and events such as "stop the violence" campaigns organized by local community groups, or gang-intervention work of local police and/or public schools, therefore, have become a central feature in urban ministry. In this societal milieu, it becomes essential for the urban-ministry practitioner to be clear about the theological underpinnings that motivate and ultimately give these conflict resolution aims the real potential for success.

Reconciliation as a Preemptive Process

It is important to stress that the theological goal of urban ministry in reducing stress, tension, and conflict is, in essence, the fundamental goal of the gospel of Jesus Christ: the ministry of reconciliation (2 Corinthians 5). In urban ministry, however, this ministry of reconciliation is demonstrated in behavior among believers that embodies the ideals of divine compassion and justice promotion in tandem, regardless of hostilities that seek to confront, compete, and destroy emotionally, physically, or spiritually. Reconciliation in this context must be preemptive. By preemptive, I refer to an understanding of conflict resolution that involves *forgiveness that precedes or comes before repentance*. This is the theological precondition the urban practitioner must reflect and project to contending enemy factions before reconciliation can become possible.

Ordinarily, we think of reconciliation as involving "repentance" or a change of perspective on the part of the "enemy" or "adversary" before rapport or relationship can be favorably established. In preemptive reconciliation, love and respect are bestowed upon the person in conflict *prior to* his or her repentance or change of attitude in an effort to restore, initiate, or otherwise create a sense of community within the believer in Christ. Just as God initiated salvation for us through Jesus Christ's life and death because of divine love, even before we repented, we must also preemptively affirm love and forgiveness for others. Divine love initiates action based on love rather than waiting for the requirements to be met for repentance, justice, or correctness (Genesis 12:1-3; Exodus 3:1-8; Ruth 1:15-18; 1 Samuel 2:1-10; the birth narratives in Luke). It involves a process whereby the humanity of the "enemy" is affirmed in spite of his or her offensive behavior. Although the actions of the adversary may be out of control, the preemptive posture of reconciliation enables the urban practitioner or believer in Christ not to respond in kind by losing her or his humanity. In this process, as we shall see below, the urban Christian does not surrender her or his fundamental opposition to oppression, but is able through this opposition to insist on affirming the humanity of the "enemy" by not allowing the opponent's dignity to be devalued.

Deconstructing the "Enemy Status"

As Thurman pointed out, the first step in creating an enemy is to remove the person from their status of being human.[24] In order to do this, the individual has to be categorized or objectified so that he/she is no longer a person in our eyes, but an object. It is always easier to dislike objectified categories: liars, sexists, thieves, and so on. Once the "offending" personality has been replaced by the *objectified label* of wife beater, welfare mother, Black male of medium complexion, Republican, Liberal, lesbian, gang member, or whatever, then it is easier to construct the psychological, spiritual, and physical parameters of alienation. The individual is no longer human, but has become objectified. This is why, for example, our society finds it relatively convenient, albeit very costly, to "get tough on crime" by arresting and incarcerating literally millions of people whom we view not as humans, but as *criminals*. Humans make mistakes, need education, rehabilitation, or another chance, but criminals are dangerous: they are not human.

Preemptive reconciliation does not involve passive acquiescence to unacceptable behavior. On the contrary, it requires active resistance to dysfunction and injustice or, more accurately understood, it involves the proactive deconstruction of negative realities through a process of identifying and disengaging destructive behaviors and circumstances. In sports terminology, it has been suggested that the "best defense is a good offense." This is the methodology of proactive reconciliation. It seeks to deconstruct the enemy status and restore the opponent to the human family. To deconstruct the enemy status, therefore, one fundamentally has to respect the opposing individual's status as being human in order to proactively initiate activities, attitudes, and situations that will neutralize hostility.

In this way, we demonstrate our respect for the fundamental humanity of drug dealers, pimps, out-of-control police officers, or redlining banks by forgiving them preemptively. We affirm their humanity by refusing to cooperate with their dysfunctional behavior. This is the altruism of agape. Because we *love* them so much and have *preemptively forgiven* them, we are no longer able to ignore their unjust and community-destroying actions and must oppose their negative behavior in an effort to restore them to just relationships within the community. We become duty-bound to identify and preemptively disengage their destructive behaviors, thereby working to block and neutralize their abuse. Once this is done, restorative justice efforts enable the wider community to engage the offending and the aggrieved parties with one another as appropriate to repair the harm, allow communal healing, and affirm the common humanity of all.

As a core value, preemptive reconciliation is the spiritual determination to engage confrontation with the intent of dismantling the enemy status that so pervasively characterizes society in general and finds some of its most overt manifestations in the urban arena. One of the most significant examples of the potential of preemptive reconciliation to influence public policy was evidenced in South Africa following the collapse of apartheid in that country when, through the leadership of Archbishop Desmond Tutu, that nation established its Truth and Reconciliation Commission to help reduce lingering hostility that could have given rise to full-scale civil war. Clearly, preemptive reconciliation is not easy—nor is it without its own brand of tension and conflict. Much courage is required to implement this core value, but because this is a guiding principle that ultimately produces positive systemic change, it is critical to lasting and effective change in urban ministry. The list of successful stories arising from utilization of this core value is long and varied, ranging from Moses confronting Pharaoh, Joshua facing the walls of Jericho, Daniel in the lions' den, Jesus' numerous challenges to systemic evil and illness, and, in the wake of the Resurrection, Paul finally beginning to work with the other apostles. Extrabiblical and postbiblical examples stretch from Socrates to Polycarp and Athanasius, Luther to Sojourner Truth and Mary McLeod Bethune, Marian Anderson, Mohandas Gandhi, and Martin Luther King, Jr.

Core Value 7: HOPE

The seventh core value in urban ministry for enhancing the quality of life-affirming realities in the metropolitan context is *hope*. Living in an environment where the prevalence of chronic health challenges such as HIV/AIDS, substance addiction, diabetes, asthma, gunshot wounds, and hypertension are the norm in the absence of even minimal health insurance coverage, it is difficult to feel hopeful about life. Where ineffective school systems, pervasive unemployment, squalid living conditions, and rampant violence define the neighborhood, apathy and despair and even hatred of oneself and others are to be expected. In such contexts, urban ministry must present an alternate positive vision of what is possible, no matter how improbable such a vision may initially appear to community residents when presented against the backdrop of ugly sociopolitical and economic realities. Some of the most beautiful and uplifting passages of scripture were written against a background of painful social contexts. The idealized vision of Psalm 37; Isaiah 65:17-25; and 1 Corinthians 12 are just a few examples. What these scriptures share in common is a view of reality that transcends crisis by focusing on God's capacity to help the believer redefine problems as possibilities. The gravity of the negative reality is not ignored or glossed over, but is taken seriously and fully engaged in a manner that seeks to acquaint the burdened individual(s) with options for both survival and positive transformation. This is what the core value of *hope* in urban ministry seeks to accomplish.

Frequently, core-city neighborhoods, with social conditions that mirror some of the poorest contexts of two-thirds-world slums, are virtually written off even by those who live there. Effective urban ministry must be energized by an indefatigable spirit that is able to perceive not only that which is present, but also that which is possible. The famed writer George Bernard Shaw wrote the now well-worn but potent statement: "You see things as they are and ask 'why?' I dream things that never were and I say 'why not?'" It is this attitude and temperament that is required for effectiveness in the urban reality. Although the writer in Hebrews summarized faith as the *"assurance of things hoped for, the conviction of things not seen"* (11:1), the inner conviction and aspiration imbedded in this definition of faith also constitute the essence of this core value we call *hope*. The story of Tyrone is an example of the power of hope.

At the annual church picnic, Mrs. Thompson (not her real name) seemed withdrawn and oblivious to all the fun everyone was having around her.

Strangely, her son Tyrone, who never missed these events, was not present today, although he seemed to have fully recovered from the pneumonia that had caused his hospitalization a few weeks earlier. Finally, the pastor approached her as she sat alone on an isolated park bench and asked if she was all right. Mrs. Thompson said, "No, I'm not all right. Yesterday, a friend told me that Tyrone planned to kill himself, and this morning, I found a loaded gun in his closet. I emptied the gun and brought it with me. It's in the car." She said Tyrone was upset because his flu-like symptoms had returned, forcing him to miss work again. The pastor immediately arranged to talk with Tyrone, and the young man told him that he had tested positive for AIDS. Following prayer, the pastor encouraged Tyrone to get medical attention, professional psychological counseling, and to seek out an HIV/AIDS support group. Within a short time, Tyrone's medications helped him recover his strength. The loving support he received from his family and his extended family of the church, along with his involvement in individual and group counseling services, helped Tyrone feel more hopeful about life in spite of his illness. This hope ultimately manifested itself in Tyrone's return to a positive approach to life. Soon, he was working again and bringing members of his HIV/AIDS support network to church with him on Sunday.

By hope, we are not referring to some syrupy idealism that is so ethereal and unrealistic that it only serves to reinforce the sense of apathy that frequently is well entrenched in depressed communities. Hope, as a core value in urban ministry, is essentially the vision, investment, and time required to bring the potential of core-city residents and their communities to fulfillment. In order to translate the values of a theistic lifestyle, defined by love and a sense of justice that is not afraid of preemptive reconciliation, one must possess a faith capacity and will that give rise to a creativity that can only be divinely borne of an indefatigable hope. These are seven of the core values that will characterize any urban ministry that seeks to truly enhance the quality of life-affirming realities in the city as reflected in the gospel of Jesus Christ.

Conclusion

In our overtly individualistic culture, urban ministry's theological emphasis on communal welfare is often difficult to translate. Moreover, analysis of the theological hermeneutic that interprets scripture toward an individual and nonurban perspective (where communal considerations are ignored) is often manifested through characteristics that are very different in their behavioral outcomes from those having urban-focused or community-centered interests. In urban ministry, core values are largely defined not by theological rhetoric, but by behavioral outcomes. According to scripture, Jesus taught, "Beware of false prophets. . . . You will know them by their fruits" (Matthew 7:15-16), and in other teachings placed a heavy emphasis on behavioral outcomes that ultimately reflected some semblance of life-affirming realities like faith in God, agape/love, justice, creativity, reconciliation, and hope (Matthew 7:21-23; Mark 3:33-35; 11:12-14). Without a clear understanding of these essential or core values, much of our effort in the sphere of urban ministry will amount to little more than "a noisy gong or a clanging symbol" (1 Corinthians 13:1).

Chart 5: Core Values, Strategies, and Action Steps

CORE VALUE A reality that is considered important	STRATEGY Plan/method to achieve a desired goal	ACTION STEPS Behavior(s) initiated to attain a specific outcome
1. THEISM	PERSONAL ASSESSMENT	DECISION/COMMITMENT
The *theist* is one who believes in the existence of God. By contrast, the *atheist* does not. In urban ministry, *theism* refers to a God-consciousness based upon *faith* rather than on the exclusive use of scientifically objective or observable data. It reflects an *affirmation of divine involvement in life* as well as in all aspects of existence that gives the believer a unique perspective on reality, encompassing both the physical and the metaphysical. (Genesis 1:1; John 1:1)	The process of: (1) daily checking and affirming personal reasons for passion regarding a particular focus in life; (2) analyzing factors that prompt you to think there is something divinely inspired or affirming about your opinions or motivations with regard to your identified life focus (philosophy of life); (3) discerning how one's life focus helps promote human dignity, compassion, and justice in society; (4) seeking clarity on how your actions help others to become more appreciative of God's involvement in their own lives; (5) identifying and examining subsurface motives that may indicate selfish proclivities and preparing oneself to accept inconvenience, if necessary, in efforts to be compassionate in work for justice.	• Cultivate your spiritual and biblical faith grounding. • Identify your ministry strengths. • Confront your weaknesses. • Clarify your own sense of call. • Identify prayer-partner(s)/mentor(s) whose faith in God and spiritual integrity you respect.

CORE VALUE A reality that is considered important	STRATEGY Plan/method to achieve a desired goal	ACTION STEPS Behavior(s) initiated to attain a specific outcome
2. LOVE *Love* (*agape*) is the divinely gratuitous relationship of devotion or commitment experienced by a conscious being directed toward another living being that seeks to enhance the quality of existence and well-being for its target without regard to merit or any expectation of reward. (John 3:16)	CONGREGATIONAL ASSESSMENT Clarifying the congregation's identity and mission. Process involves assessing: (1) *demographic information* (membership employment, education, age-groups, income level, family structure); (2) *history/heritage* (key events, e.g., church founding/ naming; significant milestones; "saints"/ leading figures in history of the congregation; theology, denominational identity); (3) *rituals, symbols, programs* (worship, Christian education, spiritual nurture, stewardship, community outreach and service, and publicity activities); (4) *the story* (prayerfully summarize the above information in an effort to clarify the character, strengths, and challenges of the congregation in the broader community context); (5) *the mission* (discerning the central mission-focus or purpose of the congregation in light of its community context).	INFORMATION GATHERING • Identify coordinating group within congregation to focus on congregational assessment goal. • Surveys. • Interviews. • Focus groups. • Identify congregation's missional focus.

CORE VALUE A reality that is considered important	STRATEGY Plan/method to achieve a desired goal	ACTION STEPS Behavior(s) initiated to attain a specific outcome
3. JUSTICE *Justice* is a moral and spiritual virtue whereby God-conscious persons implement or experience *agape/love* among human beings through the behavioral manifestation of equity and fairness with regard to the welfare of others. Justice is the vertical/spiritual dimension of goodness that is manifested through implementation of equity and fairness in the horizontal/communal dimension of social and environmental interaction.	EDUCATION The process of sharing information concerning the issue you seek to address with others in such a way that they become as informed about the topic as you are. This includes informing persons directly affected/oppressed by the issue, those who will be opponents of your perspective, and persons in the general public who are not aware or directly involved pro or con. Education takes place when information is presented fairly and simply so that your position is easily understood and clear.	LEADERSHIP DEVELOPMENT • **Share the vision** concerning the focus of ministry chosen and its theological basis as an issue of love and justice with others. • **Structure worship and liturgy** to: (1) emphasize divine presence among people and share the gospel; (2) celebrate God's love, justice, forgiveness, and liberation with invitation to Christian discipleship. • **Establish regular Bible study** that: (1) connects people's faith in God with the issue to be addressed; (2) exposes the ministry focus and planned methods to address it; and (3) builds relationships among those affected by the issue. • **Establish a study** of the specific ministry-focus issue whereby participants gain strategic expertise regarding the identified issue/challenge.

CORE VALUE A reality that is considered important	STRATEGY Plan/method to achieve a desired goal	ACTION STEPS Behavior(s) initiated to attain a specific outcome
4. COMMUNITY	RESEARCH/ANALYSIS	INFORMATION GATHERING
Community is the experience of being together in an environment or group where common interests, concerns, values, and beliefs shape the context of the shared social vision and expression of common life and well-being. In the faith community, it is the revealed presence of God that informs the common life.	**RESEARCH:** (1) Define your circle or community to which you are divinely called; (2) identify the people impacted; (3) find the "invisible people"; (4) analyze the intangible factors; (5) listen to your community. **ANALYSIS:** (1) Engage individuals or organizations that have expertise in the community and knowledge of its issues; (2) seek to determine where strengths and needs are evident in the information you have gathered; (3) verify your information to be sure it accurately represents the phenomena you are seeking to document; (4) if possible, compare your information with other research on this issue; (5) prayerfully seek God's guidance in identifying your focus of ministry in light of the facts.	• **Neighborhood mapping** (identifying key places, resources within the neighborhood) • **Interviews** • **Surveys** • **Focus groups** • **Ethnographic studies** • **Congregational assessment** (interviews, surveys, focus groups, etc.) • **Bible study** • **Select a ministry focus** regarding a specific issue.

CORE VALUE A reality that is considered important	STRATEGY Plan/method to achieve a desired goal	ACTION STEPS Behavior(s) initiated to attain a specific outcome
5. CREATIVITY	ORGANIZATION	RELATIONSHIP BUILDING
Creativity is the process of intentionally using one's faith in God to examine a challenge or opportunity and then plan, implement, and evaluate activities that are able to transform or replace negative reality with positive and life-affirming experiences.	Involves: (1) refining/sharpening the focus of ministry to be undertaken; (2) program/activity planning and methodology selection with special attention to how desired outcomes are to be achieved, documented, and evaluated; (3) negotiation with partners or opponents where appropriate to clarify and strengthen proposed methodology; (4) resource development; (5) recruitment, screening, and training of volunteers; (6) identification of future follow-up activities in anticipation of successful achievement of desired outcomes.	• **Identify potential leadership** for steering or advisory committee. • **Become a mentor** among target community. • **Convene coordinating/planning group** from among identified leaders to: (1) help strategize, plan, and coordinate activities; (2) be activity and prayer partners; (3) recruit and train volunteers. • **Cultivate resource partners:** human expertise, financial, organizational, and community agency collaborators. • **Implement coordinated training and *mentoring*** of volunteers to encourage actions that promote human dignity.

CORE VALUE A reality that is considered important	STRATEGY Plan/method to achieve a desired goal	ACTION STEPS Behavior(s) initiated to attain a specific outcome
6. RECONCILIATION	DIRECT ACTION	MINISTRY
Reconciliation is the conscious and intentionally preemptive deconstruction of the "enemy" or oppositional status and, in its place, the establishment of a relationship of cooperation or friendship.	The implementation of a specific ministry that: (1) proactively takes steps to intervene and stop oppressive realities by calling attention to their hurtful consequences; (2) presents alternative measures that are corrective and intended to alleviate suffering and injustice; and (3) structures activities that promote human dignity and demonstrates moral issues involved.	• **Establish a timetable for the ministry** that includes: (1) regular schedule of ministry activities or actions; (2) publicity of ministry-related events; (3) leadership-coordinating meetings; and (4) recruitment and training of new volunteers through building positive relationships, mentoring, and promoting accountability. • **Cultivate resource partners:** human expertise, financial, organizational, and community agency collaborators. • **Evaluate ministry results:** With the assistance of an independent (neutral/not directly involved) evaluator, assess the results of ministry activity. • **Analyze and reflect** on ministry results and refine ministry goals/activity as appropriate to more effectively achieve desired outcomes.

CORE VALUE A reality that is considered important	STRATEGY Plan/method to achieve a desired goal	ACTION STEPS Behavior(s) initiated to attain a specific outcome
7. HOPE	RECONSTRUCTION	DECISION/COMMITMENT
Borne of love and commitment to justice, *hope* is the combination of (1) the God-given *capacity to envision* a better reality than the one that presently exists, and (2) the *determination to invest* creatively in its realization. (Hebrews 11:1)	Based on ministry outcomes, *reconstruction* is the process of implementing the above six urban ministry strategies again in light of new opportunities and/or challenges that arise as a result of the newly redefined context of ministry. It moves beyond typical follow-up type activities (responding to the past) and engages in planning strategies that set the stage for creation of a new and more life-affirming future reality.	• **Cultivate your spiritual and biblical faith grounding** • **Identify your ministry strengths.** • **Confront your weaknesses.** • **Clarify your own sense of call.** • **Identify prayer-partner /mentor(s)** whose faith in God and spiritual integrity you respect.

TWO SPHERES OF URBAN MINISTRY: PARISH AND PUBLIC

If you ask typical church members why their church exists, you'll get a wide
variety of answers. Most churches do not have a clear consensus on this
issue. . . . Unless the driving force behind a church is biblical, the health and
growth of the church will never be what God intended. Strong churches are
not built on programs, personalities, or gimmicks. They are built on the
eternal purposes of God.

—Rick Warren[1]

It's alright to talk about 'long white robes over yonder,' in all of its
symbolism. But ultimately people want some suits and dresses and shoes to
wear down here. It's alright to talk about "streets flowing with milk and
honey," but God has commanded us to be concerned about the slums down
here, and his children who can't eat three square meals a day. It's alright to
talk about the new Jerusalem, but one day, God's preacher must talk about
the New York, the new Atlanta, the new Philadelphia, the new Los Angeles,
the new Memphis, Tennessee. This is what we have to do.

—Martin Luther King, Jr.[2]

A Christian physician who specializes in cardiology as a result of what she strongly feels is a divinely inspired faith commitment was pleased to accept the pastor's invitation to be one of the inspirational speakers at the youth retreat for fifty high school juniors and seniors. Having grown up in a poor neighborhood in the heart of the city, she could appreciate the issues these young people faced as the possibility of high school graduation became more real. She thought about all the challenges they now faced in today's cynical, post–9/11 world where metal detectors, drive-by shootings, school suspensions, drugs, getting the "hook up," or jail was more likely an option than college or a good job with decent pay. She felt that sharing her faith journey and how it ultimately led to her present vocation as a cardiologist might help some of these young people come to know God's power in their lives. God willing, her faith story might prove to be one of several factors leading others to confess faith in Jesus Christ. She enjoyed participating in evangelistic events like these because helping people to grow toward faith in Christ was a rewarding part of her Christian ministry.

The day after the youth retreat, the physician found herself once again in the midst of open-heart surgery on a patient who, without this procedure, faced the grim probability of an imminent and potentially fatal heart attack. In performing the surgery, her immediate priority was clearly the physical salvation of the patient whether or not he was a Christian. Although her life and profession, including her skills in open-heart surgery, are part of her Christian ministry, her skills during that particular operation, taken independently of other aspects of her life, did not overtly reflect Christian evangelism in the way her involvement in the youth retreat did. In fact, her technical expertise and behavioral conduct and conversation during the surgery, unlike the youth retreat, were virtually indistinguishable from those of a Hindu, Muslim, or Jewish physician performing the exact same procedure.

This scenario, in brief, sketches for us the basic differences between two very distinct but intimately related spheres of Christian ministry that are helpful in examining urban ministry. The two spheres are *parish ministry* and *public ministry* and should be understood not as separate components, but as two directional areas on a single continuum of ministry. The youth retreat is an example of parish ministry; the surgery is an example of public ministry. Like all Christian ministry regardless of locale, urban ministry may be broadly categorized as falling into these two overall spheres of endeavor, each with its own emphasis but leading toward common functional goals: inspiring the best in human and ecological relationships. In actual practice, many of their individual functions overlap and are often indistinguishable one from the other, but parish ministry and public ministry represent two very different types of ministry. For purposes of concept clarification, however, these constructs help in the urban context of ministry.

Parish Ministry

Parish ministry is essentially declarative and evangelistic. Parish ministry seeks to declare the tenets of faith to assist people in becoming more aware of and responsive to God's involvement in their lives and, thereby, invites a response of faith. For our purposes here, parish ministry should not be understood as exclusively referring to pastoral ministry within the setting of a local congregation, but to all forms of ministry that are overtly *evangelistic* in nature and seek to encourage people into faith in God as revealed in Jesus Christ. While it can certainly be argued that all Christian ministry is essentially evangelistic, as we have seen in the above story about the physician, not all of it is overtly or directly evangelistic. By parish ministry, I refer to that type of ministry activity that overtly evangelizes.

In its most generic forms, parish ministry may be further characterized by two general approaches: *corporate* and *personal* (see chart 6 below). Parish ministry that is corporate in approach is ministry that is essentially directed toward the local congregation of believers as a collective unit. By contrast, parish ministry that is more individually focused is referred to as *personal*. Both approaches seek to heighten awareness within people of God's involvement in their lives so as to elicit a response of faith. This is why parish ministry is viewed as essentially declarative. It does not seek to impose or legislate faith beliefs upon others; it merely presents the facts of the believer's or the believing community's faith experience. It is this testimony of faith in conjunction with the behavior of the confessing Christian that constitutes the evangelistic activity of parish ministry and invites a response on the part of those receiving this testimony.

Chart 6

PARISH MINISTRY
Evangelistic ministry that declares the gospel with the goal of having nonbelievers declare their faith in Jesus Christ and strengthening faith among Christian believers

Corporate	Personal
Ministry in the Congregation	• Individual church members
• Worship services	• Christians who are not affiliated with a congregation
• Bible study	• Non-Christians in the church's neighborhood or in the general public
• Sunday school	
• Stewardship campaigns	• Individuals working in various positions in the community (barber, beautician, schoolteacher, police officer, politician, community activist, etc.)
• Mission outreach	
• Denominational activity	
• Special events	

Within the congregation, parish ministry addresses the collective needs of constituent members who are part of the social institution specifically organized as a body of Christian believers within society. Corporately, parish ministry functions to strengthen the ministry and witness of the local congregation within the wider society from its faith center as expressed in its ecclesiastical and denominational traditions. Outside the congregation, parish ministry addresses the spiritual needs of individuals who, while not united with the ministering congregation, view themselves as believers in Christ, nonetheless.

Personal parish ministry is generally, but not exclusively, focused on strengthening the individual's faith, Christian spirituality, and lifestyle or personal choices.

Parish ministry is best understood as evangelistic and nurturing ministry because it is designed to elicit within the individual or covenant community behavioral responses to faith. It is evangelistic in the sense that it seeks to call nonbelievers into the faith. It is nurturing in that it seeks to strengthen and support those already included among the adherents of the faith. Ministries of worship, education, nurture, stewardship, and service are a means of modeling faith so that the believer is encouraged to focus on strengthening his or her relationship to God and helping others (believers and nonbelievers) also to be aware of their relationship with God, strengthening faith among believers and inviting nonbelievers toward faith. The evangelistic focus of parish ministry invites people to become part of the community of believers as a means of strengthening the declarative witness of the covenant community to the public at large. The ultimate aim of parish ministry is to enable the saints to embrace behaviors, lifestyles, and demeanor in all areas of life (private and family life, the covenant fellowship of the church, and in the wider society) that will enhance the quality of life in society in general.

Corporate Parish Ministry

As previously mentioned, the corporate focus in parish ministry seeks to evangelize by enhancing the congregational life and witness of the local church. For six consecutive weeks, the pastor of a small Black Presbyterian church in a poor section of Pittsburgh officiated at a funeral every week of a teenager who had died from neighborhood gun violence. Unemployment in the church's community has been over 60 percent for years, and 93 percent of the children in the local elementary school come from homes that are below the federal government's poverty level. Substandard housing, drug violence, and single-parent homes characterize this residential area. In this neighborhood, like many other inner-city areas facing similar challenges, corporate parish ministry must project at least four qualities: *a sense of divine call, incarnational compassion, alternative vision of the community,* and *contextual integrity.*

Sense of Divine Call. In socially challenged neighborhoods where the prevailing social and spiritual ethos is one of oppression, congregations must have a clear sense of their own *divine call* to ministry and service to this particular community and to its people. Otherwise, churches in such areas will either move to another location or eventually close. The high stress and alienation that typify urban life in poor communities give rise to rampant fear and hopelessness. Frequently, churches in these communities reflect the economic and social realities of the neighborhood; their human and financial resources are stretched. Typically, the congregation is served by a limited volunteer staff aside from the pastor. The fear and hopelessness that are evident in the community can infect the spiritual life of the congregation if left unchecked. Corporate parish ministry uses every gathering of the congregation to emphasize the church's sense of divine call to serve this particular context through its teaching and worshiping ministries. The scriptural focus of God's concern that people who believe in God work to uproot injustice and alleviate suffering must undergird the congregational sense of divine call (see Exodus 3:7-10; Leviticus 25:1-55; Psalm 40:1-11; Isaiah 58:6-7; Amos 5:23-24; Luke 1:46-55; 4:18-19; John 1:14; 10:10; Acts 4:32-35; James 2:1-7; Revelation 21:1-4). More will be said about how this sense of *divine call* manifests itself behaviorally in the section below on *contextual integrity*.

Incarnational Compassion. The evangelistic focus of corporate parish ministry in this context must interpret the "good news" of the gospel by identifying with the people in the community. Identifying with people who live in an ethos of oppression, danger, and rejection means to stand with them in the midst of their pain and affirm their value as human beings in a society that typically ignores or undervalues them. This is what is meant by *incarnational compassion:* respecting and recognizing the value of people whose social, economic, educational, and political locations in society make them vulnerable to abuse and oppression by standing with them against injustice and oppression. Incarnational compassion in this sense is to be distinguished from the old-school missionary paternalism, which, in many cases, tended to look down on the cultural context and setting of those the missionaries sought to serve. Corporate worship, Sunday school, Bible study, and other collective activities of the congregation become opportunities for spiritual bonding with the brokenhearted and celebrating God's capacity to transform circumstances of grief into joyful realities. Worship services include music and preaching that are creative, celebrative, intellectually informative, and inspiring, exposing people to new possibilities that faith in Christ offers. "And the Word became flesh and lived among us, and we have seen his glory" (John 1:14) is what this type of ministry seeks to model behaviorally.

Alternative Vision of the Community. An *alternative vision of the community* means exactly that: instead of the dreary ethos of oppression that typifies so many inner-city communities and renders residents apathetic and cynical, corporate parish ministry invites people to an understanding of the gospel that includes a new vision of what a redeemed and revitalized community could look like. Instead of the usual stereotypes of social, economic, and political dysfunction that constitute the expectations of the oppressed in poor core-city neighborhoods, corporate ministry's evangelism lifts a vision of creative alternative community realities: safe streets, beautiful and safe parks, recreational facilities that are functional and state-of-the-art, schools that actually educate children, beautiful homes, and legal business enterprises that employ residents and are owned by the people who live in the neighborhood. Scripture is full of examples in which people of limited circumstances were able, in faith, to realize incredible accomplishments. The story of Nehemiah (Nehemiah 1–7) is but one example of a beleaguered and oppressed community's struggle, perseverance, and eventual success in overcoming opposition to achieve positive goals through faith and determined vision. Corporate parish ministry in poor communities is most helpful if worship, preaching, and other educational activities are able to inspire an alternative, positive vision of what life in the neighborhood should look like and what the local congregation can do, through faith in Jesus Christ, to help the community realize this alternative vision.

Contextual Integrity. Corporate parish ministry in the urban context does not ordinarily pretend to be universally applicable. Urban pastors are usually quite clear that their focus is specifically designed for ministry in a particular type of urban setting. They also tend to focus on a specific context or subculture within the urban arena: the African American neighborhood, Hispanic ministry, Korean, Chinese, or any of several other varieties of immigrants. Unfortunately, there is a relative paucity of resources on corporate parish ministry to assist pastors, and churches in these contexts hone their leadership skills in ways that are specifically designed for their particular ministries. Many urban pastors, therefore, necessarily utilize evangelistic tools available in the wider society and simply try to adapt them for the inner-city context.

One of the most popular such resources in this vein in recent years has been the work of the suburban Orange County, California, Baptist pastor Rick Warren. His book *The Purpose Driven Church: Growth Without Compromising Your Message and Mission*[3] is based on his twenty-five-year experience as the founding pastor of Saddleback Church in Lake Forest, California. Warren's focus is evangelistically targeted toward enabling pastors and other church leaders to grow their congregations through a style of evangelism that is solidly rooted in bringing nonbelievers to faith in Christ. Kennon L. Callahan is another popular writer and church growth consultant whose work typifies the parish corporate or congregational focus in ministry. In 1986, Callahan published what has become a classic in parish ministry enhancement resources, his book entitled *Twelve Keys to an Effective Church.*[4] Both these approaches represent excellent evangelical strategies of corporate parish ministry for a "broad cross-section" of North American society, but reflect a universalized type of ministry that is assumed to have merit for any social context. Nonetheless, they are drawn from a White, mostly suburban sociocultural frame of reference that knows little about drive-by shootings, drug raids, failing schools, exceptionally high incidences of HIV/AIDS, disproportionately high incarceration of men and women in jails, or neighborhoods where 50 percent of the people have no legal employment or health insurance.

Contextual integrity in the evangelical focus of corporate parish ministry, like the sense of divine call mentioned above, must reflect a unique perspective of mission-grounding that is peculiar to the specific context of urban ministry. Clearly, there are strategies drawn from other contexts of ministry that may provide some useful insights regarding evangelism in core-city areas where the ethos of oppression dominates, but the most successful evangelistic efforts in these areas are designed with the assets and challenges of these particular contexts in mind. Carlyle Fielding Stewart's *African American Church Growth: 12 Principles for Prophetic Ministry*,[5] Samuel D. Procter and Gardner C. Taylor's *We Have This Ministry: The Heart of the Pastor's Vocation*,[6] and James Stallings's *Telling the Story: Evangelism in Black Churches*[7] represent some such resources. For example, in summarizing the history of African American engagement in evangelism, Stallings notes that a critical factor in faith matters for this population has been the conviction that God, as revealed in Jesus Christ, was able to assist oppressed Africans in overcoming spiritual and physical degradation.

> Black Christians for much of their history pursued evangelism because they saw a vital connection between embracing the Christian faith and realizing racial progress. They did not transform Jesus' message into a political theology or ideology. However, they firmly believed that Christianity helped people to overcome their spiritual and physical degradation.[8]

Samuel Freedman's book about Pastor Johnny Ray Youngblood, *Upon This Rock: The Miracles of a Black Church*, is a classic example of this principle.[9] Based upon the experience of Pastor Youngblood at St. Paul Baptist Church in the Bronx, New York, this book reveals how the congregation's ministry was aimed at enabling African American men to strengthen their relationship to God as revealed in Jesus Christ. Eldin Villafañe's *The Liberating Spirit: Toward an Hispanic American Pentecostal Social Ethic*[10] and Arlene Sanchez Walsh's *Latino Pentecostalism*[11] are other examples of this type of evangelistic focus in corporate parish ministry.

Personal Parish Ministry

As mentioned previously, personal parish ministry is directed toward persons *outside* the local congregation who still consider themselves believers in God as revealed in Jesus Christ. This may include a teacher at the school down the street from the church, the local Tennants Association president, the postal worker who delivers the church's mail, or the widow who lives across the street from the church. All these persons may consider themselves to be Christians who believe in Jesus Christ and acknowledge the importance of the local church, but for any number of reasons they shy away from official affiliation with a particular congregation. Many people outside official church membership visit different congregations on occasion or watch television evangelists like Bishop T. D. Jakes, one of the best-known of the televised Christian leaders. Personal parish ministry is to be distinguished from traditional notions of pastoral care that are framed around pastoral visitation or lay visitation activities within the local congregation. This personal form of parish ministry generally refers to what seminaries call *spiritual formation*. Spiritual formation consists of activities designed to deepen the individual's faith and Christian spirituality as a means of enabling the believer to live a more spiritually rewarding life.

As mentioned in chapter 7, alienation is a prominent characteristic in society and often manifests itself in the way many people in urban society appreciate the relative anonymity this cultural setting allows. In the highly stressful and dangerous environment of many core-city communities, it is just common sense to keep unnecessary social contacts, especially with people you do not know personally, to a minimum. The subtle and overt fears that are endemic in poor, stressful, and crime-ridden communities encourage people to remain apart, alone, and disconnected from the broader social context. Churches are places where lots of people, known and unknown, gather. As such, urban dwellers, especially in core-city areas, are able to comfortably remain apart from various social connections, including the church. Urban Christians actively affiliated and involved with the local congregation often do not realize the full potential of their Christian discipleship because of the prevailing sense of alienation and fear that characterizes the spiritual ethos of oppression in many urban communities.

Personal parish ministry in this context reflects an evangelistic quality that seeks to help both individuals who are actively involved with the congregation and those who are not better connect their faith convictions to their behavioral practices in ways that help alleviate fear and alienation. Jesus' encounter with the woman at the well in Samaria (John 4:7-30) is an example of personal ministry with an individual whose behavior clearly reflected great dissonance from her articulated faith understanding. Many people in urban communities believe in God, but are engaged in activities that certainly bear little reflection of their articulated faith convictions. The alienation and fear with which they cope is more than social, it is also spiritual. The evangelism of personal parish ministry aims to help people strengthen their relationship to God as revealed in Jesus Christ so as to enable them to live more personally fulfilling lives.

As with corporate parish ministry, the ultimate aim in personal parish ministry is the overall betterment of society to the glory of God. This aim is consistent with the goal articulated in the model prayer scripture reports as having been taught by Jesus to his followers: *"Thy kingdom come . . . on earth as it is in heaven"* (Matthew 6:9-13 and Luke 11:2-4 RSV). This prayer teaches that the idealized values of compassion and justice as represented in God's eternal reign ("the kingdom") are seen as appropriate behavioral and policy goals to be sought in the real world of temporal existence ("on earth"). In short, the goal of parish ministry is to teach believers the tenets of faith so as to equip them to model life-affirming values to the broader society.

Public Ministry

Public ministry is essentially behavioral: it acts to address particular justice issues or ethical challenges in the broader society beyond the local congregation with no expectation of a response of faith in Jesus Christ from the beneficiaries of this activity (see chart 7 below). Warren Dennis has succinctly described public ministry as referring "to those places where the ordering of church life has an influence on matters of civic importance" and asks the question "What are the public policy challenges that truly test our understanding of faith and action?"[12]

Chart 7

PUBLIC MINISTRY
Service and/or public advocacy activity that seeks to address particular justice issues/ethical challenges in society with no expectation of a response of faith in Jesus Christ from the beneficiaries of this activity.

Service	Advocacy
Direct service to those in need within or outside the congregation. Examples include: • after-school tutoring • food pantry, free meals • shelter provision • clothing assistance	Raising public awareness concerning injustice, ethical issues in society. • Community research and fact-finding • Discerning justice issues • Relationship building • Community organizing

---

The goal of public ministry is service and advocacy in the public arena, drawing attention to justice issues in society based upon beliefs rooted in the faith community. Four aspects of public ministry are sometimes difficult for

Christians to understand and should be noted: *altruism modeling faith, spiritual maturity, interpretation,* and *courage.*

Altruism Modeling Faith

In the best understanding of agape love, the practical or behavioral outcomes of public ministry for broader society are intended as altruistic but not evangelistic. Ministries of service, education, and justice advocacy are expressions of faith that do not seek or overtly anticipate that the beneficiaries of ministry will become part of the community of believers. The aim is to enhance the quality of life for the public good. This is a reality that is understandably difficult for many Christians to comprehend because faith in Christ is intrinsically evangelistic. People who come to the awareness of God's involvement in their lives naturally want to share this joy with others. Suggesting that the converted Christian not share her or his faith with others is perceived as asking people to withhold the centerpiece of their faith. Yet, in some situations, the best testimony of faith in Jesus Christ is behavior rather than verbal testimony.

There are two reasons for stressing altruism over evangelism in public ministry beyond the local congregation. First, the urban context is one of religious pluralism. Since the goal of public ministry is to enhance the quality of life in the public arena, the cooperation of people from a variety of religious traditions, including those who are non-Christian, will be needed. A drive-by bullet is not concerned with the faith tradition of its victim nor is HIV/AIDS. In order to effectively address such public issues as these, interfaith cooperation is needed. The urban Christian, therefore, must be able to participate in coalition-building for the promotion of justice causes, based on his or her faith in Jesus Christ, but without attempting to proselytize others who may be comfortable with their own non-Christian faith tradition.

Second, talk is cheap, and many people who verbally testify about their faith in Jesus Christ and love for humanity also engage in behaviors that send very contradictory messages of hostility and meanness. Jesus' words "you will know them by their fruits" (Matthew 7:16-18) are an effort to help people distinguish between those who are God-fearing insofar as rhetoric is concerned, but whose actions reveal something else. In public ministry, where the goal is to build a consensus of activity that promotes justice, the aim is to model godliness so that evidence of faith in Christ will be revealed in behavior and demeanor ("they shall know we are Christians by our love"). In doing this, the covenant community becomes the paradigm of altruistic and egalitarian value (love and justice) implied in Jesus' Sermon on the Mount: "You are the light of the world" (Matthew 5:14), wherein believers are to model appropriate behavior and values for the entire society. In essence, the goal of public ministry is not to proselytize people into the faith, but to engage in activities that seek to bring about improved social outcomes in the public arena for the betterment of society as a whole.

Spiritual Maturity

Public ministry demands spiritual maturity because the focus of this type of ministry reaches outside the local congregation and seeks to address the needs of persons who may never become part of the local congregation. This does not mean that the needs of the local congregation or faith community are not considered. Nor does public ministry imply that church members cannot be evangelistic, but it does require that congregations recognize the difference between parish ministry (evangelistic/declarative) and public ministry (altruistic/behavioral). Inviting someone to take part in Bible study is clearly an act of parish ministry because it is evangelistic, but tutoring children in math and offering food to the homeless are clearly public ministries because they are altruistic.

In public ministry, the expectation is that the spiritual needs of the covenant community have been sufficiently met (e.g., awareness of faith traditions, spiritual growth, motivation, resources), so as to enable this community to address issues in the wider society in a helpful way. The ministry challenges beyond the local congregation do not always require that churches be wealthy or have huge memberships in order to do public ministry. All that is needed are the faith and desire to reach out and help those in need. A faith community that is too spiritually anemic to engage in altruistic ministry beyond its own walls and into the wider community is a congregation that will not long survive.

Interpretation

Although the incident prompting public ministry may originate in a specific urban community, the justice issue related to the incident will have relevance for social contexts beyond the urban environment. For example, while the incidence of social promotions[13] may be more frequent in poor inner-city schools, the justice issue regarding students who are moved to higher grade levels without having attained the required skill level is a matter that has ethical implications for environments beyond inner-city neighborhoods. Urban Christians engaged in public ministry will often be called upon to interpret justice issues originating in their local neighborhood in the broader context of society.

Courage

Sometimes the ethical norms, social customs, or even civil codes in society may not resonate with the church's understanding of historic teachings about justice drawn from scripture, theology, and church traditions. In such situations, public ministry's twin aims of service and advocacy often prove controversial. Challenging prevailing social customs that are wrong takes courage. In many instances, crimes go unreported because of fear. Throughout history, people of faith have engaged in service activities to assist victims of injustice and advocated in the public square on behalf of the oppressed based upon their interpretations of what faith in God implies regarding civic responsibility. Personalities like Frederick Douglass, Sojourner Truth, Jane Addams, Dietrich Bonhoeffer, and Desmond Tutu are but a few examples of advocates involved in public ministry service. The activities of these individuals were clearly rooted in justice and compassion values drawn from the gospel. Yet, their actions were altruistically designed to improve the quality of life in the public square.

When this is done effectively, the parish (or covenant community) is influenced by its public witness, and the public arena is able to tangibly benefit from the parish's faith tenets. Behaviorally, this overlap sets the context for systemic change or spiritual growth both in the parish and in the public sector (see diagram 3 below). *Within the covenant community,* parish ministry is valued because it is nurturing for believers; public ministry is valued because its *theological* function is pedagogical: it seeks to teach by precept and example. *In the public arena,* parish ministry is respected because of its motivational importance to its adherents; public ministry is valued because its social function is egalitarian: it seeks to enhance the welfare of society.

Diagram 3: Two Spheres of Urban Ministry

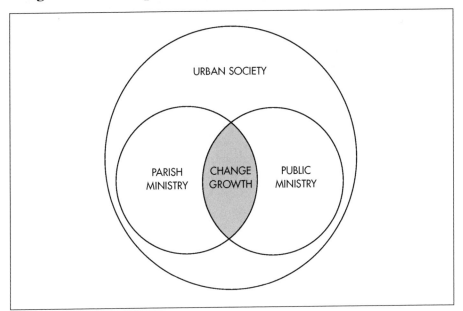

The Role of Public Ministry in American Society

The role of faith beliefs in shaping the values of American society has never been in dispute. Today, over 85 percent of Americans claim to believe in God, and more than half report that they attend worship at least once a month.[14] Much of the Southern region of the nation is, with good reason, euphemistically referred to as the "Bible Belt." In many ways the term could be applied to many areas outside the South as well where religiously promoted values play a large role in society. The 2004 presidential campaign in the United States offered proof-positive of the continuation of religiously articulated public policy debates in the nation. In spite of serious questions concerning his administration's handling of the war in Iraq, George W. Bush won reelection largely due to his public stands on issues like homosexuality, gay marriage, and abortion, positions he regularly articulated using religious language. The president attracted 78 percent of the vote among the one-quarter of the electorate who were Euro-American evangelical Christian, and he took 52 percent of the Catholic vote.[15] This election was not alone in being influenced by religious debate on public issues. As long ago as 1928, one of the factors that received much attention prior to the defeat of New York governor Al Smith's bid for the presidency was the fact that he was a Roman Catholic. Again in 1960, the public dialogue that preceded the election of John F. Kennedy as the nation's first Roman Catholic president also evidenced the significance of religion in American public life.

Among the poor in America, by no means exclusively found in cities but whose presence therein is statistically staggering, the importance of religion has been well documented, especially in subgroups like the African American or immigrant communities where the church is disproportionately influential when compared to other segments of the population.[16] As previously mentioned (chapter 2), the witness of the urban church has figured prominently in many of the major social movements that have taken place throughout history, and not just in the United States. The history of European society is one piece of experiential cloth tightly interwoven with the church, principally in its cities. The import of religious activity in the sixteenth through the twentieth centuries in Africa, Asia, South America, and Oceania is inextricably bound with the story of colonialism as well as the liberation movements therefrom. All of these activities have been anchored in the cities.

Addressing the Urban Myth

Why, then, is there a persistent myth that the city is somehow foreign territory for Christian witness? In attempting to debunk this long-standing myth of the city as a hostile environment for church growth, Lyle Schaller, that great documenter of American congregational life, opened his 1993 book

Center City Churches with a reminder that this belief has received wide attention for many years, even globally:

> In preparation for the first assembly of the World Council of Churches, to be held in Amsterdam in 1948, one document summarized the spread of Christianity during the previous one hundred years. It included this provocative statement: "There are three great areas of our world which the churches have not really penetrated. They are: Hinduism, Islam and the culture of modern cities."[17]

The myth persists in spite of the long history of effective witness for Jesus Christ that has been conducted from urban centers. As is well known, no matter how divergent the myth from reality, for those who believe the myth, it is perceived as real. Yet, the plaintive question of ethicist Harvey Cox reveals the frustration of those who love and live in the city when faced with such stubborn and misguided beliefs, yet are not dissuaded by them:

> Is there anyone left who remembers that the city is its people, and that everything from its postcard skylines to its tunnels of electrical wiring should be there to help its people make it a civitas, a community of citizens?[18]

The answer to this question is clearly yes. There are countless people who live, work, and engage in all types of ministry in cities with their efforts aimed at enhancing the quality of urban life. Their activities ultimately reach toward that grand vision of the writer in Revelation: *"Then I saw a new heaven and a new earth. . . . And I saw the holy city, the new Jerusalem . . . and heard a loud voice . . . saying, 'See, the home of God is among mortals' "* (Revelation 21:1-3). If there is anything that typifies the best in all of the world's great religions, it is the focus on hope as a means of inspiring in human relationships life-affirming behaviors that are just, loving, and always in opposition to exploitation and hatred. Christian ministry, at its best, anchors its hope in the reality of God as revealed in Jesus Christ, who became *"flesh and lived among us"* (John 1:14). This identity with the human condition (becoming "flesh"/human) reveals, at the same time, both the source of the negative myth about the city and the hope that shows the myth to be without merit.

Identification with the human condition is risky business because, frankly, there is much about human relationships that is unlovely, depressing, and dangerous. Poverty, bad schools, domestic abuse, abandoned neighborhoods with dilapidated and dangerous housing, unemployment, AIDS, and drug addiction are not pretty. These are depressing and dangerous realities. While not exclusively urban issues, with more than 75 percent of the nation's population situated in its metropolitan centers, the fact that these issues are essentially urban in nature substantially impacts public debate and policy decisions that leave their imprints on all of society, regardless of the locale.

On the other hand, when people are able to identify with one another in a way that enables them to appreciate and affirm their common God-given humanity, it is possible to experience change in human relationships that is both positive and systemic. In such a circumstance, poverty need not be permanent or intergenerational, schools can be excellent, domiciles can be nurturing rather than abusive, core-city neighborhoods can be redeveloped with safe and attractive housing, meaningful employment, and good public health. Such environments are borne from a common human identity that is modeled in the incarnation of Jesus Christ. It is this type of human identity that forms the basis of behavior that is empathic; that seeks justice, the mitigation of inequities, and remedies for pain, and enables sustainable lifestyles that are fulfilling and reflect a divinely inspired presence of mercy and compassion. It is this type of urban ministry that addresses negative urban myths and enables realization of the goal posed in Cox's question: assisting people in recognizing the city as a "community of citizens."

Conclusion

As mentioned earlier, parish and public ministry are not mutually exclusive. Yet, because of its grounding in the holistic nuances of corporate life, urban ministry tends to focus heavily on issues related to public ministry. This is not to suggest that parish ministry, especially in the city, has less to do in public ministry. On the contrary, congregations with effective urban ministries typically structure the teaching of the faith within the parish to enable believers to live empowering lives in the urban context in a way that inevitably enhances the quality of city life in the public sector. In order to engage in effective urban parish ministry, however, one has to take seriously the public realities of city life. Urban ministry, therefore, evidences a strong orientation in the values and interests that inform effective public ministry. But how are these goals achieved? What are the means by which they are accomplished? In the next chapter, the nature of this ministry in the city in the early twenty-first century is examined.

CHAPTER TEN

SEEING WITH A DIVINE LENS: ISSUES AND NETWORKS IN THE CITY

And the city has no need of sun or moon to shine on it, for the glory of God is its light, and its lamp is the Lamb. The nations will walk by its light, and the kings of the earth will bring their glory into it. Its gates will never be shut by day—and there will be no night there.

—*Revelation 21:23-25*

And God stepped out on space,
And He looked around and said,
"I'm lonely—I'll make me a world."
And far as the eye of God could see,
Darkness covered everything.
Blacker than a hundred midnights,
Down in a cypress swamp.
Then God smiled,
And the Light broke,
And the darkness rolled up on one side,
And the light stood shining on the other,
And God said, "That's good!"

—*James Weldon Johnson from "The Creation," 1922*

A lens is a transparent object that focuses rays of light in such a way that they converge to give vision and perception to physical realities around us. In urban ministry, lenses are the perspectives or method-ological starting points from which the city or any community may be viewed or interpreted. Here, the metaphor of the lens refers to an approach to under-standing cities and their constituent communities that is essentially a *system-atic analysis of the city*, meaning an *examination of various relational networks (or systems) operating in all communities*.[1] This *systematic approach* enables the urban-ministry practitioner to better understand key relationships and networks that underlie the social organization of an urban (or any communal) context and its group dynamics.

The metaphorical symbolism of the lens as a means of focusing on various relational networks in urban ministry has religious significance. In scripture, light is often indicative of God's presence (Genesis 1:3-5; Exodus 13:21; Psalms

78:14; 89:15; Daniel 2:20-22; John 1:4-5; 9:5; Acts 9:3-4; Revelation 21:23-24). Scripture also interprets the capacity to see or perceive, whether by the natural abilities of the physical eye (2 Kings 6:18-20; Isaiah 42:7; Matthew 9:27-30; 20:29-34; John 9:3-7), or by insight or spiritual revelation from experience (Exodus 3:1-4; Isaiah 6:1-8; Luke 24:13-32), as a blessing from God. As a means of understanding the city, therefore, the lens metaphor is important for the urban-ministry practitioner as a means of helping him or her remember that his or her approach to social realities must not only involve social analysis of the empirical nature, but must also take into account religious implications of spiritual reflection. This is the essence of Christian ministry or any type of faith-based urban ministry: it takes appropriate advantage of the best in empirical data collection and social analysis, but recognizes that its contribution to addressing social issues must involve a more comprehensive perspective than empirical data analysis alone can provide. The classic James Weldon Johnson poem, "The Creation," does not pretend to divulge any scientific insights about the genesis of the universe, but only a theological assertion about its origin. Similarly, in urban ministry, rather than the exclusive language of sociology in referring to relational networks or a systems analysis, we refer to what is called the lenses or *focus-areas* in urban ministry as a means to emphasize a component of theological reflection on that which is observed empirically.

Because of the gamut of competing issues, priorities, and opportunities that are found in the city, the task of sifting through and discerning how to best respond to the urban challenge can be overwhelming. In reality, the city is an intricate matrix of relational networks or systems that complement, collaborate, and sometimes compete with one another as part of the social process of urban life. Taken together, these networks or systems of relationship can be too complex to fathom; by utilizing the symbolism of a lens that can focus on a particular network or system of relationships, it is possible to gain greater insight into the varying layers constituting the urban multiplex.

It is important to remember that while analysis of relational networking systems is a useful means of examining social realities, this "systematic" approach is a hypothetical construct (like "artificial intelligence") that helps explain other realities. Systematic analysis of urban realities is comparable to systematic theology, which is but one methodological orientation in attempting to comprehend divine realities. The fact is, God cannot be systematized, but only our limited methods of trying to understand God. Although scripture is consistent in acknowledging that the Holy Spirit defies human logic and is broader than the capacity of human imagination (see Job 38–39; Isaiah 40:12-14; 1 Corinthians 1:18-21), we still embrace a strategy for trying to understand God known as *systematic* theology. In a similar manner, the urban arena is much larger than our ability to fully understand its complexities as a whole would demand. The metaphor of the lenses assists us in focusing on specific relational and organizational networks that function within all human communities and in the contiguous aggregations of these communities we call cities.

The Eight Lenses and Focus Areas in Urban Ministry

There are eight focus areas that are generally addressed by urban ministry regardless of the locale (see diagram 4). They represent themes that characterize the urban context of ministry. These focus areas relate to public issues that tend to characterize urban ministry globally in all regions and cultures and comprise organizational networks common to metropolitan areas whether the city is Addis Ababa, Bogotá, Chicago, or Shanghai. They are not all-inclusive nor are they listed in order of importance, but they are all interrelated and affect one another as all are vital to the physical and spiritual health of the city. These eight urban ministry foci invariably include *economic life, educational systems, family life, public health, ethnic/racial relations, religious culture, restorative justice* (civil and political rights), and *the environment.* Few urban ministries will address more than one or two of these, but the character of urban society virtually guarantees that elements of all eight issues will be integral to the context of ministry in any city.

Diagram 4: Urban Ministry Focus Area Lenses

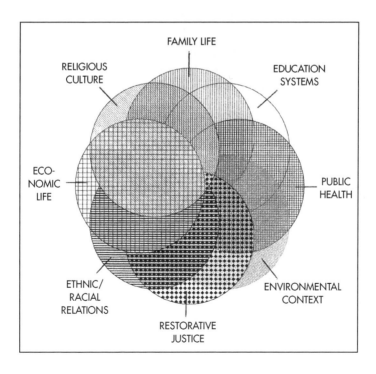

1. Economic Life

First, the church in the city cannot practice that does not, in some way, touch upon the great social realities of poverty and wealth: the challenges of *economic life*. Urban ministry necessarily involves city churches in participation with other community-based groups or organizations as well as business and political decision makers to seek remedies to extant economic disparity and disenfranchisement in light of the compassion and justice tenets of the gospel as a means of creating conditions for economic reconciliation. The study of urban ministry, therefore, must include analysis of economic issues. This requires consideration of core resources or industries that provide for the physical sustainability of the community: finance and business resources with particular attention to the chief industries that help define the core values and identity of the community. Urban ministry, in this focus, addresses issues of poverty, unemployment, adequate housing, homelessness, investment, incubator businesses, and taxation, as well as local, regional, and global markets and the effects of market and governmental policy decisions on local urban communities. All of these factors collectively define the economic life of the city or any community within the metropolitan area.

2. Educational Systems

Second, whatever the urban context, the resources that evolve around *public educational systems* are always stretched at best, or in crisis at worse. Any study of urban ministry must include them. Systems of formal education include public and private institutions of elementary, middle, and high school, as well as colleges, universities, trade schools, and so on. The urban church must address issues of access to quality schools and strong educational systems, inequity in the quality of education received between the wealthy and the poor, as well as the costs of education. Apathy and hopelessness regarding public education in urban areas are symptomatic of alienation from society; those who perceive themselves as able to do well educationally are set apart from those who do not. Again, the gospel mandate of reconciliation, rooted in divine zeal for compassion and justice, warrants action that seeks to mitigate educational dysfunction and the elimination of educational disenfranchisement.

Education is viewed as a discipline or field of study that deals with methods of teaching and learning in schools. Yet, the whole process of how people learn in society and how information is shared with others within families, neighborhoods, a city or region, or even globally is a much broader issue than dealing with methods of teaching in local schools and/or urban school systems alone. The educational ministry of the church must address a variety of media, both within and without the local schools that are part of a matrix of educational systems impacting urban life. These include the Internet, mass media, and local peer groups in the hood in addition to formal in-school activities. It is perhaps more precise, in fact, to speak of ministries that address *information systems* in the urban arena. Yet, because the issue of how people gain information, skills, and expertise—that is, how people learn—is the essence of the process we call "education," we continue to use the term *educational systems* in urban ministry to identify the variety of information networks that influence the quality of city life.

Three different types of educational (informational) systems influence all geographical regions in society, but profoundly shape urban life. These are *schools (formal educational systems), electronic media (organized communication systems including mass media, entertainment, and cyberspace)*, and *subculture (nonformal educational systems)*. The urban church must take all three into account as it seeks to strengthen its educational ministry. All three spheres will determine how the urban church's ministry must respond to the needs of the communities it serves.

3. Family Life

Third, *family life* in the metropolis is always challenged. The broad varieties of social relationships that comprise family life are included here. Survival and keeping body and soul together are always tested by each of the other realities (economics, housing, unemployment and/or underemployment, educational challenges, public health considerations, and restorative justice). Parents working two and three jobs and the impact of long work schedules on the quality of family life are two aspects of this problem facing urban churches. Youth and youth culture issues are a central focus of urban family life: from preschool and child-care realities to preteen and teen culture issues; adolescence and the disproportionately high incidents of violence and death among urban youth; the influence of media and music, including hip-hop; and young adulthood challenges. Urban lifestyle issues, therefore, inform urban ministry: work and/or unemployment and family life, parenting, the capacity to lead fulfilling single lifestyles, sexual orientation, single-parent concerns and challenges, families in crisis, abusive relationships, extended family supports, and quality of life issues for urban families (wholesome recreational activities, entertainment, sports, cultural activities). The challenges facing senior adults in the city are also part of this focus, including increased health-care needs, support systems for basic survival, and companionship. Because the family is the basic social unit of any society, strengthening the spiritual quality of the urban family's ability to perceive and reflect divine compassion and justice in its faith life is central to the gospel of reconciliation and the cornerstone of effective urban ministry.

4. Public Health

A fourth area of urban ministry is *public health*. Jesus' most prominent public ministry involved healing the sick of their infirmities. Yet, too many in the Christian community have largely ignored this aspect of the gospel's witness of reconciliation. The interactive role of faith in God and lifestyle behaviors, so critical in the ministry of Jesus and throughout the witness of scripture, is virtually ignored in many Christian discussions of faith and health today. In so doing, believers unwittingly have defined health ministry as outside the norms of faith praxis as if it were the exclusive domain of biomedicine, rather than acknowledging a partnership with biomedicine as an appropriate expression of God's healing power. Such a posture frequently limits the scope of faith and health ministry to empty religious ritual and symbolism. Consequently, several "faith and health" discussions in the urban community refer to "miracle cures" and "prayer cloth" ministries that can deter seriously ill persons from seeking substantive medical help when needed, as if to do so were the opposite of faith in God rather than a component thereof. Effective urban ministry must address faith and health from the perspective of a faithful lifestyle. This enables the gospel message of compassion and justice to address reconciliation in the public health arena in a proactive manner, acting to prevent negative health realities. Issues of healthy (faithful) lifestyle in the urban context must address diet and behavioral habits, immunizations, violence, substance abuse prevention, smoking cessation programs, medical screenings, elimination of health disparities among racial/ethnic populations, and improving access to quality medical care for the poor and elderly.

5. Ethnic/Racial Relations

Fifth, *ethnic/racial relations* must be at the core of urban ministry because people who come from a variety of ethnic and cultural backgrounds form the core of the city and its life. Indeed, the word *urban* is often a code word for Black, Brown, or whoever "those people" (the non-European people) happen to be depending upon whether the city is Atlanta, Los Angeles, Seattle, New York, Chicago, or Miami. In a social context where individual rights are supposed to be respected, code language is often used by people who wish to remain evasive about the subject of race to camouflage group stereotyping or racial profiling.[2]

In most U.S. cities, visible ethnic/racial groups (e.g., African, African American, Arabic, Asian, Latino) are more vulnerable to subtle and overt forms of social or racial discrimination. This is also true in Pittsburgh where I live and teach at the seminary. While it is certainly true that poverty and African American ethnicity are not synonymous, the fact is that in the city of Pittsburgh there is a disproportionately high correlation between these two factors, suggesting a connection between poverty and discrimination. One

assessment found that as many as 75.6 percent of African American house-
holds in Pittsburgh earn less than $25,000 annually.[3] Other arbiters of quality
of life (employment, housing, public education, or incarceration)[4] reveal the
unique social and political challenges to this population.

Dealing with the reality of the varieties of persons of non-European ethnic-
ities has never been easy in North American or any society, but it has always
been part of the urban reality. In the United States, persons of the African
Diaspora (native-born Americans or those from the African continent such as
Kenya, Ghana, Nigeria, Senegal, Malawi, or Zimbabwe, and from South
America); from the Arab world (Egyptians, Jordanians, Palestinians, Saudis,
Kuwaitis); of Asian descent (Chinese, Indian, Korean, Japanese, Vietnamese,
and others); Jews, Native Americans (Choctaw, Navaho, Sioux, for example);
or those from the varieties of Latino cultures (Cuban, Guatemalan, Mexican,
Puerto Rican, and others), to mention but a few, are all part of the fabric of
urban life: not just the Dutch, English, French, German, Italian, or Polish. As
mentioned earlier, urban neighborhoods ordinarily develop around racial
housing patterns (African American neighborhoods, Chinatown, the Italian
section, and so forth). In the urban arena, the plurality of ethnicities invariably influences ministry.

Despite its obvious futility, one of the most frequent coping strategies with
regard to ethnic or racial issues utilized by most Christians in the United
States, regardless of ethnic identity including persons of color, has been a tendency to try to ignore the uniqueness of different ethnic groups and function
as if, somehow, the characteristics of European culture (aesthetic norms, values, beliefs,) can apply to all. Urban ministry seeks to help believers approach
interethnic relationships more realistically in a manner that affirms the gifts of
each as a means of contributing to the positive spiritual, cultural, and economic mosaic that is urban life for all.

6. Religious Culture

Religious culture is the sixth focus area and has to do with understanding the
network of relationships that exist around various sets of theological beliefs
within society. This focus is primarily concerned with issues of parish ministry
and understanding how the urban context informs and shapes the church's
mission and sense of purpose even as the church seeks to affect the culture of
the community it is called to serve. This lens will involve congregational studies and other sociological data as well as theological analysis of church positions to better comprehend and strengthen ministry potential and success in
reaching the wider communities of the city.

Different congregations and groups foster different and sometimes conflict-
ing values, yet their social accountability and the authority they attribute to

their respective traditions contrast markedly with the individual moral auton-omy assumed in the wider secular culture.[5] These differing faith traditions, sects, or denominations are all part of understanding the religious life and cul-ture of the city. According to sociology of religion researcher Lowell Livezey:

> Since congregations are specifically religious, their cultural innovation is in part theological. Their central symbols are about their god or gods and the meanings they share and the authority they exercise almost always include some claims about their relationship with the Divine.[6]

Whether the religious tradition is Roman Catholic or Muslim, the effect of the faith community's interaction with the community as well as with the vari-ety of ecumenical and/or interfaith groups in the city is an important influence on the urban neighborhood's character. Designed as it is to bring human awareness of God, urban ministry is tied to a pragmatic morality that finds its roots in the undeniable relationship between the community of believers and the larger community.

7. Restorative Justice

Restorative justice is a seventh focus area for urban-ministry preparation. This focus must consider those areas of city life and institutions responsible for ensuring that society's laws are enforced and how justice is administered. It must also consider not just matters of crime and law enforcement, it must address the holistic matters of community and *the loss of community* that results when crime occurs. This communal loss affects the victim of crime, the culprit involved, and the community as a whole and is not addressed by the mere incarceration of the accused culprit. Restorative justice ministry must deal with enabling society to restore justice in a more communally inclusive man-ner and relegate this matter to police and legal functionaries alone.

The burgeoning prison industry in the United States is a matter that signif-icantly affects city life and, therefore, is a matter of special concern in urban ministry. The United States imprisons more of its citizens per capita than any other country in the world. Recent statistics reported by the federal govern-ment outline the scope to the challenge:

> The country's prisons, jails and juvenile facilities held 2,166,260 persons at the end of December, 2002 and seventeen states reported increases of at least 5% in their prison populations during that year. The 2.6% growth in the number of inmates under state and federal jurisdiction during 2002 was more than twice the 2001 growth (1.1%) and was equal to an additional 700 inmates every week during the year. As a result about 1 in every 143 U.S. residents were in state or federal prison or a local jail, as of last December 31, 2002. The total number of persons incarcerated in federal or state prisons alone (not counting county jails)

at that time included 97,491 women, accounting for 6.8% of the total. Since 1995, the number of female prisoners has grown 42%, while the number of male prisoners has increased 27%. Black males from 20 to 39 years old accounted for about a third of all sentenced prison inmates under state or federal jurisdiction although African American men nationwide account for less than 6% of the population. Currently, 10.4% of the country's black males between the ages of 25 to 29 are in prison, compared to 2.4% of Hispanic males and 1.2% of white males in the same age group.[7]

Without question, racial/ethnic minorities fare poorly with regard to their ability to participate as full citizens in society in the expression of their civil rights. In five states that deny the vote to ex-offenders (Alabama, Florida, Iowa, Kentucky, and Virginia), one in four Black men are permanently disenfranchised.[8] The disproportionate incarceration of African Americans in the U.S. prison population is a glaring example of this fact: 48 percent of all prisoners are African American males, although they account for less than 6 percent of the nation's population.[9]

Imprisonment has devastating effects on inmates' family lives. Nationwide, more than two million children have a parent incarcerated (in state or federal prisons and local jails). Of all incarcerated parents 93 percent are male and are held in state prisons (89 percent), and of this number, 55 percent report having minor children. Among female prisoners (6 percent of state prison population), 65 percent report having minor children. Nearly six out of ten (58 percent) minor children of incarcerated parents in the U.S. today are less than ten years old.[10] The effects of these situations upon family life and the children of the incarcerated are usually overlooked in society. Compassion and justice ministries of reconciliation in the urban arena must address these issues and deal with departments of municipal government such as courts, law enforcement, prisons, and all levels of judicial systems and their personnel.

8. The Environment

Finally, the urban *environment* must be considered. This means taking into account the state of natural resources (soil, air, water, drainage and waste services, pollution control) and all ecological factors affecting the quality of urban life. The interrelated factors of unsafe air, substandard drinking water, environmental pollution (toxic waste released into the air and waterways), inadequate or nonexistent recreational facilities, substandard housing, and unsafe streets all contribute to the poor health statistics affecting urban dwellers in disadvantaged neighborhoods. Poor prenatal care and higher-than-average infant mortality, children with learning disabilities, and the higher frequencies of several child and adult diseases are realities that characterize certain areas within urban environments.

Studies have documented the disproportionate placement of toxic-waste dump sites in urban areas heavily populated by the poor and people of color.[11] A representative description of health challenges facing many inner-city communities nationwide is given by physicians W. Michael Byrd and Linda A. Clayton as they discuss realities that involve more than social behaviors, but environmental problems as well:

> Since 1950, violence, crime, and drug abuse have become epidemic in urban Black neighborhoods. Moreover, this has been exacerbated by the fact that they are differentially utilized as sites for toxic wastes such as lead, mercury, arsenic, and steroids—known carcinogens and toxins with known harmful effects on childhood mental development.[12]

David M. Satcher, former United States Surgeon General and Assistant Secretary for Health, reports that 71 percent of African Americans across the nation live in counties that violate federal air pollution standards compared with 58 percent of Euro-Americans.[13] Satcher also identifies urban environmental realities as contributing to negative health disparities among Black and Hispanic children as compared to their Euro-American counterparts:

> Environment makes a major contribution to [health] disparities. For example, we know that Black and Hispanic children are more likely to be exposed to toxic substances or lead-based paint than their white counterparts. Other toxins relate to the fact that Black and Hispanic children are most likely to grow up close to hazardous waste sites where the toxins are not as well-defined.[14]

Compassion and justice considerations are the prerequisites for the type of reconciliation ministries needed to strengthen the quality of life in the city by creating a more healthful urban environment.

Conclusion

It cannot be emphasized too strongly that these focus areas are not separate and distinct aspects of ministry in the city, but are interrelated spheres of ministry activity that touch and overlap at numerous points. They are listed separately as a means to help us consider the theoretical basis of urban ministry's core values and how they are applied to its practice through these eight focus areas. Just as the broad discipline of law has several areas of concentration (civil, criminal, corporate, family, and so on), or the area of medical practice has many areas of specialization (cardiology, neurology, obstetrics, and so on), and the same is true of basic theological studies (Bible, church history, theology, pastoral care), when we come to the discipline of urban ministry, it also is more easily examined in light of these eight focus areas.

Overtly, these urban-ministry focus areas appear to fall outside the sphere of what is normally thought to be the realm of the religious practitioner and more in line with a bevy of other disciplines, all scientific in nature rather than faith-based. Indeed, the potential gamut of sciences to be encompassed in this multidisciplinary approach to ministry includes everything from economic theory to the environmental sciences. Yet, as we have discussed earlier, the essential orientation of the urban-ministry practitioner is her or his faith in God. Psalm 24:1-2 boldly affirms that *"the earth is the LORD's and all that is in it, the world, and those who live in it; for he has founded it on the seas, and established it on the rivers."* From scripture, church history, and its traditions, the strong affirmation of the gospel is that God is the Creator and sustainer of all things, and nothing is outside divine capacity or scrutiny. The bifurcation of all reality into the empirical sphere (for science) and the metaphysical sphere (for faith) is an approach that does not serve the context of ministry well. In collaboration with the science-based disciplines, the urban-ministry practitioner becomes the *theologian in residence*, the interpreter of the gospel and its ethical or evangelistic implications regarding the public issue(s) related to a particular focus area.

CHAPTER ELEVEN

THE EGALITARIAN METROPOLIS

Our witness is for the sake of the good news of God's reign; the good news is not just to be preached but lived. Thus our life and work style must conform to the kingdom norms and values. We cannot proclaim a reign of justice, love and peace, while at the same time contradicting its inclusive, non-dominating character in our mission practice and structures. If the kingdom is our focus, then a more collaborative, egalitarian, ecumenical effort in mission will be a more compelling witness.

—*Virginia Fabella and Sun Ai Lee Park*[1]

Sometimes I am tossed and driven, Lord. Sometimes I don't know where to roam. I've heard of a city called Heaven. I've started to make it my home.

—*African American Spiritual*

In 1998, Pittsburgh Theological Seminary received a gift that established an endowed faculty position for the director of its program of urban theological education, the Metro-Urban Institute. The endowed position was named after Henry L. Hillman, the man who had established the foundation that underwrote the gift to the seminary. The seminary's board of trustees appointed me to occupy this newly endowed faculty position, and I was later installed in the Henry L. Hillman Endowed Chair in Urban Ministry. Many people in various quarters of the city of Pittsburgh, unacquainted with academic terminology and the relatively few African American faculty occupying endowed chairs in seminaries throughout the nation, asked me a question: "What is this business of 'an endowed chair' in urban ministry all about?" Indeed, several folk with whom I interacted in the urban community were not familiar with what the seminary did at all.

The questions raised by my friends outside the academic community concerning the nature of an endowed chair were not irrelevant. They spoke to the very heart of issues I believe urban theological education must address. The fact was that the theological school of which I am a part sits right in the middle of the inner city, and many people living in the neighborhood around the seminary did not know about the institution or even that it existed! Even more interesting, I sometimes used to get the impression that there was a certain comfort level with this situation on both sides of the iron fence that surrounds our seminary campus. We in the academy and those on the outside often appeared basically

"OK" with our mutual ignorance of each other, a situation that, sadly, also typifies the relationship between many a church and its surrounding community.

This brings me back to the dinner table question raised by the young woman I mentioned in the introduction who, upon learning that I was a seminary professor who teaches urban ministry, innocently asked, "What is urban ministry?" It is not possible to respond to this question and to the informational gaps it represents only by way of descriptive definition. Direction is also needed: urban ministry really cannot be adequately defined without responding to the eschatological issue of its directional aims. Where does urban ministry seek to take us?

I believe that the African American spiritual entitled "A City Called Heaven" gives us a clue. That song lifted a vision of an alternate reality from the one the original singers experienced. They envisioned a place, perhaps somewhere in Canada or back home in Africa, where the conditions of slavery did not exist. Encouraged in their thinking by images drawn from scripture, they nurtured a mental picture of what freedom would look like: a city called heaven. This vision inspired them to continue working toward achieving that goal, however challenging its realization might prove to be.

One of the main challenges in urban ministry today is that many people in core-city areas have no hopeful visions. Many people in our churches and seminaries, all their God-talk notwithstanding, evidence behaviors and actions that seem bereft of a hopeful future. It is against this backdrop that I have often wondered what idealized vision provides a suitable alternative to the realities of alienation, fear, and violence that typify the ethos of oppression in so much of metropolitan life today. Although it is an eschatological question, its basis is in the present and its value is in the fact that its answer provides directional guidance for immediate behaviors. I believe that the vision in urban ministry must lead us toward achieving an egalitarian metropolis.

The notion of an *egalitarian metropolis* is a concept that is often associated with utopian, idealistic, and unachievable realities. Unfortunately, there is much that characterizes society in general and urban communities in particular that suggests lofty social agendas where egalitarian principles are the standard and equitable practices are the norm can be hard to promote and harder still to implement. On the positive side, the historical record has no shortage of examples where grand social ideals have been promoted as found in the writings of the Old Testament prophets or in Plato's *Republic* or Augustine of Hippo's *The City of God* or, as has been already noted, in more recent social justice movements—for example, Martin Luther King, Jr.'s frequent reference to the notion of the "beloved community" during the civil rights era.[2] Even in politics, candidates for public office as well as office holders often articulate their political platforms or agendas in terms of visionary goals, as in the case of Franklin D. Roosevelt's "New Deal," Lyndon B. Johnson's "Great Society," or George W. Bush's federal policies concerning public education entitled "No Child Left Behind."

Socially visionary language, in the main, does not attempt to ignore depressingly tragic social realities, but usually is spawned by such circumstances. Typically, it is an effort to assert corrective ideals that are intended to ameliorate unfortunate conditions. This is why writings like those found in Isaiah 40:1-5 or 65:17-25 reveal such beautiful idealized notions of social reality. These are scripture verses that were written during times when, in fact, the wonderful social visions they described did not exist. That we live during times where many people seem to be somewhat cynical about lofty social ideals should not deter the urban-ministry practitioner from borrowing such concepts. Indeed, this is the main purpose of the church in society: to preach the gospel—the good news—rather than succumb to the overwhelmingly bad news that characterizes that which is most often reported as "news" in the public square. Sadly, public discourse seems to be overly punctuated not with expansive and uplifting images, but with depressing ones. The nation's response to Hurricane Katrina's devastation of the city of New Orleans in 2005 is a primary example. Now, social realities of downsizing, layoffs, cutbacks, tribalism, and constituency-based interest groups dominate our social landscape. Public scandal and petty partisan politics have replaced lofty social goals. The type and quality of relationships in society these days tend to be disconnected and competitive rather than interconnected and cooperative. How can we bridge the barriers that separate us into tribes not only ethnically and culturally, but also religiously, politically, economically, and educationally when our primary social institutions of church, government, and business are primarily focused on institutional infighting and maintenance?

By egalitarian metropolis, the goal in urban ministry is to work toward a social order that seeks to recapture lofty ideals that are encapsulated in Jesus' descriptions of the kingdom of heaven (Matthew 25:31-32), where people see to the needs of the most vulnerable members of society without even thinking about reward. Compassion and justice are not idealistic concepts in this kingdom of heaven description, but are behavioral norms built upon faith in God. The notion of the egalitarian metropolis encompasses even what politicians, however inadequately, sought to accomplish, using elevated language that reached for something more than existed at the time their ideas were presented: visions like "a Great Society" or what Martin Luther King, Jr., may have had in mind theologically when he envisioned "the beloved community." The egalitarian metropolis is one that is preoccupied with justice, encourages mutual affirmation of persons, is ecologically uplifting and safe, and is characterized by an order of love and respect. It is an environment where true reconciliation, restitution, and right relationship are taken seriously as public policy. While such may seem to be a broadly utopian social agenda, it is no more expansive than the claims of the gospel that boldly assert that *"God so loved the world that he gave his only Son, so that everyone who believes in him may not perish but may have eternal life"* (John 3:16). The writer in Revelation 21:1-4 did not think such a vision too outrageous when he perceived a metropolis where *there would be no crying, no pain, all tears would be wiped away.* The notion of an *egalitarian metropolis* is not foreign to our theological heritage and certainly is not too far-fetched scripturally, but grows right out of our identity as children of God as revealed in Jesus Christ.

Challenges to Achieving the Egalitarian Metropolis

There are at least five challenges that immediately engage the task of lifting such a vision in our time. First, in suggesting an *egalitarian metropolis* as an accepted goal in society, we are presupposing, in some sense, a communal consensus of values regarding the "common good." If there is any one characteristic that defines the urban context, however, it is diversity, and getting a broad consensus on shared values and goals among varying communities, cultures, and constituencies is clearly a major challenge.

A second challenge has to do with giving the notion of an egalitarian metropolis substance. It is insufficient that our goal simply be some ethereal utopia far removed from reality in its practical dimensions sociologically, economically, politically, culturally, or physically. In the egalitarian metropolis the values of justice, compassion, integrity, forbearance, forgiveness, communal welfare, and reconciliation are embraced as public policy. Yet, translating this ideal into practical realities of everyday life is a major undertaking.

Third, although in many quarters there is a renewed interest in the role of faith-based approaches to communal concerns, this new openness is set against a backdrop of deep skepticism regarding the ultimate efficacy of faith beliefs in the public arena. The fact is that as we approach a new millennium, ours is a world where, increasingly, God-talk in the public arena is perceived as ideological, schismatic, and constituency-based propaganda rather than that which truly seeks to enhance the quality of public life. Stephen Carter's book *The Culture of Disbelief*[3] ably documented, in an analysis of legal jurisprudence, the growing intolerance of religiously motivated zeal in the public arena.

Fourth, defining a collective consensus for the egalitarian metropolis from the starting point of any individual particularity, religious or not (but especially religious), calls for determined efforts. Several years ago Robert Bellah documented the difficulty mainstream faith traditions have experienced in moving beyond denominational and theological boundaries in society: Christian/Jewish, Roman Catholic/Protestant; fundamentalist, liberal, evangelical.[4] Yet, as the United States (and especially its cities) becomes more diversified ethnically and culturally over the next few years, the common good that has historically been expressed almost exclusively in the moral and theological language of the Judeo-Christian heritage will no doubt begin to reflect aspects of other religious traditions. For example, today we blithely refer to the motto printed on our national currency, *"In God We Trust."* How will this understanding in the public sphere be altered by other religious traditions finding voice in society such as Buddhism, Hinduism, Islam, Native American sacred rituals, Santeria, Sikhism, or Taoism?

Finally, some of the most intimidating factors to be addressed in defining the elements for creating the egalitarian metropolis come not from realities outside the seminary. On the contrary, the most difficult challenge to building an effective urban theological educational curriculum that will contribute toward the realization of the egalitarian metropolis has to do with the academy's preoccupation with White upper- and middle-class culture and values and its tendency to be aloof from core-city church and community needs. Eleanor Scott Meyers noted the difficulty most seminaries have in dealing with the urban context long ago in her book *Envisioning the New City.*[5] While the need for a more substantive approach is being carved out in many theological schools, the fact remains that even as our nation and the world are becoming more urbanized with most of the people on the face of the globe living in cities, urban theological studies in most of the academy are yet viewed as tangential to the core of the theological discipline and, therefore, optional.

A Lesson from History: Valuing Formal and Informal Educational Strategies

How can we help society move from modalities of disconnectedness, cynicism, and distrust toward more cooperative strategies of hope and faith? How do we teach reconciliation in a way that inspires a more "egalitarian" process in society that moves beyond mere theological dogma and into the arena of broad public discourse, eventually to be embraced as public policy? What curriculum can best assist seminaries to equip graduates so that the gospel of Jesus Christ becomes a strategy for reconciliation adapted into public policy and help us move "egalitarianism" from the ideal into real arenas of society?

One factor seems critical: our understanding of education. It is important to note that *not all education and learning occur in the formal setting of the classroom.* Again, the context and perspective of the "bottom-up/out-group," the context of slavery, is helpful. It was illegal to teach people of African descent to read or write in English. Slaves had to learn the oral language and customs of their captors in their oppressed condition. Both slaveholders and slaves recognized the *value* of education; they differed concerning *desired outcomes* (or what they wanted the results of education to be). The slave owner's formal educational priorities and procedures for the enslaved were clearly the making of a "good slave" (the value for slave owners). This did not include teaching slaves to read and write. By contrast, the central goal of education in the slave's mind was physical survival and ultimate freedom (the value for slaves). Slaves realized that if they were to ultimately survive and overcome their oppressed condition, the ability to master reading and writing the slaveholder's language was critical. This learning, however, had to take place outside the formal educational structures put in place for slaves. Over time and often in clandestine contexts, slaves acquired the capacity to speak, read, and write the English language outside formal schools, that is, through nonformal pedagogical strategies.

This analogy concerning the differences between formal and nonformal education has significance for our understanding of theological education for urban ministry. This reality helps explain, at least in part, how many inner-city congregations and various other types of urban ministry flourish with great effectiveness without the benefit of credentialing from institutions of formal theological education. It is one thing to have "the paper on the wall" (the credentials), but it is quite another to have the skill necessary to engage in ministries that spiritually and physically transform and uplift urban communities in systemic ways. Too many seminary graduates, when faced with the challenges of the urban context (or even the suburban or rural contexts), only know how to lead congregations into moving away from communities of need rather than being the balm in Gilead as we believe Jesus has called and empowered us to be.

Essentials in Urban Theological Education

Three essentials are necessary for an effective urban theological curriculum. First, *the seminary must welcome* **community partnership**. The cloistered retreat of the monastery is a perception that still stalks the seminary (sometimes referred to off campus as a "cemetery"). This misperception can easily be dislodged when the seminary takes steps to open its classroom, library, and other facilities in an affirming way to theological researchers from the urban arena. The seminary's repository of information on the Christian faith through its formal programs of theological inquiry is its strongest asset for urban ministry. Urban theological education must take partnership with churches, educational institutions, and other community agencies seriously. Eldin Villafañe sees this pedagogical model as representing a diverse partnership or, more specifically, an urban spirit of *communion* and fellowship based upon New Testament notions of *koinonia* (communion, fellowship, participation). He calls this curriculum of urban theological education an *urban koinonia*, comprised of solidarity and community in the midst of diversity: "[seminaries becoming partners with] . . . diverse neighborhood congregations, grass-roots parachurch organizations, and service agencies."[6]

Second, *there must be theoretical and **interdisciplinary analysis** of urban ministry*. In order to embrace the goal of preparing leaders for a truly egalitarian metropolis, the seminary must see the city as text, according to Warren Dennis.[7] He argues that systems, institutions, communities, and people of the city must be engaged in the educational process as subject rather than as object. The egalitarian metropolis, by definition, reflects the aspirations of a broad spectrum of various constituencies, institutions, and individuals. What is implied here is a collaborative method of pedagogy. Presently, when we speak of interdisciplinary approaches in the seminary, we are referring to joint efforts within theological disciplines: *Bible* and *pastoral care or ethics* and *church history*. This is *intradisciplinary* theological analysis. In urban ministry, interdisciplinary theological analysis involves dialogue with disciplines outside the traditional ones offered in seminary: civil and criminal law, sociology, business, medicine, public education, and urban systems analysis. This type of interdisciplinary theoretical analysis, however, must also involve the contributions of practitioners, not just other academics. This is where collaboration with off-campus partners (churches, courts, schools, businesses, prisons, social services) is critical.

Finally, **mentoring** *is necessary in urban theological education*. The theoretical inquiry of the classroom and the library must be undergirded with opportunities for practical application in the actual context of the urban setting. Urban-focused students should be assigned to off-campus ministry mentors who can help students process their reflections on both theoretical and experiential or practical challenges in ministry related to urban theological education. The mentoring process assists urban-focus students with the spiritual formation task that must provide the grounding in theological education necessary for success in the urban context.

Collaboratively Lighting the Way

Our faith heritage as revealed in Jesus Christ raises the notion of a safe environment, a healthy living space, and an affirming community built upon love and justice. Jesus wept for Jerusalem (Luke 19:41-42) because its inhabitants *did not recognize "the things that make for peace,"* which grew out of the context of their own faith heritage. The vision of pluralism outlined in Revelation 7:9-17 is one of people (verse 9) *"that no one could count, from every nation, from all tribes and peoples and languages,"* who have worked through great difficulty to create a better environment, a better living space. Indeed, the concept of the "new Jerusalem" is lifted in Revelation 21:1-4 wherein God's presence is in the city with people, wiping away tears, alleviating death, crying, and pain. This vision results from the Holy Spirit working among the people described in Revelation 7:9 who have helped to achieve this egalitarian metropolis where the reign of God in heaven has become the reign of God on earth. We are referring not only to the "great beyond," but also to God's presence among God's people in the here and now, "which no man could number, from every nation, from all tribes and peoples and tongues" (Revelation 7:9, RSV).These are the ones who, through the power of the Holy Spirit, are becoming involved in wiping away tears and alleviating pain.

The city is a plural and complex setting, but it is a microcosm of God's creation. The "Pentecost" event (Acts 2) provides evidence of what can be achieved relationally amid the pluralism and diversity represented in the urban context. At Pentecost, differing constituencies, ethnic groups, economic strata, and traditions were reconciled in a fashion that completely redefined their relationship with one another—no longer disconnected, but interrelated. The gospel lifts this ideal of reconciliation as being possible when faith, love, and justice motivate behavior. A metro-urban approach to congregational ministry and to theological inquiry in the academic setting of the seminary requires that our curriculum take seriously the scriptural paradigm of reconciliation. The plurality of the metropolitan arena cannot be a sideline to formal theological study; rather, there must become a comprehensive curricular approach that models reconciliation through interdisciplinary, on-campus/off-campus educational collaboration and partnership with other faith-based and secular sectors of the city. It is this multidimensional and holistic approach that invites the blessing of the Holy Spirit, which can assist us in realizing an egalitarian metropolis.

The egalitarian metropolis is, in fact, just another way of conceptualizing what South Africa's archbishop Desmond Tutu pressed toward in helping his nation through crisis when, from a theological basis, he helped formulate a public policy entity known as the Truth and Reconciliation Commission. This is no different from what Martin Luther King, Jr., popularized when he talked about the theological notion of a "beloved community" that could amend public policies about racial segregation or voting rights. In these instances, there was a heavy reliance on the efficacy of altruistic love (*agape*) as the basis of justice claims for the social order where people live together in a mutually affirming way.

The vision of the egalitarian metropolis emerges out of the imagery of a city set on the hill (Matthew 5:14-16) called to be a model (light) because the presence of God empowers those who believe to become reconcilers and creators of a social order in which justice, love, and peace are manifested in the educational curriculum of our theological schools and in the everyday life of our congregations and wider community. The *egalitarian metropolis* emerges because the presence of God empowers people to be reconciled to God and to one another, resulting in a social order in which these qualities are manifested. The *egalitarian metropolis* emerges because church institutions are centers for community organization, educational uplifting, medical and spiritual healing, and strengthening families. The *egalitarian metropolis* emerges because women and men of all races and creeds, instead of competing with one another for declining resources, work together to address issues of poverty, widening economic and educational gaps in society, injustice, racism, sexism, and violence. The *egalitarian metropolis* emerges because there are seminary graduates who possess the intellectual capacity and skills base that will encourage ministries of service, advocacy, and the promotion of systemic change.

Amid widespread cynicism, fear, and a pervasive sense of resignation that seems to numb the human spirit, in the face of an apparent loss of personhood and human connectedness that appears alien to a technologically focused global and market-driven culture, the urban ministerial emphasis on agape/justice becomes all the more vital and necessary. Agape/justice must anchor urban-ministry efforts in this so-called postmodern era where values are in flux and moral confusion abounds and distrust, hostility, and injustice frequently characterize our culture. Youths, like adults, have become so disconnected that some shoot one another almost randomly while others bring guns to school, feeling otherwise unsafe, uncared-for, or unprotected. Clearly, our social, economic, ideological, and spiritual disconnections seem so strident at times that they appear impervious to any efforts at reconciliation. This dismal state of affairs is much akin to what Martin King once referred to as the moral and social "midnight hour." The old spiritual is appropriate: "Sometimes I'm tossed and driven; sometimes I don't know where to roam." But it does not stop there; it goes on to assert: "I've heard of a city called Heaven. I've started to make it my home."

Could it be that it is just now dark enough for people of faith to come out and let the light of faith shine in this challenging cultural context so clearly epitomized in city life? Perhaps it is just now dark enough for the light of faith that God has placed in the practitioners of urban ministry to begin to shine so that all social and spiritual contexts and communities may be more able to see relational affinities both materially and spiritually. Perhaps this is why, long ago, a people bound in the terrible social, legal, and economic travail of chattel slavery could envision a better reality as they sang:

> *This little light of mine, I'm gonna let it shine.*
> *This little light of mine, I'm gonna let it shine.*
> *This little light of mine, I'm gonna let it shine.*
> *Everywhere I go, I'm gonna let it shine,*
> *Let it shine, let it shine, let it shine.*

NOTES

1. An Introduction: The Information Gap and Discerning the Right Questions

1. Harvey Gallagher Cox, *The Secular City: Secularization and Urbanization in Theological Perspective* (New York: Macmillan, 1966), 3–4.

2. United Nations Web site: http://unstats.un.org/unsd/demographic/products/dyb/DYB2002/Table06.xls (accessed April 7, 2005).

3. Robert Kemper, *Journal of Theological Education*, vol. 34, no. 1 (Pittsburgh: Association of Theological Schools, Autumn 1997): 52.

4. R. B. Y. Scott, "The Book of Isaiah," in *The Interpreter's Bible*, vol. 5 (New York: Abingdon, 1956), 205.

5. In January 2000, a Memphis, Tennessee, grand jury determined that King's death could not have resulted from the individual effort of James Earl Ray, the convicted assassin, but was the result of a conspiracy with the real killer(s), as of that time yet unidentified.

6. President John F. Kennedy was assassinated along a parade route on November 22, 1963, in Dallas, Texas; El Hajj Malik El Shabazz (Malcolm X) was murdered February 21, 1965, at the Audubon Ballroom while addressing a rally in Harlem, New York City; and Senator Robert F. Kennedy, the brother of the late President Kennedy, was killed June 5, 1968, at the Ambassador Hotel in Los Angeles, California, just after winning the California Primary. Conspiracy theories were associated with all three assassinations.

7. "God-talk" is another way of referring to theological discussions or conversations where the topic involves consideration of religious, ethical, or moral issues from a faith perspective.

8. "Redlining" refers to a discriminatory practice of the banking and/or insurance industries in which home-loan financing or insurance coverage is withheld from persons living in certain inner-city neighborhoods considered to be a poor financial risk. Typically, the practice involves persons who, but for their ethnicity or location, otherwise would be granted such economic support from these institutions.

9. Andrew Davey, *Urban Christianity and Global Order* (Peabody, Mass.: Hendrickson, 2002), 14.

10. Statistics from the U.S. Census Bureau: http://www.census.gov/ipc/www/worldpop.html (accessed April 7, 2005).

11. Roger S. Greenway and Timothy M. Monsma, *Cities: Mission's New Frontier*, 2nd ed. (Grand Rapids: Baker, 2000), 67.

12. All population statistics quoted in this chapter, except as noted, are from the United Nations Web site: http://www.un.org/unsd (accessed January 21, 2004).

13. U.S. Census Bureau Web site: http://www.census.gov/ipc/www/world.html (accessed April 7, 2005).

14. Statistics 1800–1990: U.S. Census Bureau Web site: http://www.census.gov/population/census data/table-4.pdf (accessed April 7, 2005); 2000 U.S. population statistics: United Nations Web site: http://unstats.un.org/unsd/demographic/products/dyb/DYB2002/Table06.xls (accessed April 7, 2005).

15. Harvey M. Conn and Manuel Ortiz, *The Kingdom, the City and the People of God* (Downers Grove, Ill.: InterVarsity, 2001), 378.

16. For years, there has been available a series of excellent resources discussing the topic and highlighting best-practice examples of urban ministry as a means of defining the subject. Lyle Schaller's *Center City Churches* (Nashville: Abingdon, 1989); Eleanor Scott Meyers's *Envisioning the New City* (Louisville: Westminster, 1992); and Nile Harper's *Urban Churches: Vital Signs* (Grand Rapids: Eerdmans, 1999) are good examples of this approach to defining urban ministry.

2. Pitfalls and Potentials: The City as a Paradigm of Human Relationships

1. The story of Nimrod (Genesis 10:6-12) clearly associates physical power and skill, not intrinsically negative but often abused resources, as factors in the construction of cities, including Babylon.

2. Howard Thurman, *Jesus and the Disinherited* (Richmond, Ind.: Friends United, 1949; reissued 1981), 75–76.

3. In distinction to the destructive associations of the reality described as "evil" and inevitably culminating in death or nonexistence, the ideas of *reconciliation, love/justice,* and *cooperation* are realities associated with life and the generative and regenerative capacities of God.

4. James Cone, *Martin, Malcolm, and America* (Maryknoll, N.Y.: Orbis, 1991), 126.

3. Bridging the Chasms in Urban Ministry

1. Quoted in Eldin Villafañe, Bruce W. Jackson, Robert A. Evans, and Alice Frazer Evans, *Transforming the City: Reframing Education for Urban Ministry* (Cambridge: Eerdmans, 2002), 173.

2. *Figures on the Metropolitan Statistical Area* (MSA) of Pittsburgh, Pennsylvania, are from the U.S. Census Bureau Web site: http://www.census.gov/population/cen2000/phc-t29/tab01b.xls (accessed April 7, 2005). MSA is a geographic entity defined by the federal Office of Management and Budget for use by federal statistical agencies, based on the concept of a core area with a large population nucleus, plus adjacent communities having a high degree of economic and social integration with that core. Qualification as an MSA requires the presence of a city with 50,000 or more inhabitants, or the presence of an Urbanized Area (UA) and a total population of at least 100,000 (75,000 in New England). The county or counties containing the largest city and the surrounding densely settled territory are central counties of the MSA. Additional outlying counties qualify to be included in the MSA by meeting certain other criteria of metropolitan character, such as a specified minimum population density or percentage of the population that is urban.

3. See http://pghbridges.com/index.htm (accessed January 24, 2005).

4. For an excellent examination of the urban-rural connection regarding poverty, see Gary E. Farley, "Poverty: The Urban-Rural Linkages," in Eleanor Scott Meyers, *Envisioning the New City: A Reader on Urban Ministry* (Louisville: WJP, 1992), 109–24.

5. In Harvey M. Conn and Manuel Ortiz's book *The Kingdom, the City and the People of God* (Downers Grove, Ill.: InterVarsity, 2001), 335–36, relocation is the term applied to persons who undertake "to rearrange" their lives geographically to live among people who are different from themselves or from their native contexts in order to advance the evangelistic goals of ministry (also referred to as an "incarnational" style of ministry).

6. There is broad consensus among social and medical scientists that race and/or ethnic distinctions in the human family of homo sapiens document culturally learned differences rather

than substantive genetic variations within the species, a position affirmed in a variety of other disciplines as well. Representative articulations of this perspective are found in W. Michael Byrd and Linda Clayton's book *An American Health Dilemma, vol. 1, A Medical History of African Americans and the Problem of Race: Beginnings to 1900* (New York: Routledge, 2000), 46–47; Kevin J. Christiano, William H. Swatos, Jr., and Peter Kivisto, *Sociology of Religion: Contemporary Developments* (Lanham: Rowman & Littlefield, 2002), 154–59; Matthew Anderson, Susan Moscou, Celestine Fulchon, Daniel R. Neuspiel, *Journal of Family Medicine* 33 (6): 430–34; and Cornel West's "The Geneology of Modern Racism" (chap. 2) in *Prophesy Deliverance: An Afro-American Revolutionary Christianity* (Philadelphia: Westminster, 1982), 47–65.

7. Michael Eric Dyson, in his book *I May Not Get There With You: The True Martin Luther King, Jr.* (New York: Free Press, 2000), 47–48, discusses the use of evasion strategies with regard to Blacks and American history. He observes that color coding is a tool by which racial evasionists (people who claim to be "color blind" about race) attempt to ignore history and thus avoid dealing with the existence of social inequities. For example, Dyson argues that there is a "stinging paradox" for Blacks in being judged as a group and yet being expected to act individually. Dyson states: "The color coding of black identity is a historical process that occurred without black input. Blacks had little choice in how they were perceived by whites and even less choice about what features of their culture would be lauded or lambasted. In a culture where race has shaped the criteria by which blacks have been judged; where blacks have been denied the possibility of enjoying the fruits of their talents in a national vineyard they helped to plant and nurture to greatness; and where the rules of fair play have been rigged against blacks until less then forty years ago, it is disingenuous for racial evasionists to ignore that history and blame blacks for social conditions they had no hand in creating."

8. Peter Marcuse and Ronald van Kempen (2000) approach the spatial considerations of global urbanization while Lowell Livezey (2001) examines urban ministry in its social dimensions and Robert Lithincum (1991) is a good example of a symbolic focus on the city.

9. See Bakke (1987); Conn and Ortiz (2001); Linthicum (1991); Scott-Meyers (1992); and Wallis (1981).

10. Conn & Ortiz (2001), 22, 159–60;

11. Harper (1999); Schaller (1989); Scott-Meyers (1993); Livezey (2001).

12. Bakke (1987); Day, Dennis, and Peters (1997); Harper (1999); Scott-Meyers (1992); and Villafañe (1995).

4. Looking Back: Ancient and Modern Urban Ministry

1. Kenneth Scott Latourette, *A History of Christianity* (New York: Harper & Row, 1953), 75.

2. Current expressions of this hermeneutic can be seen in public debates that even until this day seek to pit biblical authority against the teaching of Darwinism in public school curricula, as if these two were mutually exclusive approaches to education.

3. While there is no dispute concerning the urban character of the Roman Empire in which Christianity first appeared, the theological significance of the urban arena in Christian history is an underrepresented topic in analysis of the Christian movement until the seventeenth through nineteenth centuries and the emergence of the Enlightenment era in Europe. Even during this time of growing urbanism and sweeping sociopolitical change, theological emphasis was not on the city itself, but was given to delineating new interpretations of faith in light of the rising authority of science and new disciplines it created, like sociology or psychology. It was not until the late nineteenth century and early twentieth century and the advent of the Social Gospel movement that the urban context received special attention as a resource for understanding the

implications of faith. Fortunately, focused attention to the biblical, theological, ethical, and pastoral care significance of the city per se in interpreting Christianity is a growing but recent phenomenon and, even now, certainly is not a dominant theme in Christian reflection.

4. Quoted in Richard Sennett, *Flesh and Stone: The Body and the City in Western Civilization* (New York: Norton, 1994), 56.

5. Harvey Gallagher Cox, *The Secular City: Secularization and Urbanization in Theological Perspective* (New York: Macmillan, 1966), 2.

6. Ibid., 3–4.

7. John Inge, *A Christian Theology of Place: Explorations in Practical, Pastoral, and Empirical Theology* (Burlington: Ashgate, 2003); Edward S. Casey, *Getting Back Into Place: Toward a Renewed Understanding of the Place-World* (Indianapolis: Indiana University Press, 1993).

8. Inge (2003), 58, 100.

9. Bakke (1987); Villafañe (1995); Conn and Ortiz (2000); Diop (1986); Mumford (1961); Adams (1966).

10. Lewis Mumford, *The City in History: Its Origins, Its Transformations, and Its Prospects* (New York: W. Harcourt, Brace & World, 1961), 8.

11. Ibid., 10.

12. Giorgio Buccellati, *Cities and Nations of Ancient Syria*, 1967, quoted in Conn and Ortiz (2000), 34.

13. Conn and Ortiz (2000), 35.

14. Ibid., 35–36.

15. Cheikh Anta Diop, *Precolonial Black Africa*, trans. Harold Salemson (New York: Lawrence Hill Books, 1987), 18.

16. Ibid., 19–20.

17. Bernard W. Anderson, *Understanding the Old Testament*, 2nd ed. (Englewood Cliffs, N.J.: Prentice-Hall. 1966), 145.

18. Robert Linthicum, *City of God, City of Satan* (1992); Wayne Meeks, *The First Urban Christians* (2003); Justo L. González, *The Story of Christianity*, vol. 1 (1984).

19. Adolf von Harnack, *The Mission and Expansion of Christianity in the First Three Centuries*, trans. and ed. James Moffatt (New York: Putnam, 1908); and Wayne A. Meeks, *The First Urban Christians*.

20. Biblical city figures from Rodney Stark's *The Rise of Christianity* (Princeton: Princeton University Press, 1996), 131–32. U.S. city figures from http://www.city-data.com (accessed March 2006).

21. Robert C. Linthicum, *City of God, City of Satan* (Grand Rapids: Zondervan, 1991), 21.

22. Ibid., 21.

23. Andrew Davey, *Urban Christianity and Global Order* (Peabody, Mass.: Hendrickson, 2002), 16–17.

24. Richard Batey, *Jesus and the Forgotten City* (Grand Rapids: Baker, 1992). Quoted in Harvey M. Conn and Manuel Ortiz, *The Kingdom, the City and the People of God* (Downers Grove, Ill.: InterVarsity, 2001), 120.

25. Conn and Ortiz (2001), 120.

26. Quoted in ibid., 121.

27. See ibid., 121.

28. Stark (1996), 149–50.

29. Ibid., 152.

30. Several writers have commented on Luke's interest in matters that seem to highlight the cosmopolitan aspects of the gospel from various points of view, including Richard J. Cassidy, *Jesus, Politics, and Society: A Study of Luke's Gospel* (Maryknoll, N.Y.: Orbis, 1983); Richard J.

Cassidy and Philip J. Scharper, eds., *Political Issues in Luke-Acts* (Maryknoll, N.Y.: Orbis, 1983); Conn and Ortiz (2000); and Bonnie Thurston, *Women in the New Testament: Questions and Commentary* (New York: Crossroad, 1998). It is significant that half of all New Testament references to the city occur within the two volumes Luke authored: the Gospel of Luke and Acts. Conn and Ortiz (2000, 124) list several instances wherein Luke regularly uses the Greek word polis (city) where other Gospel writers do not.

31. Quote from video entitled *Portrait of a Radical: The Jesus Movement* (color/50 minutes), featuring Huston Smith, Richard Rohr, and Allen Dwight Callahan (Westport, Conn.: Four Seasons Productions, 2000).

32. Conn and Ortiz (2000), 121.

33. Justo L. González, *The Story of Christianity*, vol. 1, *The Early Church to the Dawn of the Reformation* (New York: Harper & Row, 1984), 20.

34. Kenneth Scott Latourette, *A History of Christianity* (New York: Harper & Row, 1953), 75.

35. Justo L. González, *The Story of Christianity*, vol. 1, *The Early Church to the Dawn of the Reformation* (New York: Harper & Row, 1984), 20.

36. Deissmann (1957); Judge (1960); Meeks (2003).

37. Stark (1996), 57.

38. González (1984), 18.

39. Ibid., 40.

40. Ibid., 50–51.

41. Gustav Deissmann, *Paul: A Study in Social and Religious History*, trans. William E. Wilson (New York: Harper, 1957); Wayne Meeks, *The First Urban Christians: The Social World of the Apostle Paul*, 2nd ed. (New Haven: Yale University Press, 2003), 51–52; E. A. Judge, *The Social Pattern of the Christian Groups in the First Century* (London: Tyndale, 1960); and Rodney Stark, *The Rise of Christianity* (Princeton: Princeton University Press, 1996), are representative of this school of thought.

42. Meeks (2003), 53–55.

43. Ibid., 76. See also Clarice Martin, "The Haustafeln (Household Codes) in African American Biblical Interpretation: 'Free Slaves' and 'Subordinate Women,'" in Cain H. Felder, *Stony the Road We Trod: African American Biblical Interpretation* (Minneapolis: Fortress, 1991).

44. See also Deissmann (trans. William Wilson, 1957); and Rodney Stark (1996).

45. Quoted in Stark (1996), 30.

46. González (1984), 61.

47. Ibid., 41.

48. Ibid., 62.

49. Ibid. 174.

50. Quoted from Ibid., 165.

51. Ibid., 22.

5. Urban Theology: A Bottom-Up Perspective

1. James H. Cone, *God of the Oppressed*, 2nd ed. (Maryknoll, N.Y.: Orbis, 1997), xix.

2. A phrase used by Howard Thurman to describe socially vulnerable or oppressed people. See Thurman's *Jesus and the Disinherited* (1949; repr. Richmond, Ind.: Friends United, 1981), 11.

3. Alister McGrath, *Christian Theology: An Introduction* (Cambridge, UK: Oxford, 1994), 117–18.

4. John Macquarrie, *Principles of Christian Theology* (New York: Charles Scribner's Sons, 1966), 4.

5. Western thinkers often emphasize the role of reason as a separate source of revelation. Widely associated with the emergence of the scientific revolution (e.g., Francis Bacon, Galileo Galilei, René Descartes) and/or Enlightenment-era writers (e.g., John Locke, Baruch Spinoza, Jean-Jacques Rousseau, Immanuel Kant, Georg Wilhelm Friedrich Hegel), reason is found as a source of revelation in writers as far back as Thomas Aquinas and among prominent theologians from a variety of perspectives (Tillich and Gutiérrez, for example). Nonetheless, all human understanding and reason are conditioned by personal experience and context (e.g., Ludwig Feuerbach, Søren Kierkegaard, Howard Thurman, James Cone, Jacquelyn Grant) and are recognized herein as part of the broader source of revelation, referred to simply as *experience*.

6. James Cone, *A Theology of Black Liberation* (New York: Lippincott, 1970), 51.

7. Howard Thurman, *Jesus and the Disinherited*, 2nd ed. (1949; repr. Richmond, Ind.: Friends United, 1981]), 11–12.

8. A contemporary of Thurman, H. Richard Niebuhr, referred to such tendencies as a promulgation of a "Christ of culture" rather than a Christ who transforms culture among a list of five ethical typologies that he observed in Christianity in his classic work entitled *Christ and Culture* (San Francisco: Harper Collins, 2001).

9. William Julius Wilson, ed., *The Ghetto Underclass: Social Science Perspectives* (Newbury Park, Calif.: Sage, 1993), 26–27.

10. Michael Northcott, ed., "Introduction: Theology in the City," in *Urban Theology: A Reader* (London: Cassell, 1998), 2.

11. Tavis Smiley, *The Covenant with Black America* (Chicago: Third World Press, 2006), 53.

12. Warren Dennis, "The Challenges of Africentric Ministry in Urban Theological Education," in Ronald Peters and Marsha Snulligan Haney, eds., *Africentric Approaches to Christian Ministry* (Lanham: University Press of America, 2005), 138.

13. Northcott (1998), 5.

14. James H. Cone, *Black Theology and Black Power* (1968).

15. Gustavo Gutiérrez, *A Theology of Liberation* (1971).

16. Howard Thurman, *Jesus and the Disinherited* (New York: Abingdon, 1949), 11–12.

17. Northcott (1998), 5.

18. Northcott (1998).

19. William Pannell, *Evangelism from the Bottom Up* (Grand Rapids: Zondervan, 1992).

20. Pannell (1992), 118.

21. Quoted in ibid., 118.

22. I draw heavily on the resources of what is typically referred to as Liberation and Womanist theologians in defining the perspective of the bottom-up theological approach, and especially on ideas gleaned from writers including James Cone, James Evans, Jacquelyn Grant, Delores Williams, Gustavo Gutiérrez, and Gayraud Wilmore as well as the communitarian-focused and classic works of Howard Thurman, especially *Jesus and the Disinherited and Meditations of the Heart*.

6. Antecedents of a *Top-Down* Theological Perspective

1. Cornel West, *Prophesy Deliverance! An Afro-American Revolutionary Christianity* (Philadelphia: Westminster, 1982), 27.

2. John Calvin, *Institutes of the Christian Religion*, vol. 2, trans. Henry Beveridge (Grand Rapids: Eerdmans, 1966), 206–7.

3. This is a point made by a variety of ethicists and theologians writing from different

perspectives, including Robert L. Stivers, Dean H. Lewis, Jack L. Stotts, Ronald H. Stone, Gordon and Jane Douglass, Preston N. Williams, and others. See Robert L. Stivers and Dean H. Lewis, eds., *Reformed Faith and Economics* (Lanham: University Press of America, 1989).

4. Preston N. Williams, "Calvinism, Racism, and Economic Institutions," in Robert L. Stivers, ed., *Reformed Faith and Economics* (Lanham: University Press of America, 1989), 50.

5. It must be noted that the Enlightenment critique of Christian orthodoxy, which relegated awareness of God to an option in human thought rather than a component of all existence, was primarily a phenomenon of Western European and North American culture where Christianity was numerically strong. Religious beliefs in regions and cultures outside of this context, such as in Africa (African Traditional Religions or the Ethiopian Coptic Church, or North/North East African Islam), Asia (e.g., Buddhism, Hinduism, Islam), Australia, Central and South America, or Eastern and Southern Europe, were unaffected by its approach to issues about faith in God. As Alister McGrath has noted, the Enlightenment addressed Christian beliefs: "It was Christian sacred writings—rather than those of Islam or Hinduism—which were subjected to an unprecedented critical scrutiny, both literary and historical, with the Bible being treated 'as if it were any other book' (Benjamin Jowett). It was the life of Jesus of Nazareth which was subjected to a critical reconstruction, rather than that of Mohammed or the Buddha" (Alister E. McGrath, *Christian Theology: An Introduction* [1994], 81–82).

6. Alister E. McGrath (1994), 94.

7. Kevin J. Christiano, William H. Swatos, Jr., and Peter Kivisto, *Sociology of Religion: Contemporary Developments* (Lanham: Rowman & Littlefield, 2002), 4; and Kenneth Scott Latourette, *A History of Christianity* (Harper & Row, 1953), 1072.

8. According to Christiano, Swatos, and Kivisto, Émile Durkheim's *The Elementary Forms of the Religious Life,* published at the end of his career, saw religion as maintaining social order or equilibrium. Weber's *The Protestant Ethic and the Spirit of Capitalism* viewed religion as a vehicle for social change. In *The Social Teaching of the Christian Churches,* the theologian Ernst Troeltsch sought to relate types of religious experience to the varieties of social teachings with which they might be correlated. See Christiano, Swatos, and Kivisto (2002), chapters 1 and 4 and pages 4, 94.

9. Among the classic treatises dealing with this phenomenon are Max Weber's *The Protestant Ethic and the Spirit of Capitalism* and Ernst Troeltsch's *The Social Teaching of Christian Churches*.

10. As we have seen, several European nations (including England, many German provinces, Switzerland, the Netherlands, Scotland, etc.) had already become aligned with the Protestant movement as a top-down theological and cultural norm. However, as Kevin J. Christiano, William H. Swatos, Jr., and Peter Kivisto observe in their book *Sociology of Religion: Contemporary Developments,* "The uniqueness of the . . . emergence of the United States was in its 'having its religious roots as a nation virtually entirely' framed within the Protestant theological context" (Lanham: Rowman & Littlefield, 2002), 92. In this context, the Protestant theological norms were established as part of the top-down sociocultural template in the new republic.

11. T. Harry Williams, Richard N. Current, and Frank Freidel, *A History of the United States [To 1876]* (New York: Alfred A. Knopf, 1961), 55.

12. First Amendment to the U.S. Constitution.

13. Quoted in T. Harry Williams, Richard N. Current, and Frank Freidel, *A History of the United States [To 1876]* (New York: Alfred A. Knopf, 1961), 677.

14. Quoted in Christiano, Swatos, and Kivisto (2002), 92.

15. Christiano, Swatos, and Kivisto (2002), 95.

7. Antecedents of a *Bottom-Up* Theological Perspective

1. Howard Thurman, *The Search for Common Ground* (New York: Harper & Row, 1971), 86–87.

2. Ralph E. Luker, *The Social Gospel in Black and White* (Chapel Hill: University of North Carolina, 1991), 4–5.

3. J. Phillip Wogaman, *Christian Ethics: A Historical Introduction* (Louisville: Westminster/ John Knox, 1993), 194–95.

4. Cited in Wogaman (1993), 196.

5. Ronald E. Peters (Sept. 1994). "Afrocentrism and Mainline Denominations." An unpublished paper delivered to Vanderbilt Divinity School, Nashville, Tenn., p. 3.

6. Gunnar Mydral, E. Franklin Frazier, Carter G. Woodson. Melville J. Herskovits.

7. U.S. Constitution, Article I, Section 2 (altered after the Civil War by the Fourteenth and Sixteenth Amendments).

8. West (1982), 48. For a very thorough synopsis of this phenomenon, the reader is referred to West's "Genealogy of Modern Racism" (chapter 2, from which this excerpt is drawn) in *Prophesy Deliverance! An Afro-American Revolutionary Christianity* (Philadelphia: Westminster, 1982), 47–65.

9. West (1982), 61–63.

10. John Calvin, *Institutes of the Christian Religion*, vol. 2, trans. Henry Beveridge (Grand Rapids: Eerdmans, 1966), 206–7.

11. Quoted in Eric L. McKitrick, *Slavery Defended: The Views of the Old South* (Englewood Cliffs, N.J.: Prentice-Hall, 1963), 86–87, 95. It is significant that more than 140 years after this theological rationale was in circulation, African American biblical scholars still find it necessary to address themselves correcting the misuse of scripture involving these texts. For example, see Cain Hope Felder, *Troubling Biblical Waters* (Maryknoll, N.Y.: Orbis, 1990), and Clarice J. Martin's "Haustafeln (Household Codes) in African American Biblical Interpretation: 'Free Slaves' and 'Subordinate Women,'" in Cain Hope Felder, ed., *Stony the Road We Trod* (Minneapolis: Fortress, 1991), 206–31. Also see Renita Weems's *Just a Sister Away*.

12. Albert J. Raboteau, *Slave Religion: The "Invisible Institution" in the Antebellum South* (Oxford: Oxford University Press, 1978), 96.

13. James H. Cone (1972), *The Spirituals and the Blues*; Melva Wilson Costen (1993), *African American Christian Worship*, 93–98; William E. B. DuBois (1903), *Souls of Black Folk*, chapter 1: "Our Spiritual Strivings"; James Weldon Johnson and J. Rosamond Johnson (1925, 1926), *The Books of American Negro Spirituals*; Benjamin E. Mays (1933), *The Negro's God*; Wyatt Tee Walker (1979), *Somebody's Calling My Name: Black Sacred Music and Social Change*.

14. Sister Thea Bowman, "The Gift of African American Sacred Song," in *Lead Me, Guide Me: The African American Catholic Hymnal* (Chicago: G.I.A. Publications, 1987). See the first of the unnumbered pages following the book's preface.

15. John Hope Franklin, *From Slavery to Freedom: A History of Negro Americans* (New York: Alfred A. Knopf, 1980), 182.

16. See http://womenshistory.about.com/library/bio/bltruth.htm (accessed May 29, 2006).

17. Franklin (1980), 188.

18. Quoted in Wogaman (1993), 189–90.

19. *Periscope: Black Presbyterianism—Yesterday, Today and Tomorrow* (New York: United Presbyterian Church [USA], 1982), 13.

20. Frederick Binder, David M. Reimers, *All the Nations Under Heaven: An Ethnic and Racial History of New York City* (New York: Columbia University Press, 1995), 57.

21. Ibid.

22. Quoted in James Cone, *Black Theology and Black Power* (Minneapolis: Seabury, 1969), 96.

23. Ralph Luker, *The Social Gospel in Black and White* (Chapel Hill: University of North Carolina, 1991), 28.

24. Ibid., 91–92.

25. Franklin (1980), 313.

26. Milton C. Sernett, *Bound for the Promised Land: African American Religion and the Great Migration* (Durham: Duke University Press, 1997), 36.

27. Ibid., 38.

28. Ibid., 40.

29. Quoted in ibid., 36.

30. Luker (1991), 180.

31. Ibid., 157.

32. Ibid.

33. Ibid.

34. Sernett (1997), 39.

35. A perception skillfully discussed in Sernett's 1997 analysis, *Bound for the Promised Land.*

36. Fred D. Smith, "Africentric Christian Education: A Historical Perspective," in Ronald Edward Peters and Marsha Snulligan Haney, eds., *Africentric Approches to Christian Ministry* (Lanham: University Press, 2006), 110–11.

37. Quoted in Peter Paris, *The Social Teaching of the Black Churches* (Philadelphia: Fortress, 1985), 96.

38. Luker (1991), 174.

39. The African American Registry Web site: http://www.aaregistry.com/african_american_history/1751/Spiritual_charisma_Adam_Clayton_Powell_Sr (accessed May 30, 2006).

40. Thurman (1949), 11.

8. Core Values in Urban Ministry

1. Jim Wallis, *The Soul of Politics* (Maryknoll, N.Y.: Orbis, 1994), xv.

2. Because Western culture, its pluralism notwithstanding, draws its foundations so heavily from the Greco-Roman civilization of antiquity, I refer to this sense of God-consciousness in urban ministry by utilizing the Greek word for God, *theos,* or for our purposes here, the value known as theism.

3. Barna Group surveys taken in 2002 regarding Christianity and in 2004 among adherents of other faith traditions: http://www.barna.org/FlexPage.aspx?Page=Topic&TopicID=2 (accessed September 2005).

4. Howard Thurman, *Jesus and the Disinherited* (1949; repr. Richmond, Ind.: Friends United, 1981), 89.

5. Ibid., 97.

6. Quoted in James M. Washington, ed., *Testament of Hope: The Essential Writings and Speeches of Martin Luther King, Jr.* (San Francisco, Calif.: Harper), 19–20.

7. Quoted in Washington (1986), 246-47.

8. For an interesting perspective on the growing marginalization of faith beliefs from the arena of jurisprudence, see Stephen L. Carter's *The Culture of Disbelief* (New York: Basic Books, 1993).

9. In February 2004, the New York chapter of the American Civil Liberties Union filed suit in federal court on behalf of employees in government-funded social service contracts with the

Salvation Army. The plaintiffs claimed that they were subject to discriminatory or illegal employment practices that the organization felt justified in imposing based upon its religious beliefs. See http://www.nyclu.org/salvation_army_pr_022404.html (accessed March 30, 2007); also http://www.usdoj.gov/crt/religdisc/lown_opinion.pdf (accessed March 30, 2007).

10. See chapter 4, "Biblical Mandates on Justice and Social Class," in Cain Hope Felder's *Troubling Biblical Waters: Race, Class, and Family* (Maryknoll, N.Y.: Orbis, 1990).

11. Cain Felder, *Troubling Biblical Waters: Race, Class, and Family* (Maryknoll, N.Y.: Orbis, 1990), 56.

12. Ibid., 59.

13. Ibid., 68.

14. Ibid., 59.

15. Ibid., 71.

16. Ibid., 68.

17. Ibid., 71–78.

18. Dudley (1978); McCaleb (1996); Sample (1990); Schaller (1993); Stallings (1988); Stewart (1994).

19. See John Hope Franklin; Lincoln and Mamiya (1990).

20. See http://www.gangsummit.org/index.html (accessed October 10, 2006).

21. This difference usually implies ethnic divergence from overarching norms in the U.S. and Europe that are based upon European-dominated cultural and aesthetic values (see chapter 1).

22. Jeffrey Dahmer was a serial killer who tortured, dismembered, and ate his victims. On June 7, 1998, James Byrd, Jr., a forty-nine-year-old African American, was stripped, beaten, and dragged to death by a vehicle in a racially motivated crime perpetrated by three white males, John King, Shawn Berry, and Lawrence Brewer. In 1999, Columbine High School in unincorporated Jefferson County, Colorado, near Denver and Littleton, was the place where two students, Eric Harris and Dylan Klebold, brought guns to school and killed twelve students and a teacher along with wounding twenty-four other students before committing suicide.

23. The April 19, 1995, bombing of the Murrah Federal Building in Oklahoma City by Timothy McVeigh, a Gulf War veteran, killed 168 people, and the September 11, 2001, crash of airplanes into the New York City World Trade Towers and the Pentagon Building in Washington, D.C.

24. Howard Thurman (1987), 91–98.

9. Two Spheres of Urban Ministry: Parish and Public

1. Rick Warren, *The Purose Driven Church: Growth Without Compromising Your Message and Mission* (Grand Rapids: Zondervan, 1995), 82–83.

2. Quoted in James M. Washington, ed., *Testament of Hope: The Essential Writings and Speeches of Martin Luther King, Jr.* (New York: HarperCollins, 1986), 282.

3. Rick Warren (1995).

4. Kennon L. Callahan, *Twelve Keys to an Effective Church* (New York: Harper & Row, 1986).

5. Carlyle Fielding Stewart III, *African American Church Growth: 12 Principles for Prophetic Ministry* (Nashville: Abingdon, 1994).

6. Samuel D. Procter and Gardner C. Taylor, *We Have This Ministry: The Heart of the Pastor's Vocation* (Valley Forge: Judson, 1996).

7. James O. Stallings, *Telling the Story: Evangelism in Black Churches* (Valley Forge: Judson, 1988).

8. Ibid., 74.

9. Samuel G. Freedman, *Upon This Rock: The Miracles of a Black Church* (New York: Harper, 1993).

10. Eldin Villafañe, *The Liberating Spirit: Toward an Hispanic American Pentecostal Social Ethic* (Grand Rapids: Eerdmans, 1994).

11. Arlene Sanchez Walsh, *Latino Pentecostalism* (2003).

12. Warren Dennis, "Afrocentric Urban Theological Education and Ministry: A Curriculum Response to 'Is This New Wine?'" (D.Min. paper, United Theological Seminary, Dayton, OH, 1998), 16.

13. Social promotion refers to the practice of promoting a student to a higher grade level in school even though he/she has not mastered the skill competency required for success in the current grade from which he/she is being promoted.

14. Warren, Purpose Driven Church.

15. Time magazine Web site: http://www.time.com/time/archive/preview/0,10987,1022606,00 .html (accessed February 9, 2005).

16. C. Eric Lincoln and Lawrence H. Mamiya, *The Black Church in the African American Experience* (Durham: Duke University Press, 1990); Albert Robateau, *Slave Religion; George Washington Carver, The Negro Church in America*; and W. E. B. DuBois, *Souls of Black Folk* (1903) are representative examples of this documentation over time.

17. Lyle Schaller, *Center City Churches: The New Urban Frontier* (Nashville: Abingdon, 1993), 11.

18. Harvey Cox, "Foreword," in Eleanor Scott Meyers, ed., *Envisioning the New City: A Reader on Urban Ministry* (Louisville: Westminster/John Knox, 1992), 14.

10. Seeing with a Divine Lens: Issues and Networks in the City

1. Although the words *city* and *community* are used interchangeably for the purposes of this aspect of our discussion, it should be noted that there are significant differences between the two. Suffice it to say in this context that city generally refers to *an aggregation of smaller communities whereas a community is ordinarily understood as a relational network of persons in a particular locale, vocation, or organization with shared interests and values.*

2. Michael Eric Dyson, in his book *I May Not Get There With You: The True Martin Luther King, Jr.* (47–48), observes that color coding is a tool by which racial evasionists (people who claim to be "color blind" about race) attempt to ignore history. He argues that there is a "stinging paradox" for Blacks in being judged as a group and yet being expected to act like individuals. Dyson states: "The color coding of black identity is a historical process that occurred without black input. Blacks had little choice in how they were perceived by whites and even less choice about what features of their culture would be lauded or lambasted. In a culture where race has shaped the criteria by which blacks have been judged; where blacks have been denied the possibility of enjoying the fruits of their talents in a national vineyard they helped to plant and nurture to greatness; and where the rules of fair play have been rigged against blacks until less than forty years ago, it is disingenuous for racial evasionists to ignore that history and blame blacks for social conditions they had no hand in creating."

3. Esther L. Bush, "State of Black Pittsburgh," address delivered at the annual meeting of the Urban League of Pittsburgh, Inc. at Carnegie-Mellon University, Pittsburgh, PA, October 23, 2003.

4. Ralph Bangs, Statistics from the University Center for Social and Urban Research, University of Pittsburgh. Pittsburgh, PA (2000).

5. Lowell W. Livezey, *Public Religion and Urban Transformation: Faith in the City* (New York: New York University Press), 23.

6. Ibid., 22.

7. Statistics from a July 2003 report of the Department of Justice, 950 Pennsylvania Avenue, NW, Washington, D.C., taken from the Website at http://www.usdoj.gov.

8. Tavis Smiley, *The Covenant with Black America* (Chicago: Third World Press, 2006), 53.

9. Ibid.

10. Jeremy Travis, Elizabeth M. Cincotta, and Amy L. Solomon, "Families Left Behind: The Hidden Costs of Incarceration and Reentry," in *Urban Institute—Justice Policy Center* (Washington, D.C., October 2003): 1.

11. Alternative Policy Institute PAC Issue #2 (1986), "Toxics & Minority Communities" (Oakland, Calif.: Center for Third World Organizing). This 1986 report found that three out of the five largest commercial hazardous waste landfills in the United States were located in mostly Black or Latino communities and that these landfills accounted for 40 percent of the nation's estimated commercial landfill space. Additionally, the study found that three out of five Black and Latino Americans live in communities with uncontrolled toxic waste sites, and cities with large Black populations like St. Louis, Houston, Cleveland, Chicago, Atlanta, and Memphis had the largest numbers of uncontrolled toxic waste sites.

12. W. Michael Byrd and Linda A. Clayton, *An American Health Dilemma*, vol. 1 (New York: Routledge, 2000), 132.

13. Quoted in Tavis Smiley, *The Covenant with Black America* (Chicago: Third World Press, 2006), 10.

14. Ibid., 5.

11. The Egalitarian Metropolis

1. Virginia Fabella and Sun Ai Lee Park, eds., *We Dare to Dream: Doing Theology as Asian Women* (Hong Kong: Asian Women's Resource Centre for Culture and Theology, 1989), 12.

2. See Kenneth L. Smith and Ira G. Zepp's *Search for the Beloved Community: The Thinking of Martin Luther King, Jr.* (1974).

3. Stephen L. Carter, *The Culture of Disbelief* (New York: Basic Books, 1993).

4. Robert N. Bellah, "Conclusion: Competing Vision of the Role of Religion in American Society," in *Uncivil Religion*, ed. Robert N. Bellah and Frederick E. Greenspan (New York: Crossroad, 1987), 219–31.

5. Eleanor Scott Meyers, ed., *Envisioning the New City: A Reader on Urban Ministry* (Louisville: Westminster/John Knox, 1992), 24.

6. Eldin Villafañe, "A Prayer for the City: Paul's Benediction and a Vision for Urban Theological Education." An address delivered to the CUTLEEP Conference, Sheraton Boston Hotel and Towers, Mar. 28, 1998, Boston, Mass., 13–14.

7. Warren Dennis, "Urban Theological Education" (unpublished Doctor of Ministry paper submitted to United Theological Seminary).

INDEX

National Council of Negro Women, 104
National Urban League, 100, 101, 102, 104, 125
National Youth Administration's Division of Negro Affairs, 104
Native Americans, 87–88, 163, 172
negro, origin of word, 87
neighbor: concern for welfare of, 57–58, 99, 117, love of, 18, 24, 116, 118, 121
neighborhoods, 124, 145; abandoned, 155, conflicts/violence in, 129, 132, 145, 166, ethnic, 14, 147, 163
New Orleans, Louisiana, 22, 64, 73, 170
New York, 40, 97, 98, 100, 102–3, 127
Nineveh, 38
Northcott, Michael, 62, 68–69

Oklahoma City Federal Building, 129
oppression, 46–48, 86, 116; opposition to/rejection of, 94, 130, 146, victims of, 99, 100, 104–5, 146, 149, 153
orthodoxy, 50–54, 79, 82, 113
Ortiz, Manuel, 9

Palestine/Palestinians, 37, 41, 44–46, 163
Pannell, William, 70
Parish ministry, 143–50, 163; corporate, 143–44, 145–48, declares gospel/tenets of faith, 143–45, 150, evangelizes/nurtures, 143–48, 153, goals of, 144, 150, personal, 143–44, 148–50, within/outside congregation, 143, 144–48
Parks, Rosa, 127
pastoral care, 125–26, 149, 182n3
paternalism, missionary, 146
patriarchy, 48
Paul, apostle, 17–18, 24, 38, 39, 43, 44–45, 66, 85; declining right to be paid, 122, preaching gospel to Gentiles, 121, working with other apostles, 131–32
peace, 4, 12, 27, 93, 168, 174, 175
Pentecost, 11, 12, 53, 175
Pentecostals, 14, 58, 70, 148
people of color, 25, 27, 118, 163, 166; *urban* as code word for, 25–28
Philadelphia, Pennsylvania, 52, 94, 95, 97, 100, 102, 104
Pittsburgh, Pennsylvania, 5, 19–20, 124–25, 145, 162–63, 168

pluralism, 9, 25, 50, 83, 87, 151, 174, 175
police, 43, 164, 165; brutality/killings, 5, 93, 131, gang-intervention work of, 129
poor, the: identifying with, 146, importance of religion among, 154, learning from, 67–69, perspective/voice of, 55–74, welfare of, 121
poverty, 155, 160; amid wealth, 21, both urban and rural, 22–23, discrimination and, 162–63, permanent/multigenerational, 127, 156, in Scripture, 43, wide divergence between wealth and, 60–62
Powell, Adam Clayton, Sr., 100, 102–3
prayer, 6, 36, 57, 59, 101, 126, 135, 139, 141, 150
preaching, 60, 101, 111, 121, 146, 147, 170
Presbyterians, 82, 95, 104, 124, 145
prisons/prisoners, 6, 22, 55, 103; inmate statistics, 25, 164–65
probation systems, 6
Procter, Samuel D., 148
Protestantism, 52, 103; beginnings of, 75–83, principles of social action, 83, reconfigured, 86
public health, 111, 132–33, 156, 159, 161, 162
public ministry, 150–56
public policies/issues, 71, 117, 119, 170–71; challenges that test faith understanding, 150, debates, 154, 155, focus areas of urban ministry, 159–67, preemptive reconciliation influence on, 131–32
public schools: academic performance in, 23, 124–25, creating wholesome environment in, 126–27, enemy-status mindset in, 129, gun violence in 93, 128, 129, 176, poverty level/homeless students of, 126–27, 145, 163, troubled/ineffective, 6, 132, 147, 155
See also educational system; schools

Raboteau, Albert, 91
Race: code language regarding, 25–28, idea/notion of, 25, 89, riots, 98
racial profiling, 6, 25, 28, 162, 181n7
racism, 90, 100, 176
Ransom, Reverdy, 100–102
Reconciliation: as core ministry value, 111, 127–32, 134, 140, 160, in egalitarian

World Trade Center, 5, 129
worship, 57, 99, 144, 145, 146, 154; celebration in, 102, 137, social organization in, 34–35
Young Men's Christian Associations, 97

Youngblood, Johnny Ray, 148
youth. *See* children/youth

zeal, religious, 24, 99, 126, 171